THE WEST EUROPEAN ALLIES, THE THIRD WORLD, AND U.S. FOREIGN POLICY

Recent Titles in
Contributions in Political Science

Library of Congress Cataloging-in-Publication Data

Payne, Richard J.
   The West European allies, the Third World, and U.S. foreign policy :
post–Cold War challenges / Richard J. Payne.
      p. cm.—(Contributions in political science, ISSN 0147–1066 ;
no. 282)
   "Written under the auspices of the Center for International
Affairs, Harvard University."
   Includes bibliographical references and index.
   ISBN 0–313–27460–6 (alk. paper)
   1. United States—Foreign relations—1989– 2. United States—
Foreign relations—Developing countries. 3. Developing countries—
Foreign relations—United States. 4. Europe—Foreign relations—
Developing countries. 5. Developing countries—Foreign relations—
Europe. 6. North Atlantic Treaty Organization. 7. World
politics—1985–1995. I. Harvard University. Center for
International Affairs. II. Title. III. Series.
[E881.P29 1991b]
327.73—dc20   91–11334

British Library Cataloguing in Publication Data is available.

A paperback edition of *The West European Allies, the Third World, and U.S. Foreign
Policy* is available from the Praeger Publishers imprint of Greenwood Publishing Group,
Inc. (ISBN 0–275–93626–0)

Library of Congress Catalog Card Number: 91–11334
ISBN: 0–313–27460–6
ISSN: 0147–1066

First published in 1991

Greenwood Press, 88 Post Road West, Westport, CT 06881
An imprint of Greenwood Publishing Group, Inc.

Printed in the United States of America

The paper used in this book complies with the
Permanent Paper Standard issued by the National
Information Standards Organization (Z39.48–1984).

10 9 8 7 6 5 4 3 2 1

THE WEST EUROPEAN ALLIES, THE THIRD WORLD, AND U.S. FOREIGN POLICY

Post–Cold War Challenges

Richard J. Payne

WRITTEN UNDER THE AUSPICES OF THE CENTER FOR
INTERNATIONAL AFFAIRS, HARVARD UNIVERSITY

CONTRIBUTIONS IN POLITICAL SCIENCE,
NUMBER 282

GREENWOOD PRESS
New York • Westport, Connecticut • London

For Jason

Contents

Acknowledgments

I am indebted to many students, colleagues, friends, anti-apartheid organizations, and various government officials who made significant contributions to this book. I would like to thank Michele Steinbacher, Benjamin
White, Jeffrey Taylor, Amy Nichols, Michele Hermann, Colleen Gierut,
Shickere Sabbaghu, Eric Nicoll, and Troy Bollinger for assisting me with
research, and Michele Steinbacher for typing and proofreading the manu-
script. I am extremely grateful to Garold Cole and Carol Ruyle at Illinois
State University and Barbara Mitchell at Harvard University for their in-
valuable assistance in locating library materials and to Kay Gibbons of
Illinois State University's graphics department for preparing the table.

The Center of International Affairs at Harvard University provided the
ideal environment for working on this book. Several colleagues were ex-
tremely helpful. I am particularly indebted to Professors Saadia Touval,
Samuel Huntington, Jorge Dominguez, Robert Paarlberg, Jeanne Wilson,
Michael Desch, Stanley Hoffmann, Robert Keohane, Lenore Martin, and
Dov Ronen for their insights and suggestions. I would like to thank Professor
Roger Fisher of Harvard Law School for his suggestions and generosity and
Janice Rand, Alice Allen, Tom Murphy, Jean Shildneck, and Anne Emerson
of the Center for International Affairs for helping to make the year at
Harvard enjoyable and productive.

I wish to acknowledge the financial support I received from the Ford
Foundation/National Research Council and Illinois State University which
enabled me to spend the year at Harvard University to work on the manu-
script. I am grateful for the support of many friends, especially Carol and
Richard Miller, Bill and Maria Brisk, Gail Jacobson, Kandice Hauf, and
Beverly Dale. Above all, I would like to thank my son Jason for his insights
and for assisting my research efforts while in Cambridge.

Introduction

Revolutionary changes in Eastern Europe in 1989 and 1990 and the end of the Cold War—symbolized by the reunification of East and West Germany as well as U.S.-Soviet cooperation in the Persian Gulf—radically altered the post–World War II strategic environment and posed significant new challenges for American and Soviet foreign policymakers. While both superpowers squandered their resources on a rapid military build-up in the 1980s and were preoccupied with conflicts in the Middle East, Nicaragua, southern Africa, Afghanistan, and elsewhere in the Third World, Europeans were confident enough to pursue foreign and domestic policies that were largely independent of the superpowers' policies. By 1990 both the United States and the Soviet Union were committed to a new "architecture" for Europe, centered around a unified Germany.

Although neither the United States nor the Soviet Union favored the push toward German reunification, they were essentially powerless to stop the inexorable march toward a single German state. Similarly, Moscow and Washington could do little more than reluctantly adjust to the emerging East European nationalism and West European assertiveness. The combination of superpower involvement in Third World conflicts, the relative economic decline of the United States, and Gorbachev's policies of *perestroika* and "new thinking"—prompted by Soviet economic decline, political disintegration, and severe military setbacks in Afghanistan—eventually led to the emergence of new international realities that were radically different from those of the Cold War period. Clearly, the major changes in Europe were directly influenced by developments in the Third World, especially the escalating U.S.-Soviet rivalry during the renewed Cold War, as well as serious differences between the United States and its European allies on approaches to Third World issues. And the first major crisis of the post–Cold War period, Iraq's occupation of Kuwait, also affected America's relations with Western Europe and complicated European political and economic integration.

For over forty years American foreign policy focused on containing Soviet expansion and strengthening the North Atlantic Treaty Organization (NATO) alliance against Soviet military aggression. Even though the United States allocated almost 50 percent of its military budget to NATO, largely for the protection of Western Europe, the overwhelming majority of military conflicts between the United States and the Soviet Union occurred in the Third World, an area that became the battleground for ideological allies during the Cold War. While it may be argued that America's military strategy successfully maintained stability in Europe, the U.S. tendency to eschew negotiations and to emphasize military solutions to what were essentially socioeconomic and political problems in the Third World ultimately undermined American as well as Soviet power within their respective alliances without resolving underlying causes of regional instability. The 1990–91 Persian Gulf crisis underscored this reality. Although Operation Desert Storm was a military success, it created additional problems in the Middle East and forced the European allies to focus on developing their own defense organization, the Western European Union, within NATO.

Paradoxically, NATO's success in Europe influenced several West European governments to avoid collaborating with the United States in many Third World conflicts, especially when these threatened the effectiveness of the alliance in Europe. America's ideological preoccupation with Communist expansion in the Third World influenced it to concentrate a disproportionate share of its human and material resources on conflicts beyond the area covered by NATO, thereby creating tensions among alliance members, who construed Western security as being largely confined to Europe, and increasing European fears of nuclear confrontation between the United States and the Soviet Union. Furthermore, divergent American and West European interests, different perceptions of communism, varying historical experiences and ideological orientations, and conflicting objectives in, and approaches to, the Third World engendered strains within NATO, beginning shortly after its inception in 1949. The Korean War in 1950, American intervention in Vietnam in 1954, and conflicts in Angola, Nicaragua, and the Persian Gulf during the 1970s, the 1980s, and, to a lesser extent, in the early 1990s seriously eroded West European confidence in America's wisdom and ability to lead the alliance. On the other side, Moscow's expansionist policies weakened the Soviet Union's control over its Warsaw Pact allies and seriously impeded its own economic development. By March 31, 1991, the Warsaw Pact was formally dissolved, and Moscow's political and economic problems continued to escalate.

Whereas complex internal political, social, economic, and religious factors combined to provide the impetus for change in East and West Europe, Soviet and American involvement in Third World conflicts clearly served as an important catalyst for the disintegration of the Warsaw Pact, the independence of the East European states from Moscow's domination, and the erosion of the NATO alliance. The Third World factor was a constant source of friction within the Western alliance and ultimately contributed to the demise of détente between the United States and the Soviet Union. That it was the U.S.-Soviet rivalry in the Third World, not in Europe, which eventually influenced American policymakers to dismantle détente was demonstrated by the fact that détente between West Europe and Moscow, consolidated by the Helsinki Accords that emanated from the 1975 Helsinki conference on Security and Cooperation in Europe, proceeded largely unaffected by superpower competition. As case studies show, American rhetoric on common Western interests in preventing Soviet-Cuban expansion through military means was largely inconsistent with the reality of diverging West European approaches to and interests in the Third World. American actions in most of these conflicts were essentially unilateral and, with the exception of Operation Desert Storm, often collided with West European objectives and strategies.

Because the British and French democratic societies were never clearly threatened by communism, and because of West Germany's geographic proximity to the Soviet Union and Bonn's desire to unify the two Germanys, all three countries adopted varying degrees of detachment from America's preoccupation with Soviet expansion in the Third World. Having played a significant role in Spain's and Portugal's transition from authoritarianism to democracy and their subsequent integration into the European Community (EC), Britain, France, and Germany believed that nonmilitary solutions were more appropriate than military intervention in dealing with most Third World conflicts, especially when called upon by the United States to assume their share of NATO's responsibilities. Ironically, it was the United States that had restrained Britain and France from military intervention in Egypt during the Suez crisis in 1956, an experience which marked the decline of British power and the consolidation of American ascendancy. After the Suez crisis the West European allies were far more reluctant than the United States to use force as a foreign policy instrument in Third World conflicts, including the 1990–91 Persian Gulf crisis.

Europe's growing assertiveness in world affairs and its lack of confidence in America's leadership of NATO were inextricably linked to U.S. foreign policy fiascoes outside of Europe. But as successive American presidents attempted to contain Soviet expansionism, the primary motive for American actions in the Third World, Europeans became increasingly concerned about the implications of the U.S.-Soviet rivalry for their own relations with Eastern Europe, the Soviet Union itself, and with developing countries. As anticommunism became a preoccupation of American politics, the country's self-perception became intertwined with its ability to confront the Soviet threat. Thus, whereas President Carter was viewed as being "soft on communism" because he emphasized political and economic solutions to instability in Central America, southern Africa, the Middle East, and elsewhere, President Reagan was perceived as making America "stand tall" by focusing on containing communism by primarily military means. But while Reagan viewed the Third World as the testing ground of American leadership in the crusade against communism and the rapid military build-up as the most tangible way to demonstrate American strength, the West European allies openly disagreed with the United States and questioned American wisdom and unilateralism in world affairs. And when President Reagan met his Soviet counterpart, Mikhail Gorbachev, in Reykjavik in 1986 and proposed drastic reductions in nuclear weapons without consulting the NATO allies, West Europeans were convinced that America could not be trusted to safeguard Western security interests. This perception was reinforced by the Iran-Contra scandal, which demonstrated to the Europeans the unprofessionalism of U.S. foreign policy-making and ultimately undermined the Reagan presidency. Reagan's decision to testify on the Iran-Contra scandal in early 1990 marked the first time that an American president had to defend his foreign policy in a court of law. The costs of frustrating Soviet-Cuban expansion in the Third World eventually outweighed potential benefits for the United States.

As the Berlin Wall, the most tangible symbol of Soviet-American rivalry, was being demolished in 1989, the prevailing view was that the United States had won the Cold War. The Third World component of that struggle was largely overlooked until Iraq's occupation of Kuwait in August 1990 and Operation Desert Storm in early 1991 overshadowed developments in Europe and influenced the United States in particular to commit massive military resources to the Persian Gulf. Just as regional problems were frequently reduced to an East-West analysis, the complex consequences of a more than forty-year policy of containment were simplified in terms of a zero-sum game. In light of the role of economic power in contemporary world affairs, if there were to be winners in the Cold War, the Japanese and the West Germans were ahead of the other contenders. While the success of Operation Desert Storm prompted President George Bush to proclaim the establishment of a "new world order" and to assert that the next century would be an American century, the United States had to rely on Japan, Germany, and other countries for money to finance the war.

Yet, American aid to resistance movements in Afghanistan, for example, clearly influenced Moscow to reconsider its military intervention in that country and probably played a major role in Mikhail Gorbachev's emerging as the new Soviet leader instead of Grigory Romanov. An easy Soviet victory in Afghanistan could have facilitated Romanov's rise to power by confirming the military's view of the efficacy of force and, consequently, would have postponed change in Eastern Europe. Similarly, it could be argued that U.S. support for the Nicaraguan Contras weakened the Sandinista regime and contributed to the internationally supervised free and fair elections in early 1990 in which the opposition coalition, led by Violeta Chamorro, defeated Daniel Ortega and the Sandinistas. America's determination to use force against Soviet-backed Third World regimes and to expand its military capabilities undoubtedly persuaded the Soviet Union to reconsider the costs of its involvement in regional conflicts. But the Cold War, in addition to causing incalculable destruction to Third World countries, ultimately weakened the superpowers themselves and rendered them incapable of playing a major role in the new Europe.

Although the United States will remain the dominant superpower for the foreseeable future and can be seriously challenged only by a unified Europe that is capable of surmounting inherent schisms and nationalistic impulses, the East-West rivalry undoubtedly contributed to the United States' relative economic decline. Excessive borrowing from Japan and Western Europe during the 1980s to finance the extraordinary budget deficits reduced America's strength vis-à-vis its creditors, damaged its international image as far as fiscal responsibility was concerned, created unprecedented trade imbalances and trade frictions with Japan and the EC, and generally contributed to its relative economic decline at a time when economic factors were becoming paramount in global affairs. Paradoxically, it was the nuclear stalemate emanating from the rapid military build-up by the superpowers that eventually diminished the utility of military power and aided the ascendancy of economic issues in world politics. The U.S.–led coalition's military victory in Operation Desert Storm did not significantly alter this reality.

Excessive military spending and accompanying wastefulness ultimately prompted Americans to question both and to evaluate national security within the broader context of economic competitiveness overseas and economic prosperity at home. The Reagan administration's military strategy was undermined at home because it diverted resources from domestic programs, and was challenged by the West Europeans because it threatened their interest in continuing détente with Moscow at a time when Gorbachev was perceived by even Prime Minister Margaret Thatcher, Reagan's staunchest NATO ally, as a man with whom the West could do business. Furthermore, while the fight against communism may have influenced the demise of the Soviet empire and the rise of democratic regimes in Eastern Europe, the implications for American democracy remain to be evaluated.

Despite its success in frustrating Soviet objectives in Europe, or perhaps because of it, the United States often found itself disagreeing with its European allies who preferred to pursue foreign policies independent of NATO in the Third World, especially in areas such as the Middle East and the Persian Gulf where close cooperation with America, prior to Iraq's occupation of Kuwait and Operation Desert Storm, could have jeopardized significant European economic interests. Even in areas such as Nicaragua, where they had relatively few investments, West Europeans openly opposed U.S. policies. But in most regional conflicts the European allies were unable to achieve their major foreign policy objectives without U.S. support, despite progress toward the development of European Political Cooperation (EPC) in foreign policy formulation and implementation. Nonetheless, European views on these crises influenced both alliance politics and U.S. foreign policy in the Third World, a factor that was taken into consideration by those countries which wanted to pressure Washington into altering particular policies.

By focusing on how the European allies responded to conflicts in the Middle East, the Persian Gulf, Central America, and southern Africa, this book provides a comprehensive analysis of underlying tensions, as well as cooperation, between the United States and its allies in areas beyond Europe. Divergent European and American interests and strategies in the Third World significantly affected the broader issues of détente, relations between East and West Europe, America's leadership abilities, the U.S.-Soviet rivalry, and ultimately NATO itself. The interrelationship between Third World conflicts and these broader issues was demonstrated by the fact that the lessening of ideological confrontation between Moscow and Washington in southern Africa, Central America, the Middle East, and the Persian Gulf was followed by revolutionary changes in Eastern Europe. Because areas outside Europe were the main battlegrounds of the East-West conflict, West Europeans, many of whom did not share Washington's preoccupation with Communist expansion, attempted to moderate American policies toward the Third World in order to protect détente with the Soviet Union. Changes in Europe and continuing conflicts in the Third World pose serious challenges for U.S. foreign policy in a post–Cold War international system in which economic might is increasingly more important than military power in determining the strength of nations. The aftermath of Operation Desert Storm underscored these fundamental changes.

THE WEST EUROPEAN ALLIES, THE THIRD WORLD, AND U.S. FOREIGN POLICY

1

The NATO Alliance: Power, Interests, and Perceptions

Significant political and economic change in Europe in 1989 and 1990 were partly due to NATO's remarkable success in containing Soviet expansion in Europe and strengthening Western Europe's political and economic institutions. At the start, NATO was dominated by the United States, primarily because of the vast power disparities between the European countries, which were devastated by World War II, and America, which emerged from that conflict as the indisputable economic and military superpower. But this situation was temporary, a fact seemingly ignored by Washington. America's perceptions of its partners failed to adjust to their rapidly changing economic and political conditions, assisted greatly by the Marshall Plan and U.S. military protection.

Diverging American and European interests and perceptions, together with the growing importance of economic power and the decline in the utility of weapons as instruments of national power, were bound to create tensions among the NATO countries. America's problems with its allies in the Third World were only symptomatic of deeper, insidious schisms in the post–World War II international arrangements and within the Western alliance itself. As Layne observed, Western Europe's humiliating and anachronistic dependence on the United States was at the root of the turmoil in Atlantic relations. An alliance based on American superiority and European subordination fostered resentments.[1] In addition to outmoded views, America's overcommitment to NATO and growing domestic demands for shrinking resources influenced many policymakers in Washington to question the reliability of its allies, especially in out-of-area conflicts. But the United States failed to resolve the contradiction between wanting to play the dominant role and the need for a more equitable sharing of responsibility for defending Western Europe at a time when the allies were clearly more assertive politically and increasingly prosperous. NATO's military and political foundations were seriously eroded by developments in Eastern Europe (which effectively dismantled the Warsaw Pact as a military alliance), the economic and political integration of Western Europe through the Single Market, the emergence of Gorbachev and his "new thinking" in foreign policy, and the reunification of the two Germanys on October 3, 1990.

The political and cultural underpinnings of the Western alliance were weakened as the United States consolidated its trade ties with Asia and as population and political power shifted from the more European-oriented East Coast to California and Texas. Since the end of World War II the percentage of the American population living in the western part of the country doubled and the proportion of Americans of European origin rapidly declined. By 1990 the growing number of Asian-, Hispanic-, and African-Americans influenced some analysts to conclude that by the twenty-first century Americans of European ancestry would no longer be the dominant majority.[2] Simultaneously, successor generations in both the United States and Europe were relatively unconcerned with pivotal issues that had strengthened the bonds between the allies. Furthermore, NATO's emphasis on military aspects of security proved disturbing for younger Europeans, many of whom were increasingly involved in anti-nuclear weapons protests.[3] These factors combined to diminish the importance of NATO precisely when Europeans were highly skeptical of America's leadership abilities and as Americans were increasingly concerned with domestic problems.

Determined to demonstrate that "America was back" and ready to confront the "evil empire," President Reagan had emphasized the revitalization of the NATO alliance and the restoration of America's leadership of it. Assuming that strains in NATO emanated from America's lack of resolve to reassert its leadership position vis-à-vis the West Europeans and its unwillingness to compete with the Soviet Union in the Third World and elsewhere, the Reagan administration embarked on a massive military build-up even as it implemented major tax cuts. In the process of trying to achieve its objectives, the administration exacerbated tensions with its allies over issues such as Soviet–Cuban involvement in regional conflicts, the Strategic Defense Initiative, and negotiations with Gorbachev at Reykjavik in 1986.[4] Instead of strengthening the alliance, Reagan actually helped undermine it by influencing the Europeans to focus even more on improving relations with Moscow, building institutions that would provide alternatives to NATO, and reducing Europe's dependence on the United States. Overall, Reagan gave the allies the impression that American foreign policy was reactive, largely devoid of a coherent strategy for dealing with the perceived Soviet threat, unilateral and insensitive to those whose cooperation was sought, and based on economic and financial policies that made the United

States dependent on Japan and Western Europe.[5] Divergent European interests and perceptions of the Soviet threat were often ignored.

West Europeans, particularly the West Germans, viewed the Soviet threat within the broader context of détente. Their underlying interests resulted in differences between their perception of the Soviet Union and Washington's anti-Communist crusade. The renewal of the Cold War during the first half of the Reagan administration influenced many Western allies to conclude that they could not rely upon the United States to protect their interests by maintaining détente or to recognize the nuances of the evolving European political order.[6] For West Germany, superpower confrontation could have jeopardized its growing economic and political ties with Eastern Europe in general and East Germany in particular. Its own experiences with the Soviet Union were extremely complex, a reality to which Washington seemed oblivious. While West Germany and France attempted to modify Soviet behavior by creating bonds of interdependence, the United States often adopted coercive economic measures to weaken the Soviet Union as a way of influencing Soviet foreign policy. But without a common perception of the Soviet threat, it was inevitable that the NATO alliance, designed primarily to prevent Soviet expansion in Europe, would eventually be undermined as differences between the United States and Western Europe increased.[7] In the process of attempting to reassert its leadership within the alliance, America succeeded in convincing its allies to distance themselves from their leader and to adjust to the emerging strategic realities.

Far from providing greater military security, the renewed Cold War heightened tensions within the alliance and diminished security for all Europeans. Warsaw Pact and NATO countries grew increasingly concerned about the implications of escalating rearmament by the superpowers, as it was apparent that instability in the Third World, where the superpowers indirectly confronted each other, could have resulted in nuclear war in Europe itself.[8] The Soviet Union's modernization of its conventional forces and development of middle-range nuclear missiles, together with America's emphasis on a nuclear defense system based in the United States, led the West Europeans to conclude that Washington had decoupled its own defense from that of its allies. In other words, the Soviets could threaten Europe while sparing the United States. This was a widely held belief among Europeans who had been skeptical of America's willingness to honor its commitment to use its own nuclear weapons to defend its allies.[9]

THE ALLIANCE: COMMON AND CONFLICTING OBJECTIVES

Alliances are cooperative arrangements among nations designed to safeguard common interests against perceived external threats or to advance particular interests.[10] Yet allies often have conflicting interests. And given that alliances are based on political or military expediency and reflect the inability of states to achieve their objectives by themselves, the very foundations of an alliance are likely to disintegrate as some members accumulate enough power to redefine their interests, alter their strategies for securing their objectives, and reassert their national autonomy that was reduced by participating in the alliance. Although an alliance may add precision to an existing community of interests and to the general policies and concrete measures serving them, these interests are usually not identical.[11]

Military alliances may be classified as either defensive or offensive. The defensive alliance is primarily concerned with opposing external threats from specific states, but does not focus on intra-alliance disputes. An offensive alliance aims at forcibly changing the international status quo, territorially or otherwise, to increase the assets of its members.[12] Whether defensive or offensive in nature, alliances reflect the security needs of individual countries. States may attempt to increase their security by cooperating with other states, assuming that their opponents abstain from joining an alliance. Some states, believing that others will not abstain, will become a member of an alliance to avoid isolation or to preclude any of the partners from allying against them. Eventually, the emergence of an alliance will influence the formation of a rival alliance because, as Glenn Snyder observed, there is no way of knowing that the first alliance is intended only for defensive purposes.[13] Ultimately, both sides will escalate their security burdens but will achieve only marginal security dividends and perhaps even greater insecurity than they experienced previously. Because national interests are not necessarily permanent, an alliance can be weakened by factors that are extraneous to inter-alliance rivalry. Even if common security needs dominate the objectives of the alliance, there must be a convergence of policies in other areas and an ideological component to ensure its survival. However, the ideological factor can augment the alliance by mobilizing moral convictions and emotional preferences for its support, or it may weaken it by obscuring internal political dynamics and divergent interests while expectations are being raised.[14] Such contradictory forces tend to cause an alliance, especially one that is composed of democratic states, to break up.

In order to successfully deal with security threats which prompted the alliance's formation, member countries generally agree to surrender some of their autonomy and to allow one state to assume a leadership role. Yet the dual pressures of sovereignty and democratic values militate against a strictly hierarchical system, and the behavior of states essentially guarantees that alliances will eventually disintegrate. In addition to obvious disintegrative forces such as generational changes, technological advancements, political and economic developments, and poor leadership skills, alliances erode because of their success in dealing with perceived threats. If the alliance achieves its original objectives, its reason for existing begins to shift.[15] Thus, it is NATO's success, not its failure, in helping to maintain stability in Europe that undermined its existence as a military alliance.

In the aftermath of World War II, the West Europeans were faced with an unprecedented threat from the Soviet Union, their wartime ally. Neither Winston Churchill nor Harry Truman anticipated the creation of an alliance that would commit America to Europe's defense until early 1948. Churchill's conception of American involvement in Europe, articulated in his Iron Curtain speech in Fulton, Missouri, centered around a limited association between Washington and Western Europe.[16] It was Ernest Bevin, Britain's foreign minister from 1945 to 1951, who advocated the formation of NATO as a component of the Anglo-American relationship. Although widely regarded as an alliance, NATO was initially an American guarantee of Europe's security until it could defend itself. Developments in Western Europe in 1989 and 1990 were therefore consistent with the original idea of Europe's responsibility for its own security.[17]

As the Soviet threat intensified and as America assumed greater international responsibilities commensurate with its economic and military dominance at the time, NATO was transformed into a more traditional alliance. The Soviet atomic test and North Korea's attack on South Korea in 1950 heightened awareness of the need for a stronger alliance. This also required West Germany's participation and greater U.S. recognition of that country as a sovereign state. Although the other West Europeans, particularly the French, were reluctant to support rearming Germany so soon after a devastating war in which at least 50 million Europeans died, they accepted the U.S. proposal because of their desire to have American troops stationed in Europe as an "automatic trigger" for an American response to any Soviet attack.[18] Yet the escalating procurement of nuclear weapons by the superpowers, while providing security through stalemate, ultimately facilitated the West Europeans' decision to distance themselves from Washington.

Formed during an unprecedented upheaval in modern European history that disrupted the established international system dominated by European countries, the NATO alliance was increasingly strained by inherent cross-pressures.[19] Despite the fact that Soviet expansionism served to consolidate the alliance on a general level, Britain, France, West Germany, and the United States each had specific international and domestic interests that aided the emergence of intra-coalition rivalries which gradually weakened NATO. Intra-alliance rivalries became more prominent as economic considerations replaced military concerns as principal objectives of foreign policy, a development which eventually eroded America's leadership, stimulated intra-alliance competition for markets in Eastern Europe and the Third World, and generated trade friction between the European Community and the United States. The alliance could not destroy deeply rooted intra-European rivalries stemming from political calculations and parochial interests, nor could it completely bridge differences across the Atlantic.

The merging of old and new realities made alliance relations extremely complex. The division of Germany between two competing alliances influenced Bonn to play the role of bridge-builder between East and West. But West Germany's desire to reunite the two Germanys through its policy of *Ostpolitik*, though nominally supported by the allies, engendered European anxieties about a powerful, united Germany in Central Europe. France, the victim of German aggression in both world wars, hindered West Germany's desire to regain respectability in the international community by exploiting the horrors of Nazism. France also attempted to diminish American influence in Bonn as part of its general strategy of preserving its independence and remaining a "mini-superpower" outside of NATO's military arrangements. Britain, an historic rival of France, was less intensely concerned about West Germany and ties across the narrow English Channel and more preoccupied with relationships across the Atlantic. However, continuing British ambivalence about being committed to Europe reinforced French and German assumptions about the Anglo-American partnership.[20]

Significant differences in approaching NATO between the French and Germans on one hand and the British on the other may be attributed to historical, cultural, and linguistic links between the United States and Britain. More important, however, were experiences shared by the Anglo-American allies and their attempts to restructure the international economic, political, and security system following World War II. Unlike France, which was defeated and occupied for four years by Germany, Britain avoided occupation due in part to America's assistance and to Germany's decision to invade the Soviet Union. Cooperative efforts between the United States and Britain during the war prompted British foreign policymakers to emphasize a closer security relationship with Washington in order to avoid new conflicts in Europe.[21] The growing Soviet threat to Western Europe under Stalin augmented Anglo-American ties, and America's policy of containment strengthened the partnership in Third World areas where Communist-backed insurgents were viewed as inimical to Western interests. Regarding itself as a major power, Britain continued to play an important military role in the NATO alliance and to serve as a bridge between the United States and Western Europe. Furthermore, in an effort to balance its global responsibilities with its shrinking resources, Britain assumed the position of a non-ideological and flexible mentor to its relatively inexperienced but powerful American ally and deliberately transfered many of its international obligations and military bases outside Western Europe to the United States.[22]

Britain's loss of military supremacy was underscored by American opposition to the joint French, British, and Israeli intervention in Egypt in

1956 to secure the Suez Canal. But whereas the French reacted to the humiliating Suez experience by cooperating with the Germans to construct an alternative base of support, the British reestablished close links with Washington and focused on building an independent nuclear deterrent as a symbol and guarantor of Britain's world status.[23] Although similar perceptions of the Soviet threat and international roles had helped sustain the "special relationship," Britain's embrace of Washington became an American liability as structural changes in Europe—primarily the development of EPC, the Single Market, and the reunification of Germany—reduced NATO's importance. Former Prime Minister Margaret Thatcher's reluctance to participate in European integration and the loss of the privileged personal and political relationship she enjoyed with former President Ronald Reagan combined to diminish the special relationship between London and Washington. However, Britain's unequivocal support for American initiatives following Iraq's invasion of Kuwait rejuvenated the Anglo-American partnership.

Although France was seriously weakened by World War II and depended on American assistance to rebuild its economy and protect itself from Soviet aggression as well as internal Communist activities, Charles de Gaulle pursued, to the extent possible, a foreign policy that emphasized France's independence; its role as the "continental balancer" in relation to Germany, Britain, and the two superpowers; its participation in creating the postwar international order; and restoring its position as a global power that was capable of asserting control over a farflung empire.[24] Nevertheless, France was incapable of implementing policies that directly clashed with American objectives in Europe, particularly West Germany's rearmament and full integration into NATO. Determined to surmount the psychological and physical trauma of defeat and occupation, France maneuvered to restrain Germany by promoting tight European economic integration and by obtaining maximum freedom to act independently within the framework of the alliance. Furthermore, France attempted to use its limited independence to prevent either close collaboration or direct confrontation between the United States and the Soviet Union,[25] a strategy that strained relations between Paris and Washington.

Believing that the existence of the NATO alliance and the Warsaw Pact would benefit the superpowers and perpetuate Europe's subordinate position vis-à-vis the United States and the Soviet Union, France actively pursued détente with the Eastern bloc and tried to assist the fragmentation of both alliances in order to facilitate the realization of an independent, powerful Europe in which France would play a prominent role.[26] Circumscribing NATO's powers was therefore consistent with France's broader foreign policy objectives. De Gaulle's decision to withdraw French forces from NATO's command and to prohibit the alliance from having its headquarters in France seemed to have been part of a carefully calculated strategy since

1957. His proposal in 1958 for joint American, British, and French leadership of NATO, with each member of the tripartite directorate having veto power over the use of American nuclear weapons, was designed to assist in France's withdrawal from NATO. De Gaulle "brushed off a secret American suggestion in 1962 that a French general instead of an American one might command the alliance's forces in Europe";[27] by so doing, he demonstrated his intention to withdraw France from NATO's military command. France acquired its own nuclear arsenal and pursued an independent policy in Africa, China, Southeast Asia, Latin America, Eastern Europe, and with the Soviet Union.

However, France also recognized that limited cooperation with the United States would not only ensure its military protection but would also contribute to strengthening Europe's economic, political, and military autonomy.[28] Thus, Europe would eventually emerge as a "third force," one capable of challenging the United States for world leadership. In both NATO and in the creation of the new Europe, Germany was the pivotal actor.

Discredited by Nazi atrocities and denied full sovereignty, West Germany was pressured to demonstrate its loyalty to NATO and its commitment to the postwar European order. At the same time, its geographic location on the frontline of the Cold War and Bonn's desire to unite the two Germanys exposed it to tremendous political cross-pressures. Bonn had to take into consideration the interests of Paris, Washington, Moscow, and to a lesser degree, London. Given the conflicting objectives of these governments, West Germany was simultaneously an intra-alliance as well as an inter-alliance mediator. From its creation in 1949 until the early 1960s, West Germany stood firmly in Washington's shadow, even as it endeavored to reassure France that military aggression would not recur. In an attempt to guarantee Germany's commitment to peace, and to frustrate the superpowers' efforts to perpetuate Europe's division, France tried to integrate West Germany into the new West European political and economic institutions. However, Bonn wanted to maintain close ties with Washington not only to influence the United States to formulate policies that were in West Germany's interest but also to improve its value to Moscow, thereby facilitating the achievement of its principal foreign policy goal—reunification.

West Germany's role in NATO was further complicated by the paradox of superpower relations. Even though the United States regarded West Germany as vital to containing the Soviet Union, American foreign policy rested on the concept of double containment, that is, containing both Bonn and Moscow. By keeping the former firmly anchored in the Western alliance, Washington reduced the possibility of either Soviet expansion in Europe or the reunification of Germany. Despite stated American support for a united Germany, both superpowers shared the interest of preventing a powerful, resurgent German state from either joining the opponent's sphere of influence or becoming neutral,[29] a problem that both Moscow and Washington tried to resolve at Malta in late 1989, forty years after NATO was formed.

Between 1975 and 1991, conflicts between Bonn and Washington occurred with greater frequency and it was apparent that the old assumptions upon which America's postwar policies were formulated were seriously undermined by an economically powerful and politically assertive Germany. Partly because of their preoccupation with the Cold War and their allocation of significant human and material resources to it, both superpowers needed German economic assistance by the mid–1970s. When escalating oil prices in the early 1970s had a major negative impact on the American economy, Washington turned to Bonn in its efforts to reflate the Western economies. To a large extent, Moscow also depended on West Germany for economic reasons. The increasing importance of economic and financial factors, as compared to military might, as essential sources of national power worked to Germany's advantage. The shift from military power to economic power ultimately strengthened Western Europe while weakening the Soviet Union and the United States, but neither superpower faced this reality until 1989. Even though West Germany had the strongest economy in Western Europe, it remained "a political dwarf." West Germans publicly voiced dissatisfaction with the large number of American troops (about four hundred thousand in 1989) on their soil, constant military maneuvers and low flights by military aircraft, and the general compromise of West Germany's sovereignty. German sentiment was articulated by Elmar Schmahling, who noted that to younger generations of West Germans the discrepancy between economic success and political status seemed increasingly inappropriate and unacceptable.[30] When the Cold War de-escalated, West Germany was in a strong position to alter its political status, which was predicated on the existence of two rival alliances in Europe.

Spain, unlike West Germany, was relatively free from political and military cross-pressures. Although the Spanish Civil War (1936–1939) gave Germany and Italy, which helped General Francisco Franco, an opportunity to test the blitzkrieg and other military strategies that would be implemented in World War II, Spain did not fight in World War II and was essentially neutral during the Cold War. Apart from the fact that Spain was relatively isolated from major events in Europe during Franco's rule, its ambivalence about joining NATO emanated in part from its conflicting historical messages. While Franco was clearly an anti-Communist, the Soviet Union was not perceived as a major threat. On the contrary, Spain's major concern was internal violence, especially by the Basque separatist movement. Franco's subversion of democratic principles prompted West Europeans, who were also anti-Communist, to declare Spain the pariah or outcast of the West.[31] Consequently, after Franco's death in 1975, Spain attempted to integrate with Western Europe by declaring its support for democracy and

by joining NATO in 1982. Unlike the other NATO allies who were trau-
matized by World War II and distrustful of the Soviet Union, Spain's decision
to join NATO was designed to put pressure on the European Economic
Community (EEC) negotiations on Spain's membership.[32] By 1982, if conflicting interests contributed to strains within NATO, fundamental differences in how Americans and West Europeans perceived their roles in the
world, and each other, clearly threatened the alliance's cohesion.

EUROPEAN AND AMERICAN WORLDVIEWS AND PERCEPTIONS OF EACH OTHER

Historical experiences, socioeconomic and political values, military capability, and economic conditions profoundly influence the worldviews of
Americans and Europeans, their perceptions of each other, and their foreign
policy interests. More specifically, these perceptions helped to shape European and American approaches to problems in the Third World in general
and to the Soviet threat in particular. America's relative isolation from social,
political, and religious violence in Europe and its self-perception as a refuge
from such turmoil clearly distinguished it from West European countries,
which had to confront the realities of power politics and periodic mass
destruction. Unlike Europe, where morality was secondary to fashioning
temporary alliances to restore the balance of power, America regarded itself
not only as moral but also as an exceptional society with a divine mission,
a theme frequently echoed by Ronald Reagan.

Indeed, America had often viewed itself as a righteous society and, as
such, an alternative to the "evil" Europeans. As William Pfaff put it, American repudiation of Europe as a politically corrupt and dangerous civilization
was at the source of the American Revolution, and a notion of Europe as
a "used-up" civilization is at the intellectual and emotional roots of American political consciousness today.[33] However, America's splendid isolation
from the turbulence of Europe, which fostered and perpetuated its view of
international affairs, ended as it was drawn into European conflicts in the
twentieth century.

The emergence of the Soviet Union as America's global rival propelled
the latter into the fray of power politics which it had rejected as inconsistent
with its raison d'etre. Nonetheless, the fundamental premises and values
that mold America's worldview were not significantly altered, which induced
the United States to believe that, unlike ordinary countries, it exercised
righteous power on behalf of its divine mission. The transfer of world
leadership from Western Europe consolidated the United States' emphasis
on the importance of military power. Ironically, this development provided
opportunities for the West European allies to refocus their attention on
domestic problems and economic reconstruction. These changes led Henry
Kissinger to conclude that the Europeans were adopting features that were

characteristic of America, such as the belief in the pacific efficacy of economic relations, an attempt to evade the sordid details of maintaining the global balance of power, and the presumption of superior morality.[34] Additional factors shaping Americans' worldviews are their tendency to be preoccupied with economic issues and domestic problems, a belief in a harmonious world, and a congenital ethnocentrism, especially in relation to the Third World. Because of Americans' widespread self-concern, U.S. policymakers usually exaggerated the nature of the Soviet threat in order to get the nation involved in international affairs. Believing that global harmony is natural, Americans adopt a simplistic analysis of world events but react with right-eous rage when others are perceived as preventing the existence of a har-monious international society. The unprecedented bombing of Iraq and the killing of Iraqi troops fleeing Kuwait supported this view. In addition to regarding its own use of force as legitimate or even moral, the United States believes that others should concur with its policies. Western Europe's ex-periences with both power politics and the tragic consequences of the "ter-rible simplifiers" of the twentieth century influenced the allies to be more cautious and flexible when dealing with conflicts.[35] Yet the belief that Amer-ica is a global power, whereas West European countries are regional powers, contributes to each area's worldviews as well as their perceptions of each other.

America's status as a superpower influenced it to perceive its interests in broader terms when compared to its European allies. Whereas the United States was expected to play a leading role in resolving problems around the world, ranging from the Persian Gulf conflict to southern Africa, West Europeans generally attempted to either support or oppose Washington, depending on their views of American policy and their interests in a given conflict. But Europeans perceived Washington's distinction between global and regional powers as a deliberate effort to unilaterally defend so-called Western interests or to pressure European leaders to adopt America's overall strategy.[36] However, there were significant differences among Europeans themselves concerning the global power versus regional power issue. West Germany, for example, clearly preferred to define its interests largely in regional terms. France and Britain, on the other hand, maintained great power aspirations, if only because of their significant historical and eco-nomic ties to several Third World countries and their participation in in-ternational institutions they helped to develop.[37]

While the United States in the 1980s was determined to stand up to the Soviet threat in the Third World, Europeans were primarily concerned with creating the new European order, an enterprise that required a stable in-ternational environment and deliberate government actions.[38] West Euro-peans' concentration on domestic troubles and their overall approach to Third World conflicts led to their sharply divergent views of the Soviet threat.

On a general level, Europeans and Americans shared two conflicting conceptions of Soviet behavior. The first stressed the hostile and expansionist nature of the Soviet Union and emphasized containment of Soviet power. The second and more complex worldview recognized the importance of ideology in Soviet foreign policy but focused more on a variety of constraints on Soviet power and regarded Soviet behavior as being relatively consistent with that of other great powers historically. The solution to Soviet aggression was containment as well as cooperation in order to persuade the Soviet Union to behave in accordance with internationally accepted rules of conduct.[39] As détente was eroded in America by Soviet expansionism in Angola, Ethiopia, and Afghanistan, Washington abandoned the more complex worldview and stressed East-West confrontation in relation to Third World conflicts. By contrast, the Europeans moved closer to the complex worldview and openly disagreed with the U.S. tendency to oversimplify Soviet behavior.

Under the Reagan administration, America's resurgent nationalism embodied a unilateralist component that led policymakers to conclude that America would act alone to protect its interests, irrespective of how the allies perceived the problem.[40] But the fragmented way in which U.S. foreign policy is formulated and implemented, the institutional rivalries, and the intra-departmental conflicts combined to militate against a clear American articulation of the Soviet threat, even if the dominant view was one of confrontation. Electoral politics induced politicians to use the Soviet threat or risk being called "soft on communism."[41] Nevertheless, the overall American view of the Soviet Union was more belligerent than that of the West European allies.

While each European country viewed the Soviet threat differently, based on geographic location, economic interests, historical ties, and so on, the general European perception of Moscow was more conciliatory than the United States' view. Defining their interests in comparatively narrow terms, partly as a reflection of their limited military capability, West Europeans also saw the Soviet threat in limited terms. Whereas the United States took a global approach and viewed Soviet activities in the Middle East, southern Africa, Nicaragua, and the Persian Gulf as detrimental to America's interests, Europeans usually confined their concern about Moscow to Europe. Furthermore, they regarded the Soviet Union not as an implacable foe, but as a troublesome neighbor with which they shared important interests.[42] Consequently, their ideological approach to the Soviet Union was not as intense as America's. Essentially, Western Europe became a bridge between Moscow and Washington. At the same time, it was increasingly becoming an independent power that would serve as an alternative to the superpowers.

Britain's view was closer to America's, although more complex. Britain perceived the Soviet Union as a threat to European stability and was concerned about growing Eurocommunism on the continent and Communist subversion at home.[43] But unlike the United States, Britain shared its European partners' belief that the West should also assure Moscow that they posed no physical threat and that the Soviet Union could allocate more resources to its formidable internal economic problems. Confidence-building and dialogue with the Soviet Union were regarded as integral components of an overall Western defense strategy. The British government, while supporting America's emphasis on deterrence and defense, underscored the importance of fostering greater understanding between East and West.[44]

France, on the other hand, viewed the Soviet threat within the broader context of Franco-German relations and its own global ambitions. Furthermore, France was seen by Moscow in a way that reinforced French views of both alliances. The Soviet Union, determined to prevent a strong Franco-German alliance within NATO, deliberately cultivated Paris as the alternative interlocutor to Bonn in relations with the West. Even as Moscow attempted to exploit French concerns about resurgent German nationalism, France used its relationship to not only improve its bargaining power with the United States and West Germany, but also to establish its postwar global status.[45] Simultaneously, however, growing anti-nuclear sentiments and what was construed as pacificism as well as nationalism in West Germany in the early 1980s prompted France to adopt a tougher stance toward Moscow. French president François Mitterrand's problems with Communists in his own government, his dislike of Soviet socialism, and Germany's reluctance to accept more nuclear missiles induced him to move closer to the United States. Mitterrand was clearly worried about the changing balance of power in Europe that resulted from renewed Soviet spending on strategic weapons.[46]

West German perceptions of the Soviet threat were shaped by history and geography. German aggression against the Soviet Union and the Soviet occupation of East Germany inevitably led to fears on both sides and an emphasis on security. Although West Germany supported the United States (its protector), Bonn had to take Soviet interests into consideration. Apart from a divided Germany being inconsistent with West Germany's foreign policy objectives, tensions between the two alliances were acutely felt in Bonn. Cultural exchanges, trade, and the broader effort of reunification would certainly be impeded by hostility between NATO and the Warsaw Pact. More important, Germany would be at the heart of fighting in Europe, as the Central Front in Europe ran through it. Thus, America's perception of security heightened German anxieties. As Arthur Cyr noted, America's emphasis on conventional deterrence and "flexible response" seemed to undercut rather than reinforce West German security.[47] These conflicting European and American worldviews in general and perceptions of the Soviet threat in particular strongly influenced how Americans and Europeans viewed each other and seriously undermined NATO. Ironically, with the dramatic changes in Eastern Europe and Gorbachev's reforms within the Soviet Union, American attitudes toward the Soviet Union began to approximate the thinking of Western Europe,[48] thereby further decreasing NATO's relevance.

As Western Europe became more assertive and confident, its perceptions of the United States shifted dramatically. America's anticolonial policies and support for self-determination of British and French colonies created serious strains in NATO and marked the beginning of European disillusionment with the United States. It was clear that America's policies had diminished Europeans' enthusiasm for giving priority to Atlantic rather than European relations.[49] By the late 1960s and early 1970s, America was seen by Europeans negatively because of Vietnam, racial conflict, Watergate, and widespread domestic violence. The political paralysis that characterized decision-making in Congress and the inability of the president to implement important foreign policy objectives led Europeans to conclude that the American political system was inferior to their parliamentary systems, in which major decisions can be made without much difficulty. But if Europeans failed to understand the American system of checks and balances, Americans found it extremely frustrating to deal with European allies that were simultaneously sovereign countries and partners in the European Community. [50] Although their foreign policies were harmonized, there were significant differences in how they conducted their external relations.

Accustomed to dealing paternalistically with the allies, American policymakers were reluctant to accept European criticism. As Henry Kissinger stated, Americans acted as if disagreement with their views was due to ignorance, which could be overcome by extensive briefings and insistent reiteration.[51] The prevailing view among Europeans was that America acted unilaterally and expected the allies to unquestioningly support its actions. Europeans were either ignored or regarded as "junior partners whose job it was to fall in line with whatever the American design might be."[52] Increasingly, the allies saw the United States as making critical decisions that had serious implications for their interests, but viewed their ability to influence those decisions as relatively slight.[53] The most obvious example of this was the European reaction to President Reagan's negotiations at Reykjavik in 1986.

After protracted negotiations with the European allies to put missiles in their countries as part of the overall American strategic deterrent, Reagan hastily accepted Soviet proposals that would radically alter what had been concerted NATO policies on deterrence without prior consultation with the allies. The reaction in Europe and the United States was one of profound disbelief. Reykjavik confirmed the impression that Reagan, "acting out of a mixture of amateurism, moralism, and a quest for immediate political gains, was trying to define a new world beyond nuclear deterrence, and thus destabilizing a global order based on the balance of terror."[54] Instead of demonstrating American leadership, Reagan convinced the Europeans that

American leadership could not be trusted. This perception was strengthened during the Iran-Contra scandal—a situation in which a small group of unqualified and irresponsible officials circumvented American law to supply weapons to the Nicaraguan Contras. Whatever the merits or deeper ramifications of this development, it was obvious from the Europeans' perspective that the United States' credibility as a reliable partner was greatly damaged.[55] Instead of bringing the alliance together, the recklessness with which the Reagan administration approached foreign policy issues and the huge budget deficits it created only augmented European resolve to pursue an independent foreign policy through the institution of European Political Cooperation (EPC).

While Europeans were critical of America's handling of international affairs, Americans were obviously frustrated by the allies' failure to share the responsibility for defending Western security interests. From the American viewpoint, Europeans had not only abdicated their responsibility to contain communism but had also succumbed to the fatal attractions of appeasement in the guise of détente.[56] Europeans were seen as free-riders at a time when their economies were extremely strong and when America had become the world's largest debtor nation. At a more fundamental level, many conservatives were clearly disturbed by the fact that the European allies were assisting the economies of Eastern Europe and the Soviet Union through trade and other financial arrangements, even as Washington was preoccupied with weakening the Soviet Union in order to reduce its expansionist policies. Having defined its national security primarily in terms of the Soviet threat, the United States would have harmed its own interests by doing less. Retaliating against free-riders would have inadvertently undermined its containment strategy.[57] Despite the fact that Congress required the Pentagon to issue a report on allied contributions to Western arms expenditures, the impact of the report was insignificant as far as prompting Europeans to increase their military budgets. The 1990 report indicated that the United States had spent $293 billion on defense in 1988, or 60 percent of all military spending by Western nations. By contrast, West Germany had spent $35.1 billion and France $36.1 billion.[58] But Europeans focused primarily on the Soviet threat in Europe and perceived their contributions differently. In *Statement on Defense Estimates*, the British pointed out that the European allies collectively provided most of NATO's ready forces in Europe and the Atlantic, including 90 percent of the soldiers or troops, 80 percent of the artillery and aircraft, 70 percent of the tanks, and 65 percent of the major warships. It noted that many countries bear the social and economic cost of maintaining conscript forces.[59] Consistent with their worldviews in general and their interests and perception of the Soviet Union, West Europeans had cultivated détente with Moscow, a strategy that militated against rapid military expansion.

WESTERN EUROPEAN DÉTENTE WITH THE
SOVIET UNION

Divergent European and American approaches to détente, or the relaxation of tensions, demonstrated the interplay of European interest in preserving improving relations with the Soviet Union and their concern about the growing U.S.-Soviet rivalry in the Third World in the mid-1970s and throughout much of the 1980s. Relaxing tensions benefited West Europeans much more directly than it did the United States. Contrary to the view that the European attitude toward détente was little more than a desperate hope that it could keep comfortably aloof from the turbulence of worldwide conflict,[60] Western Europe's perception of détente reflected its underlying interest in creating economic and political institutions as alternatives to military alliances. More immediately, it indicated a need to address severe economic decline and high levels of unemployment. At a deeper level, détente in Europe was always separate from the general East–West détente pursued by America. The geopolitical, cultural, historical, humanitarian, economic, and ideological imperatives that prompted Europeans to develop links with the Soviets contrasted sharply with factors that motivated Americans. It was the depth and variety of those imperatives that influenced the allies to preserve détente during the new Cold War between the superpowers.[61] Far from reining in the allies with his military and rhetorical confrontation with the Soviet Union, Reagan inadvertently contributed to a wide rift in the Western alliance and isolated America from the dynamic changes in Europe. But the problems within NATO were compounded not only by Reagan's disregard of European interests but also by his early repudiation of détente, widespread American misunderstanding of it, and conflicting Soviet and U.S. interpretations of what détente was designed to accomplish.

Although American foreign policymakers, particularly President Richard Nixon and Secretary of State Henry Kissinger, clearly understood the realities of power in the international system, the deep-rooted American tendency to view the world in terms of either conflict or harmony, and not a mixture of both, ultimately resulted in an oversimplification of détente as an instrument of foreign policy. The term *détente*, popularized by Charles de Gaulle in the mid–1960s and employed by NATO in the late 1960s, was used as one element in an alliance policy that emphasized balancing defense and reduced East-West tensions.[62] But in an attempt to mobilize public support for a policy toward a country that was strongly perceived as a threat to America's very existence, Nixon and Kissinger articulated the new development in superpower relations in terms of the unrealistic and simplistic goal of a "structure for peace." As Raymond Garthoff observed, "The discrepancy between the private calculation and the public characterization, between the realistic management of power and the promise of a new era of durable peace, ultimately came to haunt détente and undercut popular support, as the excessive expectations it aroused were not realized."[63] Americans, and some of their allies, were given the impression that détente would alter Soviet behavior dramatically. When Moscow behaved otherwise, Americans were alarmed and felt betrayed by the Soviets as well as by their own leaders.[64]

By contrast, the Soviet Union construed détente as an integral part of peaceful coexistence that would facilitate their objective of encouraging change without having to contend with the United States' military force. Under these altered circumstances, the Soviets would be relatively unencumbered in their efforts to achieve revolutionary changes that would eventually result in world socialism and communism, a goal obviously at odds with the defining principle of America's postwar policy, namely the containment of communism. From the Soviet perspective, détente implied a reduction of tensions in Europe but not in the Third World, a view that was consistent with the West European allies' perceptions of their interests. Soviet expansionism in the Third World would continue, taking advantage of regional instability and eroding American power.[65]

If Americans were overly optimistic about what détente would achieve, the Soviets were incredibly naive in their assumptions about America's loss of resolve. In addition to harboring illusions about America's willingness to acquiesce in Soviet-supported changes in the Third World, Moscow apparently believed that the United States would regard Soviet contributions to "progressive" changes in the Third World as compatible with U.S.-Soviet détente.[66] The conflicting West European and American views and expectations of détente explain, to some extent, Soviet miscalculations.

Geography, history, and culture conspired to create intrinsic differences between West European and American perceptions of détente. Contradictions between the allies were inherent in the very forces that culminated in the emergence of NATO. The destruction of European economies, the division of the continent between two rival blocs, and the legacy of World War II provided the impetus for détente in Europe as well as the basis for inevitable conflicts between America and its allies on how to respond to Soviet activities beyond Europe. While West Europeans themselves had contradictory expectations of what détente would enable their individual countries to accomplish, their overarching, common objective was the comprehensive rehabilitation of Europe. Détente essentially meant the normalization of relations in Europe, regardless of what the Soviets were doing elsewhere. Détente was viewed not only as a way of preventing war in Europe but also as a prerequisite for Europe's rediscovery of its "civilizing mission" in world affairs.[67] It represented possibilities: a new and united Europe; the reunification of families; freedom of movement; increased trade; the promise of a European cultural renaissance; cultural cross-fertilization between East and West; and the emergence of the continent as the center of innovation in the arts and sciences.[68] Yet the alliance, which assisted in

Europe's reconstruction and provided stability, was increasingly regarded as an obstacle to the realization of these aspirations, despite its continued utility in the overall strategic balance between East and West. From America's perspective, however, the allies were not facing up to their responsibilities of containing Communist domination in the Third World, a factor considered by some groups in the United States as justification for a reduced American military role in Europe. In either case, the alliance was threatened.

Among the European allies, Germany and, to a lesser extent, France were the major beneficiaries of détente. For de Gaulle and successive French leaders, détente was compatible with France's domestic political goals. In addition to securing greater independence for France and contributing to its role as a "mini-superpower," détente allowed ruling political parties to outflank the French Communist party, which was extremely loyal to Moscow.[69] West Germany experienced more direct benefits as well as cross-pressures from détente. The success of Bonn's policy of Ostpolitik, primarily cooperation between the two Germanys, was clearly premised on West Germany's loyalty to the NATO alliance. Nevertheless, the Germans' concerns with everyday problems, such as pollution, reunification of families, the return of ethnic Germans from various countries in Eastern Europe, transportation, and the policing of borders influenced Bonn to improve relations with Moscow. Because the United States had a worldview which depended on Bonn's cooperation, the extent to which American policymakers could pressure West Germany's leaders was limited. From Bonn's viewpoint, American confrontation with the Soviet Union directly jeopardized West Germany's interests by assisting hardliners in Moscow, many of whom were not in favor of major alterations in Soviet foreign policy.[70] In order to further Ostpolitik, West Germany endeavored to insulate itself from the U.S.-Soviet rivalry and attempted to strengthen cooperation between members of the two alliances. Sensitive to Soviet interests and fears, Bonn distanced itself from the new Cold War initiated by Jimmy Carter and escalated by Ronald Reagan. Détente, for West Germany, became a permanent imperative, one that could not be sacrificed because of Third World hostilities. Regional détente had to be protected against the fallout of a renewed Cold War.[71] Cooperation instead of confrontation with Moscow was seen as the most effective way of restraining Soviet military aggression in Europe. In light of the success of détente in Europe, the West European allies, unlike the United States with its global concerns, were not anxious to become involved in the East-West rivalry in the Third World. Their power and interests undoubtedly influenced them to adopt positions on out-of-area conflicts that were often in direct conflict with American actions. When superpower tensions arose because of hostilities in the Middle East, southern Africa, Afghanistan, and elsewhere, the West European allies refused to jettison détente. On the contrary, West Europeans sought to institutionalize normalized relations with the Soviets through the Conference on Security and Cooperation in Europe (CSCE) in 1975.

Despite European support for various agreements between the United States and the Soviet Union to implement détente, the allies clearly favored a separate détente with Moscow that would parallel but not necessarily converge with that between Washington and Moscow. Furthermore, the Soviets had interests in Europe which did not affect the United States as directly as Western Europe. When the preparatory discussions on CSCE were initiated in November 1972 at Helsinki, Moscow had three principal goals: (1) to gain general acceptance of the territorial and political status quo in Central and Eastern Europe; (2) to reduce interstate barriers to increased economic relations; and (3) to further the regional process of East-West détente.[72] Under Leonid Brezhnev's leadership, the Soviets actively encouraged East-West trade and cooperation in many areas and obtained recognition of Eastern Europe's borders. However, human rights provisions of CSCE were largely ignored, a fact that dampened Washington's enthusiasm for the agreement. Election politics in the United States in 1976 helped to undermine American support for détente as candidate Ronald Reagan opposed President Gerald Ford's decision to sign the accord in Helsinki. Nonetheless, the West European allies and the Soviets cooperated to ensure the continuation of détente in Europe, a process that was decelerated by the weak leadership in Moscow during the early 1980s.

The significant changes in Eastern Europe in 1989 and 1990 were, in part, outgrowths of efforts by the allies to deemphasize confrontation with Moscow, even as America was challenging Soviet involvement in the Third World. Mikhail Gorbachev's efforts to consolidate Soviet ties with Western Europe were therefore a rejuvenation of a process that had atrophied in the early 1980s.[73] The West Europeans' enthusiasm for Gorbachev's "new thinking" reflected their commitment to détente. Superpower tensions in the renewed Cold War prompted Prime Minister Margaret Thatcher to launch a détente offensive in 1984, despite her ideological and personal affinity to Ronald Reagan. Thatcher, like many other European conservatives, believed that through cooperation with Moscow the West could encourage greater autonomy in Eastern Europe and decrease Soviet domination of the area.[74] Expanded trade and increased political cooperation with Eastern Europe were integral components of European détente, developments which eventually strained relations not only between the United States and its allies but also between the Soviet Union and Eastern Europe.

WESTERN EUROPE'S TIES WITH EASTERN EUROPE AND THE SOVIET UNION

Ideological and economic considerations combined to shape the divergent West European and American commercial relations with Eastern Europe in general and with the Soviet Union in particular. Weakened by World War II and highly dependent on foreign trade due to relatively small internal markets, West European countries were more strongly motivated to find markets in Eastern Europe than was the United States. With the largest internal market in the world, an abundance of natural resources, and economic prosperity unmatched by any other country or group of countries, the United States could pursue a comparatively independent foreign economic policy. More important, America used its economic power as a coercive instrument in international relations. The United States attempted to influence Soviet behavior through economic rewards and disincentives. As the ideological rivalry between the two superpowers intensified, the view that the Soviets should not benefit from Western technology, especially if it had military applications, became deeply ingrained in U.S. policy. An important component of this policy was the formation of the Coordinating Committee for Multilateral Export Controls (COCOM) in 1949. Composed of all the West European countries (except Iceland) as well as Japan and Australia, COCOM tried to adopt uniform rules on the transfer of militarily sensitive technology to the Warsaw Pact and other Communist states.[75] From the Soviet Union's perspective, significant commercial links with the West, especially the United States, would compromise its independence and diminish its maneuverability in foreign affairs. Nevertheless, conflict between the superpowers did not prevent their respective allies from developing economic ties whenever possible. The West Europeans did not subscribe to the American assumption that the East European countries under Soviet domination were essentially as hostile toward the West as the Soviet Union was. Centuries of cultural and political exchange between East and West Europeans inevitably led to contradictory American and West European ideas about the role of trade in East-West relations.

When détente was at its zenith in the early 1970s, the American position on trade with the East approximated that of the West Europeans, thereby lessening tensions within the alliance. But Moscow, while wanting normalized trade relations with Washington, clearly attempted to drive a wedge between the United States and its allies in order to exert greater pressure on Washington.[76] As Americans became disillusioned with détente and concerned about Soviet restrictions on Jewish emigration, trade between the superpowers declined. In the United States, this adversarial relationship was institutionalized through the Jackson-Vanik Amendment to the Trade Act of 1974, which tied trade with Moscow to the freedom of Jews to leave the Soviet Union. U.S.-Soviet rivalry in Angola, the Horn of Africa, Nicaragua, and elsewhere in the Third World in the late 1970s and early 1980s further reduced trade between the superpowers and exacerbated tensions within the Western alliance. Economic problems in Western Europe, which were much worse than those in the United States, sharpened the differences between the allies during the escalation of the Cold War under Reagan.

The most divisive trade issue was the construction of the Yamal gas pipeline from the Soviet Union to Western Europe. Within the broader strategic context of the U.S.-Soviet rivalry, Washington regarded the project as an attempt by Moscow to increase its economic and political leverage over the allies. Furthermore, some of the technology furnished for the pipeline was seen as being of military value to the Soviet Union.[77] Overlooked were the economic benefits that would accrue to the West Europeans. It was estimated that European companies would earn between $7 and $10 billion from equipment sales, a significant transaction in light of the high unemployment and deep recession in Western Europe.[78] In addition, Soviet gas would alleviate European dependence on Middle East oil supplies. Failure to take the allies' interests into consideration undermined America's economic sanctions against the Soviet Union.

Because of the business community's pivotal role in West Germany's economic reconstruction, government officials were extremely sensitive to business interests and generally avoided impeding economic transactions. West Germans believed that relations with Moscow could be improved through more, not less, trade. Consequently, they emphasized maintaining economic ties to Eastern Europe and the Soviet Union even during the height of the new Cold War. Increased trade with the Warsaw Pact, particularly with East Germany and the Soviet Union, not only contributed to West Germany's economic growth but also facilitated political and human contact with East Germany and demonstrated the independence of the EC in conducting a regional foreign policy and Bonn's leadership role.[79] West Germany's concentration on trade, partly because of its recent past and the structures of the postwar order, resulted in the country's dominant economic position in the EC as well as its position as Eastern Europe's largest Western trading partner. Changes in Eastern Europe in 1989 clearly placed West Germany in an advantageous situation vis-à-vis the other EC members. In addition to their concerns about the economic might of a united Germany, Bonn's Western allies were clearly worried about a partnership between the Soviet Union and Germany based on the former's vast natural resources and the latter's economic power. However, the Soviets were also fearful about the impact of the Single European Market on their ability to improve trade with the West.[80]

Similarly, France did not allow its membership in NATO to seriously affect its economic ties to Eastern Europe and the Soviet Union. Paris had consistently resisted any American effort to reduce trade and non-military technology transfers.[81] Apart from construing such attempts as violations of France's sovereignty and independence in foreign affairs, French leaders viewed trade with the East as the most effective way of reducing tensions, ending the division of Europe by both superpowers, and restoring Europe's position as a major world power. Like West Germany, France was determined to isolate commercial relations with the East from the U.S.-Soviet rivalry in the Third World.

Britain, on the other hand, was less affected by events in Eastern Europe and subscribed to American perceptions of the Soviet threat to a much greater extent than either West Germany or France. Because of its relative distance from the Soviet Union and lower stakes in the success of détente in Europe, especially when compared to West Germany, Britain was more interested in preserving the status quo in Europe. Sharing neither France's determination to unite Europe nor West Germany's aspiration of a reunified Germany, Britain was clearly reluctant to promote change in Eastern Europe that would weaken NATO and jeopardize Western security interests. [82] Yet British policymakers did not fully support America's predilection for economic sanctions against Moscow because of its involvement in Third World hostilities. Margaret Thatcher, who did not share West German Chancellor Kohl's enthusiasm for massive aid to Eastern Europe, argued that Western loans would allow the Soviet Union to continue the arms race without negative effects on economic reforms.[83] Nevertheless, British firms were encouraged to increase trade with Eastern Europe. In 1988, seven major British banks arranged a $1.5 billion loan to finance trade with the Soviet Union, an attempt to make Britain more competitive with West Germany, France, and Italy.[84]

Rapid political changes in Eastern Europe and Gorbachev's focus on perestroika, which demanded "new thinking" in Soviet foreign policy, had radically altered Western economic relations with the East and challenged many of the postwar assumptions and institutional arrangements. Both the United States and the Soviet Union were pressured to elevate economic relations above military confrontation when the Cold War ended. Gorbachev, concerned about providing much-needed consumer goods for Soviet citizens and pressured to demonstrate tangible benefits of perestroika, persuaded President George Bush at Malta to terminate economic restrictions that were an integral part of the Cold War.[85] Similarly, American business leaders and the West European allies urged Washington to remove many curbs on technology exports to Eastern Europe. And in light of the Soviet Union's decision to allow Jews to leave the country, the Jackson-Vanik Amendment was no longer necessary. Trade restrictions against Moscow were relaxed and Washington decided to support observer status for Moscow in the General Agreement on Tariffs and Trade (GATT), the Western economic organization.[86] The United States also granted the Soviets most-favored-nation treatment in trade relations in early 1990, despite widespread congressional opposition to Gorbachev's economic sanctions against Lithuania after it had declared its independence from the Soviet Union. In July 1991 Gorbachev met with the industrial countries' leaders in London to discuss Soviet economic problems and to seek Western assistance.

NEW SOVIET THINKING AND THE ALLIANCE

Gorbachev's articulation of new political thinking in Soviet foreign policy and his advocacy of a "common European house" were inextricably linked not only to serious domestic economic problems but also to the expansionist policies in the Third World of his predecessors. The failure of the Soviet Union's centrally planned economy and the enormous costs of the inefficient bureaucracy that accompanied it drew increased attention to major expenditures on client states around the world. Although largely ignored, the Third World factor was pivotal in the revolutionary changes in international politics in 1989 and 1990. As former President Richard Nixon observed, Brezhnev's militarism and expansionism gave the Soviet Union a severe case of imperial indigestion after it gobbled up Third World countries.[87] Gorbachev's "new thinking" was a deliberate attempt to address this problem.

"New thinking" was characterized by (1) emphasizing the interdependence of nation-states and their problems, (2) greater respect for international law and the use of international institutions to resolve conflicts, (3) solving Third World problems through international cooperation, and (4) rejecting the nuclear arms race as well as the idea that security can be assured by military means.[88] Thus, the reduction of East-West tensions was imperative, but relaxation could not occur without addressing the Third World component of the U.S.-Soviet rivalry. This required diminishing Soviet military involvement in regional conflicts as well as trying to find ways to resolve them peacefully, preferably through cooperation with the United States. Consequently, Moscow supported the United Nations' efforts to end the Iran-Iraq conflict and to remove Iraq from Kuwait and worked with the United States to achieve Namibia's independence as well as the gradual withdrawal of Cuban troops from Angola.[89] Indeed, Gorbachev's reforms were directly linked to the reality that unless there were significant economic and technological improvements the country would deteriorate internally as well as lose its superpower status. In order to concentrate on perestroika Gorbachev had to alter the external environment of Soviet foreign policy.[90]

Yet Gorbachev's new thinking in foreign policy was embraced much sooner by Margaret Thatcher than by Mitterrand, Kohl, and Reagan. Paradoxically, American exaggeration of the Soviet threat throughout the postwar period ultimately undermined domestic support for confrontation with the Soviet Union.[91] In fact, Reagan's strident anti-Communist rhetoric and his predilection for military solutions to essentially political and social problems inadvertently assisted Gorbachev's strategy by making the Soviet Union appear far more reasonable than the United States.

During Gorbachev's visit to Bonn in mid-1989, he issued a joint statement with Chancellor Kohl in which the two leaders declared they were "pursuing the aim of removing the causes of tension through a constructive, forward-looking policy, so that the feeling of threat that still exists can be replaced gradually by a state of mutual trust."[92] A poll commissioned by Second German Television in June 1989 indicated unprecedented positive views of a foreign leader in Germany: 90 percent of those polled believed that Gorbachev could be trusted, whereas only 58 percent said they trusted President Bush. About 84 percent of the West Germans questioned said that they did not feel militarily threatened by the Soviet Union.[93] In contrast, the British were more cautious. While acknowledging major shifts in Soviet foreign policy and the historical fears of the Soviet Union which prompted it to act aggressively, British policymakers advocated realism in setting expectations to avoid excessive optimism or pessimism; vigilance in sorting out dangers from opportunity; and openmindedness about the possibility of change.[94]

Gorbachev's advocacy of a "common European house" was a direct challenge to American foreign policy in general and to the NATO alliance specifically. When Gorbachev argued that it was "time to deposit in the archives the postulates of the Cold War period, when Europe was regarded as an arena of confrontation, divided into spheres of influence, and somebody's outpost, and as an object of military rivalry,"[95] he was skillfully changing the game played by the superpowers for most of the postwar period. By contending that "the philosophy of the common European house concept rules out the probability of an armed clash and the very possibility of the use of force or threat of force—alliance against alliance, inside alliances, wherever,"[96] Gorbachev was clearly attempting to undermine America's leadership role in Europe.

If Europeans viewed developments in Europe positively, Americans were understandably apprehensive. From Washington's perspective, Moscow intended to create even more tensions within NATO.[97] But detaching Western Europe from the United States also had important ramifications for the Soviet Union in relation to its own alliance. Similarly, American attempts to punish the Soviets culminated in weakening NATO and increased foreign policy-making independence for East as well as West Europeans. As Pierre Hassner put it, "nothing could have served Soviet aims better than the Reagan administration's heavy-handed attempts to delay seriously or even block the Soviet–West European gas pipeline project."[98] Yet the emergence of a strong, autonomous Western Europe posed serious challenges for Moscow itself. If Washington had to leave Europe, then Moscow would have difficulty justifying its grip on its own allies. Though the Soviet Union wanted to maintain the two alliances to preserve stability in Europe and keep West Germany in check, albeit with America's position in NATO much diminished, domestic pressures for economic reforms and internal ethnic and nationality problems eroded Moscow's control over Eastern Europe.[99] Unlike Britain, which was concerned about alliance cohesion, France supported the Soviet objective of creating a "common European house" and ending the division of Europe. Mitterrand pointed out that "it is perhaps one of the objectives of the Soviet leaders to achieve the separation between the American continent and the rest of Europe. Perhaps... but it is also quite a desirable objective."[100]

THE SINGLE EUROPEAN MARKET: AMERICA'S ECONOMIC RIVAL

The Marshall Plan, the economic component of America's postwar European policy, was perceived as a crucial catalyst for European economic unity. Although the United States also clearly viewed a united Europe as relieving it of many of its military and economic burdens,[101] the worldview fashioned by the postwar architects of American foreign policy would inevitably frustrate efforts to restore that country's splendid isolation. Furthermore, the very success of the U.S. economic policy in Europe allowed the Western allies a greater degree of maneuverability, precisely because their growing economic independence lessened America's leverage over them. Eventually, the United States found itself in the peculiar situation in which its military and political allies were simultaneously its economic competitors and major challengers for world power as they moved toward a single market. Consequently, America's efforts to perpetuate its traditional leadership role within the alliance were counterproductive and ultimately damaging to the United States itself.[102]

America's preoccupation with the Communist threat and its emphasis on military responses to it "expanded the military budget, distorted the economy and the direction of technological research and development, diminished the competitiveness of American goods, and condoned a debtor mentality in every sector of American public and private life."[103] In their military competition with the Soviet Union, U.S. foreign policymakers had lost sight of the real foundation of America's world leadership—its economic might. Although Samuel Huntington correctly observed that the unprecedented budget deficits, which were financed by the West Europeans, the Japanese, and others, stemmed from the weakness of Reagan's economic policies and not the American economy, it was extremely difficult to separate these realities neatly. Furthermore, Huntington's argument that since the budget deficits were produced quickly by one set of policies they could therefore "be reversed almost as quickly by another set of policies"[104] obviously ignored the pervasive lack of political will to deal seriously with the problem and the psychological barriers that would have to be surmounted in order to restore America's sense of fiscal responsibility.

America's unclear definition of its vital interests, as opposed to peripheral interests, influenced Washington to react to crises that were largely irrelevant to the protection of national interests. As Paul Kennedy pointed out, the United States suffered from imperial overstretch because it failed to balance its interests and resources.[105] Washington was unable to adequately defend all of its interests simultaneously, and the West Europeans were unwilling to allocate more resources to the military because the United States not only defended them but was also prepared to act unilaterally in regional wars. The underlying dilemma for the United States was directly related to its status as a hegemonic power. According to the theory of hegemonic stability, the costs of regime maintenance tend to fall disproportionately on the hegemonic actor. Over time, the relative power of this leading state thus tends to erode.[106] The most tangible evidence of Europe's relative strength vis-à-vis the United States was European economic integration and the movement toward a single market, ideas initially advocated by Washington. Europe was increasingly viewed as an economic locomotive in its own right, largely because of slowed American growth and reduced European economic performance on the U.S. business cycle.[107]

The creation of the Single European Market was inextricably intertwined with America's relative economic decline and a growing protectionist sentiment in Congress on the one hand and the emergence of Japan as the United States' economic rival on the other. As long as the leader of the alliance was also the dominant economic power, the allies could rely on it for advanced technology and financial leadership within international institutions it shaped, and could attempt to influence world economic policies through their close relationship with it. While dependence on the United States was not fully embraced by the allies, "to be dependent on Japan in monetary and technology matters, without integrated defense and trade ties that linked the Atlantic partners, was a different problem. The new international structure required new bargains."[108]

These new international realities influenced the movement toward a Single European Market. In 1985 Lord Cockfield of Britain submitted a proposal, "Completing the International Market," to the European Council that became the major landmark in the process of creating the Single Market.[109] The basic objective was to eliminate trade barriers between states of the EC and to combine individual national markets into one market, thereby allowing British, French, West German, Italian, and Spanish companies to compete within one huge internal market. The Single European Act of 1986 was an important step toward greater economic and political integration.[110]

From the allies' perspective, a politically fragmented and technologically dependent Western Europe would undoubtedly be relegated to a secondary position compared to the United States and Japan. The view from Europe was best articulated by Alain Madelin, who pointed out that there were already two major economic poles. "In North America, the United States and Canada have laid the foundations for a free-trade area which will be able to rely upon less costly subcontractors in Central America. In the Asia-Pacific zone, Korea, Taiwan, and the Chinese diaspora are concentrating their energies around Japan. Europe has no choice but to become a third pole of equivalent dimension."[111] By 1988 the European allies had decided to establish a Single Market in December 1992.

European cooperation in research, manufacturing, and financial services laid the foundation of the new Europe as a formidable competitor for America as well as Japan. Numerous joint ventures had been formed even before the push toward a common market to enhance Europe's ability to compete with Japan and the United States. More recent projects included Airbus Industrie, a consortium of aerospace companies from France, Britain, Spain, and West Germany that was the world's second largest manufacturer of passenger aircraft in 1989; the Joint European Submicron Silicon program, known as Jessi, designed to help Europe narrow the gap between them and the United States and Japan in semiconductor technology; Esprit, a program to improve microelectronics technology in integrated circuit design and computer-aided manufacturing; the European Space Agency; and Eurofighter, a cooperative effort among British, West German, Italian, and Spanish companies to construct new fighter aircraft.[112] The potential of Europe, whose economic growth had already surpassed that of the United States in 1989, attracted investments from Japan, the United States, Australia, and elsewhere.

Difficulties inherent in international economic cooperation threatened to impede progress toward a fully integrated European Market. Fearing that German unity would influence Western Europe's largest economic power to deemphasize European unification, France and other countries strengthened their efforts to integrate the united Germany into the Single Market. Running counter to this was concern about German economic domination. These contradictory tendencies were complicated by fears within the EC that countries such as Spain and France, which are magnets for Latin Americans and North Africans, respectively, would give workers from the Third World access to jobs throughout Western Europe. Furthermore, emigration from East European countries also threatened the EC's free movement project.[113] Finally, labor unions did not enthusiastically support unrestricted movement and the ability of companies to locate anywhere in the Single Market. West German workers feared competition from lower-paid Spanish and Portuguese workers, for example, and Spain and Portugal worried about competition from even-lower-paid workers from Eastern Europe and the increased attention that investors were giving those countries. Portugal responded by providing incentives to encourage new investments from outside the EC.[114]

By inducing competition among European firms, the Single Market raised the probability of decreased competition from outsiders in order to compensate the less-competitive companies within the market. As Lester Thurow astutely observed, in the best of cases, common markets make it more difficult for outsiders to sell their products. Reducing internal trade barriers raises the effective level of external barriers even though these external barriers remain unchanged.[115] American officials were clearly concerned about EC procurement guidelines which stipulated that governments were allowed to exclude offers containing less than 50 percent EC content. Proposed tariffs and other regulations favored European-made computer chips, telecommunications equipment, television programs, and other products

over imports from the United States and Japan. While these policies motivated American and Japanese companies to invest in European plants to
meet the local-content requirement, the U.S. government voiced strong opposition to what it regarded as trade barriers and protectionism. In an ironic
twist in international trade, the U.S. trade representative, Carla Hills, pro-
tested EC attempts to restrict entry of American-built Japanese cars. Although America had trade grievances against Japan, Japan's strategy of
"going multinational" by establishing automobile factories in the United
States resulted in American-Japanese collaboration against the West European allies in order to protect American jobs.[116]

Although many U.S. officials worried about the economic implications
of the Single Market, there was also widespread optimism about the opportunities flowing from it. American manufacturers had supported European integration and were expanding their European operations, especially
in light of surveys indicating that the Single Market would produce approximately $4.5 trillion of goods and services annually.[117] By stimulating
European growth, the Single Market was viewed as providing an outlet for
American exports. It was also seen as eventually contributing to the erosion
of nationalistic commitments to protectionism in the various European
countries, thereby promoting liberalization of trade.[118] At a deeper level,
Europe's economic integration was part of the broader movement toward
a separate European identity that was expressed by the formulation of
common foreign policies through the EPC and the development of a European security system through the reinvigoration of the Western European
Union as an alternative to NATO, especially in Third World conflicts.

EUROPEAN POLITICAL COOPERATION AND NATO

The development of EPC was directly linked to the growing economic
and political power of Western Europe and its desire to demonstrate its
independence within NATO. Although the origins of the EPC framework
can be traced to plans formulated in 1961 and 1962 by a committee of EC
diplomats chaired by Christian Fourchet, France's ambassador to Denmark,
very little serious discussion of the idea occurred until the end of 1969, and
the first meeting of the Conference of Foreign Ministers was not held until
November 1970.[119] As détente between Moscow and Washington deteriorated, primarily because of military crises in the Third World, West Europeans were under increasing pressure to differentiate their policies from
those of the superpowers. EPC reflected an effort by the West Europeans
to speak with one voice and to avoid taking actions or positions that would
impair their effectiveness as a cohesive force in foreign affairs. Harmonizing
foreign policies, to the extent possible, would allow Europeans to formulate
a regional policy toward conflicts in the Middle East, Central America,

southern Africa, and the Persian Gulf as well as to serve as a counterweight to the United States and the Soviet Union in world politics.[120]

The first major test of EPC in foreign policy was in the early 1970s as the Arab-Israeli conflict triggered an oil embargo by the Organization of Petroleum Exporting Countries (OPEC). Tensions between the United States and its allies, arising from different responses to the Middle East crisis, at first threatened to derail the EPC process but eventually strengthened it as consultations between the allies were established through the foreign ministry of the country holding the Presidency of the Conference of Foreign Ministers. Oil politics also influenced the Europeans to harmonize their foreign policies in the Middle East through the development of Euro-Arab dialogue.[121] Although not immune from national pressures resulting from governments trying to protect their interests, EPC, prior to Iraq's invasion of Kuwait, had clearly functioned to distinguish European policies in the Middle East from those of the United States, and provided the Arab states with a channel through which they could try to influence American policy in the region. Having failed to significantly influence events in the 1990–91 Persian Gulf crisis, the Europeans attempted to revive EPC in the war's aftermath.

From America's perspective, the West Europeans' failure to speak with one voice on East-West issues, Third World conflicts, and trade strengthened its own position vis-à-vis the Soviets and individual European countries. Conversely, when the Europeans acted as a unit in foreign policy and expressed views that conflicted with the United States' on the Middle East or Central America, Washington's reactions ranged from anger to derision.[122] The West European allies' independence in foreign policy was often regarded as a direct challenge to America's leadership of NATO.

West Germany's foreign policy objectives demanded that it work within the Western alliance while simultaneously cultivating its own economic, cultural, and political ties with Eastern Europe and the Soviet Union. To unilaterally formulate and implement bold foreign policy initiatives would have undoubtedly raised concerns about Germany among the Europeans themselves. Yet West Germans wanted to exercise power in international affairs commensurate with their leading economic role. Under these circumstances Bonn found that harmonized European foreign policy provided increased room in which it could maneuver. As Reinhardt Rummel and Wolfgang Wessels put it, EPC is a highly useful framework for diverting conflicting pressure away from West Germany and transferring it to an anonymous body where the blame can be put on the "group" or on other partners.[123] In Britain's case, foreign policy cooperation offered London an opportunity to assume the leadership role in the new Europe. Britain's strong international position in general, its position on the UN Security Council and in the Commonwealth, and its special relationship with the United States prompted London to influence the priorities of collective West European diplomacy. Similar to West Germany, Britain used EPC as a means of subtly dissociating itself from U.S. policy toward the Soviet presence in Afghanistan, for example, while at the same time expressing broad support for America. Without the safety of numbers, London might have found it more difficult to advocate a policy consistent with Washington's even as it resisted U.S. pressure to implement economic sanctions against the Soviet Union.[124]

THE WESTERN EUROPEAN UNION AND NEW STRATEGIC REALITIES

Despite assertions about the importance of the European-American military partnership for European stability, by 1990 it was obvious that the postwar order and American hegemony in Europe had ended. It was not coincidental that at the beginning of the 1980s European governments and public opinion emphasized the need for an independent European security system. The demise of détente and the return of the Cold War led to conflicting American and European perceptions of the Soviet threat and how to respond to it.[125] Apart from the East-West dimension of the U.S.-Soviet rivalry in the 1980s, from the West Europeans' perspective, regional conflicts directly affected their foreign policy interests. Many of the crisis areas had historical and colonial ties to Britain, Spain, Portugal, Germany, and France.

With the need for out-of-area international peacekeeping operations becoming more apparent, the allies tried to strengthen their military capability. In 1984, Claude Cheysson, the French Minister of Foreign Affairs, initiated the reactivation of the Western European Union (WEU). Composed of Britain, France, West Germany, Italy, the Netherlands, Belgium, and Luxembourg, the WEU had been established by the Brussels Treaty of 1954. Both the long-standing French objective of making Europe more independent of the United States and escalating superpower tensions emanating from regional wars contributed to the Europeans' idea that "some genuine tasks should be restored to the Organization [WEU] and that its rules and institutions should be adapted to the new circumstances and to the responsibilities proposed for it."[126]

NATO was never regarded by West Europeans as having responsibilities in out-of-area conflicts. WEU, on the other hand, allows member countries to act in concert in military operations in the Third World wearing their WEU colors. Furthermore, WEU is the only European organization in which both the defense ministers and foreign ministers of the various countries can discuss security issues that are significant for West Europeans. In 1966, France decided not to participate in NATO's Euro-Group where security matters are discussed.[127] Despite the British contention that WEU seeks to "reinforce rather than duplicate work done in NATO and to ensure that the European input into the alliance is coordinated and coherent,"[128] it was obvious that WEU was an integral part of West European integration and Europe's emergence as an alternative to the superpowers in international affairs. Far from coordinating their activities with the United States in the Persian Gulf during the Iran-Iraq war in the 1980s, the West European allies worked through WEU and stressed the separateness of their operations from the NATO alliance.

Dramatic changes in Europe in 1989 and 1990 further augmented the shift away from NATO. Germany's assertiveness in foreign affairs, its refusal to remain in Washington's shadow, the demolition of the Berlin Wall, and the rapid American military response to Iraq's occupation of Kuwait in mid-1990 as well as America's dominant role in Operation Desert Storm in early 1991 strengthened West Europeans' efforts to develop their own security system. But Chancellor Kohl's speech on German reunification, in which he outlined his plans for the integration of East and West Germany in economic, cultural, technological, and political matters,[129] caused widespread concern among both East and West Europeans. Kohl's failure to consult the four major powers (the United States, Britain, France, and the Soviet Union) who were responsible for the postwar order in Europe prior to the speech reinforced the view prevalent among Europeans and Americans that a united Germany must remain within NATO. The general view was that without NATO oversight, a unified Germany could reinvigorate the Warsaw Pact, thereby creating new insecurities in Europe.[130] Thus, despite the disintegrative effect of changes in Europe on NATO, European apprehensions of German unification pulled the allies toward maintaining NATO, albeit in a radically altered form. Following Operation Desert Storm and Iraq's civil war, WEU met in conjunction with the EC, for the first time, to discuss humanitarian aid for Iraq's Kurdish refugees. Ironically, Britain, America's staunchest ally, initiated European actions on the tragic refugee problem. The United States seemed reluctant to take the leadership role in addressing the human suffering that was a consequence of the war.

NOTES

1. Christopher Layne, "Atlanticism Without NATO," *Foreign Policy*, no. 67 (Summer 1987): 23.

2. William A. Henry, "Beyond the Melting Pot," *Time*, April 9, 1990: pp. 28–31.

3. Simon Serfaty, "Introduction," *SAIS Review* 2, no. 4 (Summer 1982): 2; and David P. Calleo, "The Atlantic Alliance: An Enduring Relationship?" *SAIS Review* 2, no. 4 (Summer 1982): 34.

4. Phil Williams, "The Limits of American Power: From Nixon to Reagan," *International Affairs* 63, no. 4 (Autumn 1987): 586.

5. David Anderson, "Statement," Hearing before the Subcommittee on Europe and the Middle East of the Committee on Foreign Affairs, House of Rep., 100th

Cong., 1st Sess., December 2, 1987 (Washington, D.C.: Government Printing Office, 1988), p. 2.

6. Michael Smith, *Western Europe and the United States: The Uncertain Alliance* (London: Allen and Unwin, 1984), p. 68.

7. William G. Hyland, "The Struggle for Europe: An American View," in *Nuclear Weapons in Europe*, ed. Andrew Pierre (New York: Council on Foreign Relations, 1984), p. 29; and James Oliver Goldsborough, *Rebel Europe: How America Can Live with a Changing Continent* (New York: Macmillan, 1982), pp. 11–12.

8. Harry Maier, "Drifting Together? New Challenges Facing the Two Alliances," in *Drifting Apart? The Superpowers and Their European Allies*, ed. Christopher Coker (London: Brassey's Defense Publishers, 1989), p. 171.

9. Henry A. Kissinger, "A New Era for NATO," *Newsweek*, October 12, 1987, p. 58; Stanley Hoffmann, "The Western Alliance: Drift or Harmony?" *International Security* 6, no. 2 (Fall 1981): 105; and Jim Hoagland, "Europe's Destiny," *Foreign Affairs* 69, no. 1 (1990): 35.

10. Robert E. Osgood, *Alliances and American Foreign Policy*, (Baltimore: The Johns Hopkins Press, 1968), p. 17.

11. Hans J. Morgenthau, "Alliances in Theory and Practice," in *Alliance Policy in the Cold War*, ed. Arnold Wolfers (Baltimore: Johns Hopkins Press, 1959), p. 186.

12. Osgood, p. 18.

13. Glenn H. Snyder, "The Security Dilemma in Alliance Politics," *World Politics* 36, no. 4 (July 1984): 462.

14. Osgood, p. 23; Morgenthau, p. 189; and Richard E. Neustadt, *Alliance Politics* (New York: Columbia University Press, 1970), p. 2.

15. Kim Richard Nossal, "The Dilemmas of Alliancemanship: Cohesion and Disintegration in the Western Alliances," in *America's Alliances and Canadian-American Relations*, eds. Lauren McKinsey and Kim Richard Nossal (Ontario, Canada: Summerhill Press, 1988), p. 36.

16. Don Cook, *Forging the Alliance: NATO, 1945–1950* (New York: Arbor House/William Morrow, 1989), p. 113.

17. Theodore Draper, "Coalition Dynamics: NATO, the Phantom Alliance," in *The Global Agenda: Issues and Perspectives*, eds. Charles W. Kegley and Eugene Wittkopf (New York: Random House, 1988), p. 158.

18. Robert R. Bowie, "The Atlantic Alliance," *Daedalus* 110, no. 1 (Winter 1981): 54.

19. Seyom Brown, *New Forces, Old Forces, and the Future of World Politics* (Glenview, Ill.: Scott, Foresman, 1988), p. 56.

20. Roger Morgan, "Preface," in *Partners and Rivals in Western Europe: Britain, France, and Germany*, eds. Roger Morgan and Caroline Bray (Aldershot: Gower, 1986), p. xi.

21. Arthur Cyr, *U.S. Foreign Policy and European Security* (New York: St. Martin's Press, 1987), p. 58.

22. Robbin F. Laird and Susan Clark, *Britain's Security Policy: The Modern Soviet View* (London: The Institute for European Defence and Strategic Studies, 1987), p. 67.

23. Christopher Tugendhat and William Wallace, *Options for British Foreign Policy in the 1990s* (London: Routledge, 1988), pp. 14–15.

24. Wolfram F. Hanrieder and Graeme P. Auton, *The Foreign Policies of West Germany, France, and Britain* (Englewood Cliffs, N.J.: Prentice-Hall, 1980), p. 97.

25. Roy C. Macridis, "French Foreign Policy: The Quest for Rank," in *Foreign Policy in World Politics*, ed. Roy C. Macridis (Englewood Cliffs, N.J.: Prentice-Hall, 1985), p. 23.

26. Hanrieder and Auton, p. 105.

27. Paul Lewis, "Scholars Acclaim de Gaulle as Leader of Great Vision," *The New York Times*, April 9, 1990, p. A4.

28. Macridis, p. 57.

29. Wolfram F. Hanrieder, "The German-American Alliance at Forty," *Aussenpolitik* 40, no. 2 (1989): 149.

30. Elmar Schmahling, "German Security Policy Beyond American Hegemony," *World Policy Journal* 6, no. 2 (Spring 1989): 373.

31. Federico G. Gil and Joseph S. Tulchin, "Introduction," in *Spain's Entry into NATO: Conflicting Political and Strategic Perspectives*, eds. Federico G. Gil and Joseph S. Tulchin (Boulder, Colo.: Lynne Rienner, 1988), p. 2.

32. Gregory F. Treverton, *Spain: Domestic Politics and Security Policy* (London: The International Institute for Strategic Studies, 1986), p. 31.

33. William Pfaff, *Barbarian Sentiments: How the American Century Ends* (New York: Hill and Wang, 1989), p. 21.

34. Henry A. Kissinger, "Reflections on a Partnership: British and American Attitudes to Postwar Foreign Policy," *International Affairs* 58, no. 4 (Autumn 1982): 584.

35. Hoffmann, "The Western Alliance," p. 116.

36. Baard Bredrup Knudsen, *Europe Versus America: Foreign Policy in the 1980s* (Paris: The Atlantic Institute for International Affairs, 1984), p. 34.

37. Francis Pym, "British Foreign Policy: Constraints and Opportunities," *International Affairs* 59, no. 1 (Winter 1982–83): 6.

38. Stanley Hoffmann, "NATO and Nuclear Weapons: Reasons and Unreason," *Foreign Affairs* 60, no. 2 (Winter 1981–82): 331.

39. Hoffmann, "The Western Alliance," p. 107.

40. John E. Reilly, "Foreign Policy in the Second Reagan Administration: Alliance Interests, Ideology, and Domestic Pressures," in *Reagan's Leadership and the Atlantic Alliance: Views from Europe and America*, ed. Walter Goldstein (Washington, D.C.: Pergamon-Brassey's, 1986), p. 106.

41. Joseph S. Nye, "Gorbachev's Russia and U.S. Options," in *Gorbachev's Russia and American Foreign Policy*, eds. Seweryn Bialer and Michael Mandelbaum (Boulder, Colo.: Westview Press, 1988), pp. 385–86.

42. Layne, p. 26; and James Chace, "Europe and America: Double Isolationism," *SAIS Review* 7, no. 4 (Summer 1982): 11.

43. Tugendhat and Wallace, p. 62.

44. Secretary of State for Defense, *Statement on the Defense Estimates of 1987* (London: HMSO, Her Majesty's Stationery Office, 1987), p. 1.

45. Angela Stent, "Franco-Soviet Relations from de Gaulle to Mitterrand," *French Politics and Society* 7, no. 1 (Winter 1989): 15.

46. Dominique Moisi, "French Foreign Policy," *Foreign Affairs* 67, no. 1 (Fall 1988): 153.

47. Cyr, p. 62.

48. Robin Toner, "Americans Are Warming to Soviet Union, Poll Finds," *The New York Times*, December 3, 1989, p. 15, and "Text of President Bush's Speech on Relations Between the East and the West," *The New York Times*, November 23, 1989, p. A6.

49. Henry A. Kissinger, "Strains in the Alliance," *Foreign Affairs* 41, no. 2 (January 1963): p. 261.

50. Reginald Dale, "U.S./Europe: More Than an Ocean Between Them," *The Atlantic Community Quarterly* 23, no. 3 (Fall 1985): 236; and Stanley Hoffmann, *Dead Ends: American Foreign Policy in the New Cold War* (Cambridge, Mass.: Ballinger, 1983), p. 181.

51. Henry A. Kissinger, *The Troubled Partnership: Reappraisal of the Atlantic Alliance* (New York: McGraw-Hill, 1965), p. 6.

52. Wolf Mendl, *Western Europe and Japan Between the Superpowers* (New York: St. Martin's Press, 1984), p. 66.

53. Lawrence Eagleburger, "Statement," *U.S. Policy Toward Europe*, Hearing before the Subcommittee on Europe and the Middle East of the Committee on Foreign Affairs, HR, 99th Cong., 2nd Sess., July 22, 1986 (Washington, D.C.: Government Printing Office, 1986), p. 3.

54. Moisi, p. 155; and James Schlesinger, "Reykjavik and Revelations: A Turn of the Tide?" *Foreign Affairs* 65, no. 3 (1986): 435.

55. Michael Howard, "A European Perspective on the Reagan Years," *Foreign Affairs* 66, no. 3 (1988): 484.

56. Robert W. Tucker, "Reagan's Foreign Policy," *Foreign Affairs* 68, no. 1 (1989): 17.

57. Gregory F. Treverton, *Making the Alliance Work: The United States and Western Europe* (Ithaca, N.Y.: Cornell University Press, 1985), p. 15.

58. Michael Wines, "Allied Arms Outlays Still Lag, Pentagon Says," *The New York Times*, April 18, 1990, p. A5.

59. Secretary of State for Defense, *Statement on Defense Estimates, 1989*, vol. 1 (London: HMSO, Her Majesty's Stationery Office, 1989), p. 2.

60. Irving Kristol, "Should Europe Be Concerned About Central America?" in *Third World Instability: Central America as a European-American Issue*, ed. Andrew J. Pierre (New York: Council on Foreign Relations, 1985), p. 64.

61. Marian Leighton, *The Deceptive Lure of Détente* (New York: St. Martin's Press, 1989), p. 104.

62. Raymond L. Garthoff, *Détente and Confrontation: American-Soviet Relations from Nixon to Reagan* (Washington, D.C.: The Brookings Institution, 1985), p. 25.

63. Garthoff, p. 29.

64. Michael Mandelbaum, "Ending the Cold War," *Foreign Affairs* 68, no. 2 (Spring 1989): 17.

65. Bowie, p. 59.

66. Garthoff, p. 52.

67. Kenneth Dyson, "European Détente in Historical Perspective," in *European Détente: Case Studies of the Politics of East-West Relations*, ed. Kenneth Dyson (New York: St. Martin's Press, 1986), p. 23; and Jolyon Howorth, "The Third Way," *Foreign Policy*, no. 65 (Winter 1986–87): 121.

68. Brown, p. 73.

69. Bowie, p. 58.

70. Josef Joffe, "The View from Bonn: The Taut Alliance," in *Eroding Empire: Western Relations with Eastern Europe*, eds. Lincoln Gordon, et al. (Washington, D.C.: The Brookings Institution, 1987), p. 151.

71. Joffe, p. 162; and Peter H. Langer, *Transatlantic Discord and NATO's Crises of Cohesion* (Washington, D.C.: Pergamon-Brassey's 1986), pp. 31–32.

72. Garthoff, p. 475.

73. Angela Stent, "The Soviet Union and Western Europe: Divided Continent or Common House?" *The Harriman Institute Forum* 2, no. 9 (September 1989): 2.

74. Langer, p. 475.

75. Axel Lebahn, "The Yamal Gas Pipeline from the USSR to Western Europe in the East-West Conflict," *Aussenpolitik* 34, no. 3 (1983): p. 259; and John P. Hardt, "Changing Perspectives Toward the Normalization of East-West Commerce," in *Controlling East-West Trade and Technology Transfer*, ed. Gary K. Bertsch (Durham, N.C.: Duke University Press, 1988), p. 348.

76. Mendl, p. 102; and William Dawkins, "Western Allies to Relax Curbs on High-tech Sales," *Financial Times*, February 17, 1990, p. 2.

77. Antony J. Blinken, *Ally vs. Ally: America, Europe, and the Siberian Pipeline Crisis* (New York: Praeger, 1987), p. 6.

78. Blinken, p. 4.

79. Sidney L. Jones, "The Integration and Divergence of German and American Economic Interests," in *The Federal Republic of Germany and the United States: Changing Political, Social, and Economic Relations*, eds. James A. Cooney, et al. (Boulder, Colo.: Westview Press, 1984), p. 125.

80. Ferdinand Protzman, "Two German-Soviet Pacts Called Vital First Steps," *The New York Times*, June 13, 1989, p. D11; and Serge Schmemann, "Bonn Declaration: Heal the Wounds," *The New York Times*, June 14, 1989, p. A12.

81. Lebahn, p. 262.

82. Edwina Moreton, "The View from London," in *Eroding Empire: Western Relationships with Eastern Europe*, eds. Lincoln Gordon, et al. (Washington, D.C.: The Brookings Institution, 1987), p. 246.

83. "Thatcher Warns Kohl on Gorbachev," *FBIS-Daily Report, Western Europe*, October 25, 1988, p. 4.

84. "Billion-Pound Sterling Credit Line for USSR," *Daily Telegraph*, October 21, 1988, p. 19.

85. Francis X. Clines, "Economic Pledges Cheer Soviet Aides," *The New York Times*, December 4, 1989, p. A9.

86. Clyde H. Farnsworth, "Tariff Offer Gives Soviets a Foothold," *The New York Times*, December 4, 1989, p. 9; and Clyde H. Farnsworth, "U.S. Set to Ease High-Tech Curb on Eastern Bloc," *The New York Times*, January 23, 1990, p. 1.

87. Richard Nixon, "American Foreign Policy: The Bush Agenda," *Foreign Affairs* 68, no. 1 (1989): 200.

88. Mikhail Gorbachev, *Perestroika: New Thinking for Our Country and the World* (New York: Harper and Row, 1987), pp. 140–41; and Boris Meisser, "New Thinking and Soviet Foreign Policy," *Aussenpolitik* 40, no. 2 (1989): p. 110.

89. Sylvia Woodby, *Gorbachev and the Decline of Ideology in Soviet Foreign Policy* (Boulder, Colo.: Westview Press, 1989), p. 15.

90. David Holloway, "Gorbachev's New Thinking," *Foreign Affairs* 68, no. 3

(1989): 78; and Valéry Giscard d' Estaing, Yasuhiro Nakasone, and Henry A. Kissinger, "East-West Relations," *Foreign Affairs* 68, no. 3 (Summer 1989): 6.

91. Lawrence Freedman, "Managing Alliances," *Foreign Policy*, no. 71 (Summer 1988): 78.

92. "Text of Soviet-FRG Statement, 13 June 1989," *FBIS-Daily Report, Western Europe*, June 13, 1989, p. 10.

93. "Poll Reveals West Germans Trust Gorbachev Most," *FBIS-Daily Report, Western Europe*, June 14, 1989, p. 9.

94. Geoffrey Howe, "East-West Relations: The British Role," *International Affairs* 63, no. 4 (Autumn 1987): 558–59; "Thatcher Speaks on East-West Ties," *FBIS-Daily Report, Western Europe*, 1989, p. 4.

95. "Excerpts from President Mikhail Gorbachev's Address to the Council of Europe in Strasbourg, France," *The New York Times*, July 7, 1989, p. A6.

96. "Excerpts from Gorbachev's Address."

97. Robbin Laird, "The Soviet Union and the Western Alliance: Elements of an Anticoalition Strategy," in *Soviet Foreign Policy*, ed. Robbin Laird (New York: The Academy of Political Science, 1987), p. 106.

98. Pierre Hassner, "The Shifting Foundation," *Foreign Policy*, no. 48 (Fall 1982): 11.

99. Jerry F. Hough, "Gorbachev's Politics," *Foreign Affairs* 68, no. 5 (Winter 1989–90): 40.

100. "Mitterrand on Economy and Foreign Policy," *FBIS-Daily Report, Western Europe*, February 13, 1989, p. 10.

101. Robert Gerald Livingston, "A Washington Look at Europe," in *Foreign Policies of West Germany, France and Britain*, eds. Wolfram F. Hanrieder and Graeme P. Auton (Englewood Cliffs, N.J.: Prentice-Hall, 1980), p. 287.

102. Lester C. Thurow, "America Among Equals," in *Estrangement: America and the World*, ed. Sanford J. Ungar (New York: Oxford University Press, 1985), p. 161; David P. Calleo, *Beyond American Hegemony: The Future of the Western Alliance* (New York: Basic Books, 1987), p. 4; Robert D. Putnam and Nicholas Bayne, *Hanging Together: The Seven Power Summits* (Cambridge, Mass.: Harvard University Press, 1984), p. 7; and Samuel P. Huntington, "The U.S.—Decline or Renewal?" *Foreign Affairs* 67, no. 2 (Winter 1988/1989): 93.

103. Wolfram F. Hanrieder, *Germany, America, Europe: Forty Years of German Foreign Policy* (New Haven, Conn.: Yale University Press, 1989), p. 324.

104. Huntington, p. 79.

105. Paul Kennedy, *The Rise and Fall of the Great Powers: Economic Change and Military Conflict from 1500 to 2000* (New York: Random House, 1987), p. 515.

106. Robert J. Lieber, "Secular Changes in the Atlantic Alliance: Will NATO Fragment or Manage to Survive?" in *Fighting Allies: Tensions Within the Atlantic Alliance*, ed. Walter Goldstein (London: Brassey's Defense Publishers, 1986), p. 179; and Robert Keohane, *After Hegemony: Cooperation and Discord in the World Political Economy* (Princeton, N.J.: Princeton University Press, 1985), p. 9.

107. Leigh Bruce, "Europe's Locomotive," *Foreign Policy*, no. 78 (Spring 1990): 74–75.

108. Wayne Sandholtz and John Zysman, "1992: Recasting the European Bargain," *World Politics* 42, no. 1 (October 1989): 106.

109. Lord Young, "Creating a Single European Market: A British View," *The World Today* 44, no. 3 (March 1988): 38.

110. Commission of the European Communities, "Single European Act," *Bulletin of the European Communities*, Supplement 2/86 (1986), p. 5.

111. Alain Madelin, "Creating a Single European Market: A French View," *The World Today* 44, no. 3 (March 1988): 41.

112. Steven Greenhouse, "Europeans Unite to Compete With Japan and U.S.," *The New York Times*, August 21, 1989, p. A1; and Steven Prokesch, "Europe Taking a Lead in Growth," *The New York Times*, January 15, 1990, p. A23.

113. Ferdinand Protzman, "The Germanys as an Economic Giant," *The New York Times*, November 1989, Section 3, p. 1; and Alan Riding "Rifts Threaten European Community's Plan to Remove Borders," *The New York Times*, April 16, 1990, p. A5.

114. Steven Greenhouse, "Workers Want Protection from the Promises of 1992," *The New York Times*, June 25, 1989, p. E2; and Patrick Blum, "Portugal Tells Investors It Is Gateway to Europe," *Financial Times*, February 15, 1990, p. 3.

115. Lester C. Thurow, "Europe: Closed Fortress," *The Boston Globe*, 27 June 1989, p. 62.

116. "EEC—United States," *Europe: Agence Internationale D'Information Pour La Presse (cited as Europe)*, May 25, 1989, p. 7; Nancy Dunne, "Call for U.S. Sanctions on EC," *Financial Times*, 7 March 1990, p. 6; and Clyde H. Farnsworth, "U.S. Backs Japan in Europe Auto Debate," *The New York Times*, February 23, 1990, p. C1.

117. Clyde H. Farnsworth, "Panel Sees Trade Threat from Europe," *The New York Times*, June 1, 1989, p. D13.

118. Barry P. Bosworth and Robert Z. Lawrence, "America's Global Role: From Dominance to Interdependence," in *Restructuring American Foreign Policy*, ed. John D. Steinbruner (Washington, D.C.: The Brookings Institution, 1989), p. 45.

119. Leon Hurwitz, *The European Community and the Management of International Cooperation* (Westport, Conn.: Greenwood Press, 1987), p. 208.

120. Wolfgang Wessels, "European Political Cooperation: A New Approach to Foreign Policy," in *European Political Cooperation: Towards a Foreign Policy for Western Europe*, eds. David Allen, Reinhardt Rummel, and Wolfgang Wessels (London: Butterworth Scientific, 1982), p. 3; and Commission of the European Communities, p. 18.

121. William Wallace, "Introduction: Cooperation and Convergence in European Foreign Policy," in *National Foreign Policies and European Political Cooperation*, ed. Christopher Hill (London: Allen and Unwin, 1983), p. 2.

122. Stanley Hoffmann, "The U.S. and Western Europe: Wait and Worry," *Foreign Affairs* 63, no. 3 (1985): p. 648.

123. Reinhardt Rummel and Wolfgang Wessels, "The Federal Republic of Germany: New Responsibilities, Old Restraints," in *National Foreign Policies and European Political Cooperation*, p. 40.

124. Christopher Hill, "Britain: A Convenient Schizophrenia," in *National Foreign Policies and European Political Cooperation*, p. 24.

125. Alfred Cahen, *The Western European Union and NATO* (London: Brassey's Defense Publishers, 1989), p. 6.

126. Cahen, p. 7.

127. David Harvey and Dexter Jerome Smith, "In Defense of Europe: The Western European Union Reinvigorated," in *Drifting Apart?*, ed. Christopher Coker, p. 136.

128. Secretary of State for Defense, p. 16.

129. "Excerpts from Kohl's Speech on Reunification of Germany," *The New York Times*, November 29, 1989, p. A11.

130. Bernard E. Trainor, "Shift in the Western Alliance's Focus: From Moscow to a United Germany?," *The New York Times*, February 18, 1990, p. A11; and R. W. Apple, "Bonn Flexes Its New Muscles in Relations with Washington," *The New York Times*, May 22, 1989, p. A7.

2

The NATO Allies and the Third World: Divergent Interests and Strategies

The Korean War, the Cuban missile crisis, Vietnam, the Soviet invasion of Afghanistan, and Soviet-Cuban involvement in southern Africa and Nicaragua had contributed to a climate that facilitated the nuclear arms race, which ultimately threatened European as well as global security and sharpened tensions within the NATO alliance. Whereas Europeans and Americans agreed on the nature of the Soviet threat in Europe, even though they sometimes had different and conflicting strategies for addressing it, American policy in the Third World disillusioned the allies and reduced their enthusiasm for giving priority to Atlantic, over European, relations.[1] Although the West Europeans had pursued their own interests in an atmosphere of détente with Moscow throughout much of the period of U.S.-Soviet rivalry, it was not until competition between the superpowers in the Third World declined that Europeans were able to realize many of their principal objectives.

The revival of the Cold War in the late 1970s and early 1980s only exacerbated problems that had been eroding alliance cohesion since the Korean War and the Suez crisis. Conflicts beyond Europe highlighted divergent American and European interests and power capabilities and heightened tensions in the alliance as the allies adopted strategies designed to safeguard their respective interests. American activities undermined European interests in China, the Middle East, Latin America, Eastern Europe, and the Soviet Union, and made superpower confrontation in Europe a likely consequence of regional wars. Europeans were only too aware of the Cuban missile crisis, a confrontation which had helped to shape a doomsday scenario that "spelled annihilation without representation" for them.[2]

If the Europeans distanced themselves from Washington's foreign policies in order to protect their own interests, Americans perceived their allies as not only disloyal but also as unwilling to shoulder their fair share of NATO's responsibility for defending Western interests, especially in Europe. While crises such as the Arab-Israeli War of 1973, and the OPEC-engineered oil shortage which grew out of that conflict, sharply divided the alliance, it was European reluctance to support U.S. policy on Afghanistan that led Americans to seriously question whether defending Europe should be a major priority. This marked a significant shift in the political context of the alliance.[3] As Henry Kissinger argued, "an alliance at odds over central issues of East-West diplomacy, economic policy, and relations with the Third World is in serious, and obvious, difficulty. Indeed it cannot be called an alliance if it agrees on no significant issue."[4]

NATO AND THIRD WORLD CONFLICTS

Whereas the Korean War may have strengthened NATO by highlighting Communist expansionism and by triggering the allies' decision to integrate West Germany into the Western alliance, it also signaled trouble for organizational cohesion and burden-sharing in areas beyond Europe. Although the Korean operation was conducted under the auspices of the United Nations, it had significant implications for NATO. Apart from the relatively minor contributions of war-ravaged Western Europe to the American-led Korean operation, the allies were concerned about directing essential resources away from reconstruction efforts in Europe for a war that, even though peripheral to their interests, could ultimately lead to another major war in Europe with the Soviet Union. By ushering in the Cold War, the Korean conflict consolidated the Soviet and American presence in Europe.[5] However, the sense of common purpose that generally characterized the alliance in Europe was not extended to the Third World.

Power discrepancies among the allies and their changing world views influenced them to define NATO's functions differently. At a very fundamental level, the Americans and Europeans believed that NATO should be limited to Western Europe in order to concentrate on its principal objective of preventing Soviet aggression and expansion there. At another level, the allies differed on how interests in the Third World should be protected, a problem that was never satisfactorily resolved. Confident of its strength, the United States could not foresee circumstances that would require allied assistance outside of Europe, and calculated that an expanded relationship with the allies would restrict its flexibility in foreign affairs.[6] The Soviet threat, largely confined to Europe in the early 1950s, was secondary, although clearly related, to decolonization in areas under the control of the European allies. Since the United States opposed continued colonization, a position also held by the Soviet Union as far as areas outside Europe were concerned, it was almost inevitable that European efforts to retain control over colonies in Asia and Africa would be resisted by Washington. Given their relative inability to defend their farflung empires, the West Europeans could either redefine their interests to match their ability to protect them or they could attempt to enlist American support.

France, to a much greater extent than Great Britain, had perceived its colonies as integral parts of its territory and was therefore very reluctant to grant them independence. But, unable to maintain control alone over its colonies in the vastly altered postwar international environment, France attempted to obtain support from its allies, particularly the United States, for its Indochina war in general and specifically for its beleaguered garrison at Diem Bien Phu in 1954.[7] Although Washington's refusal to aid Paris in its colonial wars eventually influenced the latter to retreat from Vietnam, the United States, in a tragic case of irony, found itself deeply involved in the Vietnam quagmire from which it had earlier persuaded the French to escape. Not only would Vietnam divide American society and defeat the War on Poverty at home, it would ultimately diminish America's power within the Western alliance and the world and influence Bush to use massive force in the Persian Gulf to "kick the Vietnam syndrome." Yet France did not avoid repeating many of the mistakes it made in Indochina during its war with Algeria from 1957 to 1962.

The Suez crisis of 1956 clearly demonstrated that military actions beyond Europe were potentially detrimental to alliance cohesion and that dependence on American military power could undermine the particular interests of the West European allies. Since neither the Soviet Union nor the United States perceived the continuation of colonialism in the Third World to be in their interest, the obvious attempt by France and Britain to retain their dominant position in Egypt was not perceived by America in the context of the East-West rivalry. While Britain and France believed that the nationalization of the Suez Canal and Egypt's acceptance of Soviet arms indicated collaboration between Cairo and Moscow against Western security interests, the United States, which was less dependent on the Canal for shipping and self-sufficient in petroleum, did not perceive the crisis in terms of a Soviet threat to NATO. Failing to obtain a united Western policy against President Gamal Nasser's nationalization of the Suez Canal, Britain and France, joined by Israel, decided to use their own forces that were assigned to NATO to attack Egypt. The United States not only refused to assist the allies but actually sided with Egypt and the Soviet Union to force France, Britain, and Israel to end their invasion of Egypt.[8] This crisis reinforced America's status as a superpower and underscored British and French decline. Equally important, it prompted the French to become more assertive in the area of defense, to develop their own independent nuclear arsenal, and eventually to withdraw from NATO's military command. And when the British, who were also severely humiliated by the Suez experience, resumed their "special relationship" with the United States, France was convinced that the British and the Americans wanted to dominate Western Europe. Ultimately, however, the Europeans concluded from their experience in Egypt that they should limit NATO's responsibilities to Europe, a decision that would later cause the United States to resent its allies' unwillingness to get involved in Third World conflicts that it perceived to be influenced by the Soviet Union.

In addition to the Suez crisis, a combination of factors persuaded Europeans to distance themselves from American activities in the Third World. Having for the most part relinquished their colonial possessions and having adjusted to their postwar reduced military status, the allies concentrated on finding alternative approaches to political and military domination of the former colonial areas. Both France and Britain developed political and economic power through integrating markets and pooling their resources. Germany's participation in Third World conflicts was limited not only by its preoccupation on economic issues but also by its recent past and a constitution that restricted military operations to the protection of its borders. Even Britain, which still had significant military capabilities, diminished its military presence overseas. The decline of Britain's economic might, its military and political dependence on the United States, and the emergence of well-armed, powerful Third World states combined to erode Britain's willingness to allocate significant resources beyond Western Europe.[9] Furthermore, divergent European and American interests in Europe and the Third World prompted the allies to distance themselves from the United States in regional conflicts. Many European countries, especially those with strong Communist and Socialist parties, refrained, to the extent possible, from rekindling strong anticolonial sentiments among the general public. By the early 1970s the Americans and Europeans had completely reversed positions on military involvement in the Third World.

The Europeans had consistently refused to openly cooperate with the United States, and often criticized American actions in the Third World. During the Yom Kippur War in 1973 the Europeans, with the exception of the Portuguese, refused to grant permission for the United States to refuel its planes on their territory because they did not want to jeopardize their relations with the Arab world by appearing to support the American airlift of supplies to Israel. Similarly, among the West European allies, only Britain allowed American planes to use NATO facilities on its territory during the 1986 air raid on Libya. These and other crises demonstrated not only a degree of intra-alliance rivalry and Europe's determination to pursue independent foreign policies but also profound disagreements about NATO's proper function in the Third World and how to respond to Soviet-Cuban activities there.[10] Nevertheless, the Anglo-American partnership within the alliance often resulted in British-American cooperation. When Britain retook the Falkland/Malvinas Islands from Argentina in 1982, the United States supplied essential logistical support. As May and Treverton put it, "in a war over symbols and prestige, not one for survival, no other American ally—not even Israel—could have obtained support of such extent, given ungrudgingly and with little or no sign of dissent."[11] But this degree of out-of-area cooperation was an exception. Conflicting American and West European interests in and inconsistent perceptions of the Third World created severe strains in NATO.

AMERICAN AND EUROPEAN PERCEPTIONS OF THE THIRD WORLD

A country's perception of the world is strongly influenced by its historical experiences, its power capabilities, its cultural values, and its self-perception. The United States' relations with the Third World, often characterized by paradox, reflect deeply held values and attitudes prevalent in the society. This is equally valid for European countries. And it is the fundamental difference in societal attitudes that influenced the allies to take radically different approaches to Third World problems. An equally important factor is the experience that the United States and Western Europe have had with the Third World. Regarding itself as morally superior to other countries, lacking a history of overseas imperialism, and having fought for its own independence from a colonial power, the United States could superficially identify with the Third World during the period of rapid decolonization that followed World War II. But American anticolonialism was driven not so much by concern for the people of the developing countries as it was by an effort to undermine European dominance of those areas in an atmosphere of intense competition with the Soviet Union for geostrategic gains. Paradoxically, the diminution of European power and the emergence of social-istically inclined societies throughout Europe transformed Western Europe's relations with the Third World. Although many of their previous assumptions of racial and cultural superiority remained, the Europeans were becoming more sympathetic to developments in their former colonies. It was the United States that had become more bellicose, conservative, and even reactionary in response to radical changes.

Yet the foundations of these conflicting European and American approaches had been laid much earlier in the various countries' histories and were modified by particular events over a long period. On the surface, America's revolutionary background could be seen as equipping it to deal with major social, political, and economic upheavals in the developing areas. But unlike the French Revolution, which was concerned with the immediacy of suffering, the American Revolution remained committed primarily to preserving freedoms by creating permanent institutions. The conditions that precipitated the American War of Independence and the eventual outcome made the American experience relatively unique and inherently limited beyond the rhetorical level in its application to Asia, Africa, and Latin America. This problem is best articulated by Hannah Arendt who argued that

the superior wisdom of the American founders in theory and practice is conspicuous and impressive enough, and yet has never carried with it sufficient persuasiveness and plausibility to prevail in the tradition of revolution. It is as though the American Revolution was achieved in a kind of ivory tower into which the fearful spectacle of human misery, the haunting voices of abject poverty, never penetrated.[12]

But if the American Revolution did not contain the essential ingredients that would help foreign policymakers to understand radical changes in the Third World, the problem was exacerbated by underlying social attitudes.

Although the United States perceived itself as the "beacon on the hill" and as an alternative to the "evil Europeans," its history is filled with both extremely positive attitudes toward Europeans and almost congenital hatred of nonwhites. This paradox was present from the very beginning of the country's settlement. There were exceptions to the widespread hostility toward nonwhites. The original European settlers at Jamestown and Boston demonstrated concern for the welfare, education, and spiritual well-being of the Indians they encountered. Harvard College, for example, regarded educating the Indians as a primary objective of the institution. But the predominant American attitude toward the Indians was more conducive to destruction than salvation. As Charles William Maynes put it, "to the waves of white settlers it seemed as though their civilization could survive only by subjugating and destroying the other. America's earliest history with the so-called Third World peoples was one of conquest and betrayal."[13] The forced removal of the ancestors of African-Americans from Africa and their enslavement in the United States reinforced both these attitudes of hostility and the tendency to convert. While the Europeans engaged in similar practices in Africa, Asia, Latin America, and in the United States, their own societies in recent history were comparatively free of the harshness and brutality that characterized American society. The relative European detachment from, or ignorance of, what occurred in distant colonies fostered a less antagonistic behavioral pattern in relations with the Third World.

Separated from European hostilities by the Atlantic and endowed with abundant natural resources, America provided almost limitless opportunities for the Europeans who settled the country. Not burdened by the pernicious effects of rigid social stratification so widespread in Europe, Americans of European descent could achieve extraordinary wealth through hard work, careful planning, and self-discipline. American Indians, enslaved Africans, and the few Asians who managed to circumvent the exclusionary laws governing nonwhite immigration until relatively recently did not receive the same rewards from their hard work and were excluded from access to major economic opportunities. Based upon the dominant view that anyone could be prosperous in the United States, American policymakers and the society at large eventually subscribed to the notion that poor people were inherently lazy and therefore undeserving of long-term assistance. Unlike the Canadians who came from the Tory roots of the North American colonies and who believed that poor people should be treated kindly and respectfully, the American Whigs developed a deep-seated aversion to the poor and a feeling that any help for less-fortunate members of society should be given on a strictly temporary basis.[14] These attitudes not only operated domestically but also influenced Americans' perceptions of the Third World. The Europeans' own experience led them to a different conclusion; namely, that there are structural causes of poverty that even hard work cannot surmount.

Compared to many of the Europeans, Americans lacked understanding of and empathy for the Third World. At the root of U.S. policy failures in the Third World were "deeply ingrained American ethnocentrism, an inability to understand the Third World on its own terms, an insistence on viewing it through the lenses of its own experience, and the condescending and patronizing attitudes that such ethnocentrism implies."[15] Although American foreign policy was directed toward preventing Communist expansion in the Third World for more than forty years after World War II, these attitudes have not changed significantly. Consequently, most postwar U.S. foreign policy failures have occurred in the Third World and many American presidents have been humiliated and voted out of office because of them. The Bay of Pigs fiasco, Vietnam, Afghanistan, the hostage crisis in Iran, the Iran-Contra scandal, and the Persian Gulf crisis have had a tremendous impact on recent American presidents.

Because anticommunism had been the organizing principle of American foreign policy during the Cold War and because most confrontations between Washington and Moscow were played out in the Third World, U.S. policymakers essentially viewed developing areas in strategic-military terms.[16] Radical regimes were therefore perceived as assisting Communist expansion in the East-West struggle. U.S. foreign assistance was concentrated not on the countries with greatest need but on those that were regarded as bulwarks against the Soviet threat. Thus, Pakistan, Turkey, the Philippines, Israel, and Egypt received a disproportionate share of U.S. foreign aid, a policy that was openly questioned in early 1990 by Senator Robert Dole after it was generally agreed that the Cold War was over. The reinvigorated anti-Communist crusade under the Reagan administration was largely indifferent to suffering in the Third World and was obviously at odds with the interests and policies of the allies. Western Europeans clearly did not share many American perceptions of the Third World or the nature of the Soviet threat and how to respond to it. Reagan's policies toward Nicaragua, El Salvador, and the Palestinian-Israeli conflict, and his general predilection for military solutions to regional problems were harshly

criticized by many Europeans. Rather than demonstrating strength and resolve, from the European perspective, the Reagan administration revealed
its profound ignorance of, and lack of empathy with, complex Third World
cultures.[17]

Although Europeans also suffer from ethnocentrism, their long experiences in Asia, Africa, and Latin America have given them a greater sensitivity
to developments in these areas. The cultural, economic, political, and military linkages between Europe and the Third World that were created by
colonialism inevitably influenced the allies' perceptions of these areas. Numerous institutional and family ties consolidated their commercial and political interactions. Europe's own economic problems, highlighted by
America's invitation to its "huddled masses yearning to breathe free" to
take advantage of opportunities in the New World, not only fostered economic relations with colonial areas but also gave Europeans a greater understanding of the structural aspects of poverty that are so pervasive in
Third World societies. Hardships endured during World War II heightened
awareness among Europeans of the need for government to play a central
role in economic revitalization, the allocation of resources, and redistri-
bution of benefits to assist the less-fortunate members of society. This reality
undoubtedly modified European views on the causes of poverty and the
responsibility of the poor for their condition. The social welfare systems
that emerged throughout Western Europe were more akin to embryonic
Third World social systems than to the more individualistic American society. Consequently, Europeans are more sensitive than Americans to the
social and economic foundations of regional instability.

Among the Western allies, France is most sympathetic to Third World
problems and demands for a New International Economic Order (NIEO)
that would facilitate a more equitable distribution of wealth between the
industrialized countries and the Third World. In fact, the term "Third
World" was coined by French writers as a reminder of the Third Estate, an
unprivileged majority imbued with a right to equal status.[18] If the American
Revolution focused on political rights, the French Revolution was primarily
concerned with economic issues. Consequently, French foreign policymakers
tend to emphasize the connection between poverty and conflicts in developing countries and are inclined to stress the North-South rather than the
East-West division of Third World instability. The views articulated by
French policymakers are also embraced by the general public. France's determination to maintain close ties with the Third World was strongly supported by the French political elite.[19] Furthermore, domestic pressures within
France and the other European countries for governments to provide various
services help to shape foreign policymakers' perceptions of developing
areas.[20] As evidence of France's support of Third World issues, Mitterrand
called upon the leaders of the seven leading industrialized democracies,
meeting in France during the bicentennial of its Revolution, to search for

ways to reduce Third World debt. To further demonstrate France's solidarity with poor countries, Mitterrand invited leaders from twenty-four developing nations to dinner at the New Glass Pyramid at the Louvre, to the opening of the new Bastille Opera House, and to the Bicentennial Parade on the Champs-Elysées, along with leaders from the major industrial states.[21] Perhaps equally important was France's determination to distinguish its policies from those of the United States and to underscore French independence and its role as an alternative to the superpowers in the Third World. France's search for a diplomatic solution, against the odds, to the Persian Gulf crisis on the eve of Operation Desert Storm demonstrated its sensitivity toward Third World issues.

As Washington vacillated between unilateralism and allied cooperation, the West Europeans often "found themselves relegated virtually to satellite status, their value judged according to their loyalty and their loyalty assessed by their readiness to accede unquestioningly to American demands."[22] But the allies, needing U.S. protection, were concerned about the consequences of Third World upheaval for European security, particularly the diversion of resources from Europe to regional conflicts and the likelihood that superpower confrontation could result in a war in Central Europe. Given the complex nature of the Atlantic partnership, West Europeans' attitudes toward the Third World were partly influenced by their perceptions of the United States. Unresolved conflicts between the conservative ideologues and the conservative pragmatists within the Reagan administration, epitomized by Secretary of State Alexander Haig's assertion that "a guerrilla war" was being waged against him by an official in the White House, led to confusion among the allies about the precise nature of American policy in the Middle East, Latin America, and Africa. Furthermore, America's "embrace of Pinochet's Chile, the Turkish military regime, authoritarian South Korea, and Duvalier's Haiti, even as partial allies in defense of the free world," was viewed by Europeans with some apprehension.[23] Thus, Washington's demands for European cooperation against regimes supported by the Soviet Union and Cuba were met with skepticism. From the predominant European point of view, American foreign policy in the Third World was partly responsible for the threats to Western security interests, such as the Arab oil embargo in 1973. Not all West Europeans perceived U.S. policy or the Soviet threat uniformly. Nevertheless, the dominant European view of regional conflicts and Soviet participation in them was significantly different from that of the Reagan administration.

Having defined their interests in a manner that was consistent with their limited power capabilities, many Europeans tended to focus on indigenous causes of Third World armed struggles, discounted Soviet-Cuban involvement, and regarded American policies as misguided overreactions. Moreover, there was a widespread perception among Europeans that both superpowers were engaged in a power struggle that emanated more from conflicting ideologies than from the facts on the ground. And partly because of their desire to insulate Western Europe from the U.S.-Soviet rivalry, many allies drew parallels between Soviet policies in Afghanistan and U.S. policies in Central America.[24]

As postwar power configurations elevated what were essentially nationalistic and ethnic struggles into strategic contests between East and West, the newly independent countries of Asia and Africa vied for either Soviet or American support and modified their ideological positions when necessary. However, the Vietnam War triggered a wave of anti-Americanism in the Third World that forced many countries to rethink their strategy of encouraging superpower involvement in regional wars. As Nacht observed, "the death and destruction associated with American military intervention, the demonstrated unreliability of the duration of U.S. security commitments, the decline in American willingness to provide security and economic assistance, and the liability of being associated with a power that was often accused of being supportive of the status quo were serious warning signals for Third World leaders."[25] Despite continued interest in American support, developing countries increasingly turned to Western Europeans, especially the Social Democrats, as an alternative to both superpowers.

The general Third World perception was that Europeans were more sympathetic than Americans to its interests, which included economic development and increased foreign assistance. Western European commitment to détente and economic growth coincided with developing countries' need to reduce hostilities and to focus on mobilizing human and material resources. Because the Europeans were more ideologically disposed than Americans to downplay the importance of Socialist rhetoric and to encourage changes, the former were frequently seen as champions of Third World causes and intermediaries with access to Washington. Such a role was also beneficial to the allies, particularly the West Germans, who wanted to avoid being directly involved in any problem that could have derailed détente. Furthermore, Europe's preoccupation with trade and diplomacy as instruments of foreign policy appealed to the Third World. The relative decline in U.S. economic power prompted developing states to turn their attention toward the EC and Japan. Economic power, from the Third World's viewpoint, implied power to assist but not power to assail, which made the EC more attractive than the United States.[26]

EUROPEAN INTERESTS IN THE THIRD WORLD

Even though the West Europeans recognized the United States' influence throughout the Third World, many of them believed that their historical ties with the developing countries facilitated deeper relationships with these states and that their advice and initiatives were accepted with less mistrust.[27] Primarily concerned with establishing the European economic enterprise, the allies concentrated on maintaining important economic ties with the Third World, particularly access to essential raw materials. Such a narrow definition of national interests, especially among the West Germans, often led to intra-alliance conflict. But even Britain, which retained an active military presence overseas and was careful not to strain its "special relationship" with the United States, usually collaborated with independent-minded France and commercially oriented West Germany to insulate economic cooperation with the Third World from superpower rivalries. Historical and cultural ties and commercial interest influenced Europeans to distance themselves from and sometimes oppose the United States in areas of conflict. Among the numerous examples was Europe's refusal to support the U.S. blockade of Cuba. Spain even decided to assist Castro's regime by establishing a direct-air link with Cuba. (Iberia Airlines flew weekly from Madrid to Havana.) Spain had close historical links with Cuba, and it desired to reemerge on the world stage by rejuvenating relations with Latin America. General Francisco Franco wanted to improve his bargaining power with Washington in negotiations on U.S. bases in Spain as well as to express his dislike for the United States, and Spain wanted to safeguard its growing trade with Cuba.[28]

Historical ties between Western Europe and the Third World complemented as well as frustrated American foreign policy objectives. For example, French influence in Africa, British links to South Africa and elsewhere, Germany's connections to Namibia, and Portugal's ties to Angola and Mozambique were sometimes beneficial to U.S. interests. On the other hand, Washington's penchant for taking unilateral actions without consulting its allies and its inclination to use military force led to friction in areas where there were opportunities for closer allied collaboration. But even as the Europeans pursued their own interests independently of Washington, they believed that they were helping to protect Western interests in the Third World.

Both France and Britain tended to concentrate their resources on their former colonies and dependent territories. British warships patrolled international waters in the Persian Gulf between 1980 and 1989. And Britain responded quickly when Kuwait, a former self-governing protectorate, was occupied by Iraq. Britain had forces stationed in Cyprus, the Indian Ocean, the Far East, Belize, and in the Falklands. France also maintained forces in the Indian Ocean, the Pacific, the Caribbean dependencies of Guadeloupe and Martinique, and in various parts of Francophone Africa.[29] Furthermore, both France and Britain, consistent with their objective to remain militarily strong, provided military assistance to many Third World countries, especially to those with which they had significant arms trade. The Third World arms market was comparatively more important for France because of its decision to leave NATO's military structure, which put it at a disadvantage in selling weapons in Europe.[30]

Due in part to their emphasis on the arms trade, Western Europeans often found themselves at odds with the United States in areas such as the Middle East and the Persian Gulf. Since the Six Day War between Israel and the Arab states in 1967, the divergence between European and American policies became more apparent. Rising tensions in the Middle East and the Persian Gulf fueled competition and conflict within NATO as France, Britain, and the United States attempted to increase their weapons sales in the area. Although by the mid–1980s Britain had secured the largest contract to sell arms to Saudi Arabia, the underlying frictions which characterized American-French relations surfaced between the two countries as France aggressively competed with the United States. Whereas France was concerned about maintaining the viability of its arms industry and its independent military force by selling sophisticated weapons to Arab states, thereby reducing research and development costs, the United States saw the French actions as a threat to its leverage as an arms supplier because Arab states could simply purchase advanced weapons from France. Thus, from the French perspective, America was undermining France's domestic arms industry and hence its security. But the United States perceived the French as recklessly selling weapons without serious consideration of strategic factors.[31] Although Iraq's invasion of Kuwait underscored America's view, Washington itself became the major arms supplier to the Middle East, the most volatile region, after Operation Desert Storm.

While America had encouraged the reconstruction of Western Europe, it often found itself being eliminated from markets in areas formerly controlled by its allies as they created new institutions to augment economic arrangements that existed under colonial rule. This paradoxical situation eventually created serious strains in the alliance as America became more dependent on Third World markets for the export of its manufactured products and as Western Europe and Japan emerged as its major competitors. As Serfaty observed, such competition was bound to exacerbate existing conflicts over more central issues of a weakened American security guarantee and the continued unraveling of an American-dominated international economic order.[32]

For much of the Cold War period, both France and Britain depended on markets in developing areas for their exports of manufactured products. France, for example, became the major supplier of medium-level technology to Middle East oil-exporting countries during the 1970s. Markets in the Third World were attractive to France, partly because of its inability to effectively compete in Europe with its Common Market partners, particularly West Germany. In the mid-1980s France had a trade deficit with all EEC countries except Greece.[33] Thus, Reagan's renewal of the Cold War was not very appealing to France, despite Mitterrand's distrust of the Soviet Union. Economic realities combined with other factors influenced France to eschew any foreign policy action that would worsen its economic conditions. During the height of the new Cold War, France's steel industry was devastated, with approximately thirty thousand workers unemployed. The automobile, tire, and shipbuilding industries were also severely affected.[34] If French and British economic interests in the Third World were not fully appreciated by the United States, perhaps it was partly because the inclusion of developing countries into the economic integration structures of Western Europe was perceived by the United States as part of the broader issue of Europe's emergence as an economic rival with an increasingly distinctive foreign policy orientation.[35]

In 1956, a year before the EEC was created, France requested that its colonies be integrated into the proposed institutional arrangements. Since its colonies in Africa, Asia, and elsewhere were regarded as overseas departments, and thus integral parts of French territory, the economies of these areas were closely linked to France by a system of preferential trade, budgetary and commercial subsidies, and expatriate personnel and investment.[36] Unlike Britain, which endeavored to terminate political responsibility for its overseas territories when they became economic burdens, France attempted to retain control by distributing the costs of empire among the other Common Market members. Unwilling to shoulder France's economic burdens and concerned about how preferential treatment for French colonies would affect exports from other countries to the Common Market and their own exports to these countries, West Germany and the Netherlands initially opposed the French plan. Eventually, because France insisted on the inclusion of its colonies as a precondition for signing the Treaty of Rome (which created the EEC), the Germans and the Dutch accepted association for overseas territories in order to secure European economic integration.[37]

Despite France's reluctance to grant independence to its colonies, the wave of decolonization, backed by the United States, was too powerful for the French territories to resist. But France insisted on perpetuating close links with the emerging states through bilateral and multilateral trade arrangements. Once again Germany and the Netherlands acquiesced to French designs, and negotiations between the EEC and the French-speaking African states led to the signing of the Yaounde Convention in Cameroon in July 1963.[38] However, major differences between Germany and France on trade issues ultimately facilitated Britain's entry into the EEC, which increased the number of Third World countries associated with the organization. More importantly, it weakened France's power within the EEC.

In addition to opposing France's relationship with its former colonies, Germany was a consistent supporter of broader trade and investment opportunities for German business in Latin America, Asia, and elsewhere. Whereas French commercial interests were advanced by special preferences for African states, German interests were best served by a large, loose association based on the principle of nonreciprocity.[39] Consequently, Germany championed the Commonwealth countries' special relationship with the

EEC. Although France had prevented Britain, Ireland, and Denmark from joining the Common Market in 1961 and 1967, negotiations that commenced in 1972 culminated in the signing of the Treaty of Accession, which enabled these countries to become members in 1973. British membership inevitably led to a more inclusive set of negotiations between the EEC and the former colonies of both France and Britain. These negotiations resulted in the the Lomé Convention in February 1975, an agreement that provided for a system of nonreciprocal tariff concessions to the African, Caribbean, and Pacific (ACP) countries.[40] France had suffered a major defeat.

If Germany was satisfied with the final outcome of these negotiations, the United States was apprehensive. President Nixon's special representative in Brussels, William Eberle, was charged with advocating conformity of EEC-ACP arrangements with the principle of free trade. Britain's abdication of many of its responsibilities in the Caribbean to the United States placed U.S. negotiators in a relatively strong bargaining position. Eberle reaffirmed America's desire to compete on equal terms for ACP markets and reiterated U.S. opposition to reverse preferences granted to the EEC by the ACP countries.[41] Increasingly dependent on America for trade as well as for jobs for its growing number of emigrants, the Caribbean Group was most vulnerable to U.S. pressure. Confronted with the possible loss of preferential trade with America if they granted reverse preferences to the EEC, the Caribbean states adopted a position consistent with Washington's even as they tried to secure solid arrangements with the Europeans for their exports of sugar, bananas, and bauxite.[42]

The United States was faced with the reality of interdependence, especially with developing countries. U.S. trade, both imports from and exports to Third World states, grew at approximately 6 percent annually during the 1970s. By 1981 these countries were purchasing 41 percent of America's exports—a greater share than Japan and Western Europe combined. However, economic problems in the Third World during the first half of the 1980s resulted in a decline in U.S. exports to developing countries from $88 billion in 1980 to $77 billion in 1985.[43]

The Lomé Convention established a comprehensive export stabilization program, known as STABEX, to guarantee the income the ACP countries received from their exports of raw materials and to protect EEC members from fluctuations in prices for commodities from the Third World. Apart from encouraging trade primarily with Europe, STABEX was perceived as a disincentive to international economic diversification because it brought the ACP countries under the firm grip of Europe.[44] France, for example, augmented ties with its former colonies by encouraging them to remain within the franc zone, asserting that the stability and liquidity that such an arrangement provided African currencies facilitated trade, aid, and investment beneficial to the African states.[45]

Rapid political changes in Eastern Europe also challenged traditional ties between the Third World and Western Europe. West Germany and France were understandably preoccupied with events in East Germany, Poland, Hungary, and the Soviet Union. Consequently, they allocated significant resources to Eastern Europe.[46] German reunification also resulted in the transfer of resources from West Germany to East Germany, and the other Europeans, wary of a united Germany with access to developing markets in Eastern Europe, concentrated on Europe 1992 as well as on expanding their investments in Eastern Europe to effectively compete with Germany.

From the Third World's perspective, this meant reduced European interests in the developing countries. African countries, burdened with foreign debt and mismanaged economies, were particularly worried about the shift of international economic assistance to Eastern Europe.[47] The ACP group of countries was obviously uneasy about the impact changes in Eastern Europe would have on negotiations on the Lomé Convention after initial discussions were terminated in October 1989 because the sixty-six ACP countries were dissatisfied with the EC's proposed trade concessions for farm exports and with the amount of financial aid offered. Nevertheless, in December 1989, two months before the agreement was to expire, delegates from the EC and the ACP countries signed a new convention. Under this agreement the ACP countries received a five-year renewable financial package totaling $13.7 billion, approximately $4 billion less than what they requested. The EC also provided $2.3 billion to protect the developing states from losses on the world commodity markets and an additional $1.3 billion to implement economic reforms.[48] Thus, despite the changes in Europe, the Third World continue to be important because Western Europeans have significant interests there.

Western Europe is extremely vulnerable to regional instability because of its reliance on imports of essential resources from the Third World. With the exception of Britain, which is self-sufficient in petroleum due to major discoveries in the North Sea, Western Europe imports most of the oil it consumes. Approximately half of its petroleum imports are supplied by Saudi Arabia, Libya, and Nigeria alone. It imports 79 percent of its iron ore; 81 percent of its copper; 61 percent of its aluminum; 75 percent of its uranium; and virtually all of its tungsten, phosphates, manganese, chromium, cobalt, nickel, and platinum.[49] It is highly unlikely that resources from Eastern Europe could significantly reduce this extreme dependency on critical raw materials imports.

Western Europe's Third World interests could not be easily separated from its complex relationship with the United States within the broader context of the NATO alliance. Despite its determination to preserve NATO as the cornerstone of British and West European security policy, Britain was conscious of conflicting European and American perspectives on the Third

World. Consequently, Britain assumed the role of bridge-builder between the United States and the other allies as opinions differed on strategies for dealing with Soviet actions in the Third World.[50]

EUROPEAN AND AMERICAN APPROACHES TO THIRD WORLD CONFLICTS

Myriad diverse and complex factors combined to influence European and American approaches to Third World conflicts. These included domestic and cultural factors, views of the Soviet threat, definitions of national interests, perceptions of the Third World, power capabilities, intra-alliance rivalries, a desire to pursue independent foreign policies to protect national interests, and European and American perceptions of each other. Strategies selected for dealing with problems in developing areas reflected the varied interests of each country, not only in the Third World but also in Europe. Significant disparities in power capabilities among the allies affected how they defined their interests and their choice of strategies for securing them: the greater their power, the broader they defined their interests. Thus, when Britain and France declined as major powers after World War II, they redefined their interests and attempted to change the game in a way that would enhance their international status and power capabilities.

Strategies adopted for dealing with Third World crises were determined, in part, by complex cultural values, economic problems, public opinion, and institutional cooperation and conflict. Fundamental cultural variations between Europeans themselves on one hand and between Europeans and Americans on the other inevitably led to diverse and often conflicting approaches to out-of-area problems.[51] Whereas Americans favored short-term solutions because of impatience, impulsiveness, and a desire to solve international problems quickly in order to return to domestic matters, Europeans tended to take a long-term approach and were more cognizant of the complexities of the issues in the various crises. West Europeans' emphasis on economic and diplomatic instruments and their general inability to project their military power globally clearly induced them to be more patient than Americans, who had the military capability to intervene in distant areas. America's hostility and bellicosity toward the Third World usually prompted U.S. policymakers to militarize the situation without serious concern for the human suffering involved. However, the Vietnam experience engendered a more muddled message on the use of force. Although not wanting to "lose a country to communism" or to allow dictators like Iraq's Saddam Hussein to "get away with aggression," initially there was little public support for U.S. participation in "another Vietnam." And the tragic aftermath of Operation Desert Storm dampened the euphoria engendered by a "quick, clean military victory." These contradictions contributed to the formulation of inconsistent foreign policies and confused the allies.[52] European political elites, as well as the general public, were disinclined to use force in the Third World.

Since the West Europeans could hardly have been expected to dismantle the social services of their postwar welfare states without facing serious consequences, their margin for maneuver was very narrow. Consequently, the realities of economic health and social stability took precedence over military involvement in Third World struggles.[53] But Britain and France, despite their economic problems, perceived themselves as having international responsibilities that required a military presence in areas beyond Europe, as demonstrated by their participation in Operation Desert Storm. Nevertheless, domestic economic problems influenced Europeans to emphasize economic and diplomatic instruments of foreign policy in relation to Third World conflicts. It was Britain and France that initiated humanitarian aid to Iraqi refugees following Operation Desert Storm.

Another factor affecting the choice of strategies adopted by Europeans and Americans was their perception of the Soviet threat in southern Africa, the Middle East, Nicaragua, and the Persian Gulf, and the most appropriate responses to it. Viewing détente as divisible and determined to insulate Europe from U.S.-Soviet rivalries in the developing areas, the Europeans were inevitably at odds with the Americans, who were committed to the global containment of communism. De Gaulle had consistently advocated excluding developing areas from superpower rivalry, partly because he regarded such competition as reinforcing the dependence on the superpowers of contending factions within poor countries. Perceiving France as an inspirational symbol to these new states, de Gaulle urged them "to do in their parts of the world what he was doing in Europe."[54]

As a global power, the United States saw troubles in specific regions as part of a larger test of America's global leadership, and was therefore induced to take decisive action. For example, as part of an overall policy of containing Communist expansion, U.S. policymakers provided military assistance to El Salvador to prevent the guerrillas from destabilizing the government and armed the Contra rebels in Nicaragua to undermine the Sandinista government. The complex causes of the problems plaguing Nicaragua and El Salvador were essentially overlooked. Although President Carter tried to become more attuned to local causes of regional rivalries, the Soviet invasion of Afghanistan and American presidential election politics shattered his efforts. Reagan intensified the theme to which Carter was forced to return.[55] Similarly, in trying to frustrate Soviet expansion in the Middle East, U.S. policymakers assumed that the United States could build an anti-Soviet strategic consensus by bringing the Israelis and Arabs together, despite ongoing hostilities between them over the unresolved Palestinian question and other problems. For a variety of reasons, the West European allies found it difficult to support U.S. policy in these cases. Disagreeing with America's uncritical support of Israel, the Europeans stressed longer-term strategies to solve the Palestinian problem and strengthen and stabilize conservative, pro-Western Arab regimes as the most effective way of addressing the Soviet threat in the region.[56]

Because the Europeans were actively engaged in developing areas long before the emergence of the Soviet Union, they tended to have different concerns than their American ally, whose interaction with most of the Third World was directly connected to the Communist threat during the Cold War. Although the Europeans (Britain and France in particular) worried about Soviet expansionism, they preferred to focus on indigenous factors that facilitated Soviet involvement. Their preferred strategy was to use economic cooperation with Moscow as a way to modify its behavior, as opposed to America's preference for punishing the Soviets by imposing economic sanctions. Furthermore, often in competition with each other and the United States, the Europeans concentrated on commercial relations with the Third World, assuming that economic and social problems were major causes of regional instability.[57] Further complicating the Europeans' approach to the Third World was their desire to develop a common European foreign policy through the institution of EPC and to distance themselves from controversial American actions in regional rivalries. Reagan's invasion of Grenada in 1983 and his persistent efforts to overthrow the Sandinistas by arming the Contras made it relatively easy for Europeans to contend that, as superpowers, the United States and the Soviet Union were both seeking hegemony and behaving similarly. Neither was viewed as tolerating political diversity within its sphere of influence.[58] Consequently, West Europeans felt no obligation to support their ally. The Persian Gulf crisis elicited a different European response because Iraq's occupation of Kuwait was a clear violation of international law.

As medium powers, the West European states had a vested interest in maintaining stability in international relations and to support efforts to resolve disputes through international institutions. Thus, unlike the United States under the Reagan administration, West European countries emphasized the role of international law and urged compliance with it. Believing that traditional principles of sovereignty and nonintervention in other countries' affairs should be followed, the European allies opposed America's support of the Contra rebels in Nicaragua and Jonas Savimbi in Angola. From their viewpoint, the systematic violation of international rules of conduct was inimical to Western interests and represented a dangerous development that would legitimize similar practices not only by the Soviet Union but also by Islamic fundamentalists.[59]

Apart from the question of the legality of American military support for different groups in various countries, Europeans generally believed that such a strategy was ineffective for several reasons. First, in most instances, assistance was given to militarily ineffective forces which were unlikely to achieve their objectives. Second, many of the groups supported by the United States were weak politically, had little public support, were often flagrant violators of human rights, and were internally divided. Third, Europeans believed that intensifying military conflict rendered a political settlement difficult if not impossible, thereby undermining their own diplomatic and economic foreign policy instruments. Fourth, war furthered Soviet objectives in many cases. Finally, lending American military assistance to these groups tied them to the Western alliance, a relationship that was damaging to the West's reputation and interests. Consequently, Europeans distanced themselves from the United States in most Third World conflicts.[60]

Another reason for Europeans to eschew military solutions emanated from their experiences in the Third World and the devastation they suffered in two world wars. Events in Europe and the Third World were often interrelated. Britain and France, for example, lost their colonies after their power was substantially diminished as a consequence of World War II. It was in the Third World where their loss of great power status was underscored and where America's military might was demonstrated. Even as the United States escalated its military involvement in Vietnam between 1965 and 1968, Britain was reducing its presence in the Middle East and elsewhere. But whereas many Americans concluded that Vietnam was lost to the Communists because of insufficient military power and the lack of domestic support for the war, Europeans saw Vietnam as as reaffirmation of the disutility of military force.[61] These divergent perceptions accounted for the difference between European and American views of Operation Desert Storm. While Europeans saw the war in terms of getting Iraq to comply with international law, Americans viewed the massive use of force as "kicking the Vietnam Syndrome." From the American perspective, the solution was not to rethink the policy, but to apply more military might.

With the exception of Vietnam, America's experience with military power had been successful. But, its efforts to create stability through economic assistance and political ties were less spectacular. The Europeans, on the other hand, had many failures with military force. They were relatively successful in creating economic links with their former colonies and managed to preserve good relations with them. Britain's success with diplomacy in Rhodesia, now Zimbabwe, with America's help, reinforced its commitment to nonmilitary policy instruments.[62] The case studies indicate how crises in the Third World ultimately affected not only superpower relations but also the long-standing American policy in Western Europe, the future of the NATO alliance, and the emergence of Western Europe as an economic and political rival of the United States. The revolutionary changes that occurred in Europe in 1989 and 1990 were inextricably linked to developments in the Third World, the area where the superpowers had risked direct confrontation for more than forty years. And the first major conflict of the post–Cold War period, The Persian Gulf war, demonstrated the reality of interdependence between the Third World, Europe, and the United States.

NOTES

1. Henry A. Kissinger, "Strains in the Alliance," *Foreign Affairs* 41, no. 2 (January 1963): 261.

2. Simon Serfaty, *"After Reagan: False Starts, Missed Opportunities, and New Beginnings* (Washington, D.C.: Johns Hopkins Foreign Policy Institute, 1988), p. 42.

3. Philip Windsor, *Germany and the Western Alliance: Lessons from the 1980 Crisis* (London: International Institute for Strategic Studies, 1981), p. 3.

4. Henry A. Kissinger, "Reflections on a Partnership: British and American Attitudes to Postwar Foreign Policy," *International Affairs* 58, no. 4 (Autumn 1982): 586.

5. Robert E. Osgood, *Alliances and American Foreign Policy* (Baltimore: Johns Hopkins Press, 1968), p. 49.

6. Gregory F. Treverton, *Making the Alliance Work: The United States and Western Europe* (Ithaca, N.Y.: Cornell University Press, 1985), p. 94.

7. Treverton, 94.

8. A. W. Deporte, *Europe Between the Superpowers: The Enduring Balance* (New Haven, Conn.: Yale University Press, 1979), p. 217.

9. Bruce George and Simon Davis, "Rapid Deployment and Reorganization: The Prospects for British Military Operations Out-of-Area," *The Atlantic Quarterly* 25, no. 3 (Fall 1987): 316.

10. Anastasia Pardalis, "European Political Cooperation and the United States," *Journal of Common Market Studies* 25, no. 4 (June 1987): 284; and Christopher Layne, "Superpower Disengagement," *Foreign Policy*, no. 77 (Winter 1989–90): 26.

11. Ernest R. May and Gregory F. Treverton, "Defense Relationships: American Perspectives," in *The Special Relationship: Anglo-American Relations Since 1945*, eds. William Roger Louis and Hedley Bull (Oxford: Clarendon Press, 1986), p. 176.

12. Hannah Arendt, *On Revolution* (New York: Viking Press, 1969), p. 91.

13. Charles William Maynes, "America's Third World Hang-Ups," *Foreign Policy*, no. 71 (Summer 1988): 119.

14. Maynes, p. 124.

15. Howard J. Wiarda, *Ethnocentrism in Foreign Policy: Can We Understand the Third World?* (Washington, D.C.: American Enterprise Institute, 1985), p. 1.

16. Steven R. David, "Why the Third World Matters," *International Security* 14, no. 1 (Summer 1989): 62; Shahram Chubin, "The Content and Background of U.S. Foreign Policy," in *Superpower Competition and Security in the Third World*, eds. Robert S. Litwak and Samuel F. Wells (Cambridge, Mass.: Ballinger, 1988), p. 2; and Roger D. Hansen "The Reagan Doctrine and Global Containment: Revival or Recessional," *SAIS Review* 7, no. 1 (Winter-Spring 1987): 44.

17. Michael Howard, "A European Perspective on the Reagan Years," *Foreign Affairs* 66, no. 3 (1988): 488.

18. Stéphane Hessel, "Mitterrand's France and the Third World," in *The Mit-*

terrand Experiment: Continuity and Change in Modern France, eds. George Ross, Stanley Hoffmann, and Syvia Malzacher (New York: Oxford University Press, 1987), p. 324.

19. Yves Boyer, "French Foreign Policy: Alignment and Assertiveness," The Washington Quarterly 9, no. 4 (Fall 1986): 7.

20. Marie-Claude Smouts, "The External Policy of François Mitterrand," International Affairs 59, no. 2 (Spring 1983): 155; and Dominique Moisi, "French Foreign Policy: The Challenge of Adaptation," Foreign Affairs 67, no. 1 (Fall 1988): 151.

21. Steven Greenhouse, "Mitterrand's Summit Goal Is to Help Poorest Nations," The New York Times, July 11, 1989, p. D1.

22. Howard, p. 490.

23. John Palmer, Europe Without America? The Crisis in Atlantic Relations (New York: Oxford University Press, 1987), p. 52; and Denis Healy, "Statement," in Parliamentary Debates (Commons), Sixth Series, vol. 12, sess. 1981–82, 4–13 November (1981), col. 129.

24. Richard Lowenthal, "Cultural Change and Generational Change in Postwar Western Germany," in The Federal Republic of Germany and the United States: Changing Political, Social, and Economic Relations, eds. James A. Cooney, et al. (Boulder, Colo.: Westview Press, 1984), p. 52.

25. Michael Nacht, "Toward an American Conception of Regional Security," Daedalus 110, no. 1 (Winter 1981): 3.

26. Baard Bredrup Knudsen, Europe Versus America: Foreign Policy in the 1980s (Paris: The Atlantic Institute for International Affairs, 1984), p. 36.

27. Reinhardt Rummel, "Coordination of the West's Crisis Diplomacy," Aussenpolitik 31, no. 2 (1980): 130.

28. Alistair Hennessy, "Spain and Cuba: An Enduring Relationship," in The Iberian-Latin American Connection: Implications for U.S. Foreign Policy, ed. Howard J. Wiarda (Boulder, Colo.: Westview Press, 1986), p. 363.

29. Secretary of State for Defense, Statement on the Defense Estimates, 1989, vol. 1 (London: HMSO, Her Majesty's Stationery Office, 1989), p. 3.

30. Andrew J. Pierre, The Global Politics of Arms Sales (Princeton, N.J.: Princeton University Press, 1982), pp. 86–87.

31. Charles A. Kupchan, The Persian Gulf and the West: The Dilemmas of Security (Boston: Allen and Unwin, 1987), p. 174.

32. Simon Serfaty, The United States, Western Europe, and the Third World: Allies and Adversaries (Washington, D.C.: Center for Strategic and International Studies, 1980), p. 9.

33. Julius W. Friend, Seven Years in France: François Mitterrand and the Unintended Revolution, 1981–1988 (Boulder, Colo.: Westview Press, 1989), p. 105; and Peter A. Hall, Governing the Economy: The Politics of State Intervention in Britain and France (New York: Oxford University Press, 1986), p. 145.

34. Friend, p. 106.

35. Pardalis, p. 274.

36. I. William Zartman, The Politics of Trade Negotiations Between Africa and the European Economic Community (Princeton, N.J.: Princeton University Press, 1971), p. 6.

37. Ellen Frey-Wouters, *The European Community and the Third World: The Lomé Convention and Its Impact* (New York: St. Martin's Press, 1989), p. 182.

38. Frey-Wouters, p. 14; and Emeka Nwokedi, "France's Africa: A Struggle Between Exclusivity and Interdependence," in *Africa in World Politics*, eds. Ralph I. Onwuka and Timothy M. Shaw (New York: St. Martin's Press, 1989), p. 182.

39. Frey-Wouters, p. 252.

40. Serfaty, p. 26.

41. Frey-Wouters, p. 20.

42. Frey-Wouters, p. 31.

43. John W. Sewell, "The Dual Challenge: Managing the Economic Crisis and Technological Change," in *Growth, Exports, and Jobs in a Changing World Economy: Agenda 1988*, eds. John W. Sewell and Stuart K. Tucker (New Brunswick, N.J.: Transaction Books, 1988), p. 10.

44. S.K.B. Asante, "Africa and Europe: Collective Dependence or Interdependence?" in *Africa and Europe: From Partition to Interdependence or Dependence?*, ed. Amadu Sesay (London: Croom Helm, 1986), p. 200.

45. J. Barron Boyd, "France and the Third World: The African Connection," in *Third World Policies of Industrialized Nations*, eds. Phillip Taylor and Gregory A. Raymond (Westport, Conn.: Greenwood Press, 1982), p. 46.

46. "Home Thoughts About Abroad," *The Economist*, November 4, 1989, p. 62.

47. "Head of IMF Touring Africa," *The New York Times*, December 28, 1989, p. A26.

48. "Fourth ACP-EEC Convention Signed in Lomé by More Than Half the World's Countries," *Togo Bulletin* 6, no. 1 (Winter 1990): 7.

49. Roy H. Ginsberg, *Foreign Policy Actions of the European Community* (Boulder, Colo.: Lynne Rienner, 1989), p. 166.

50. Edwina Moreton, "Britain and the Soviet Union," in *Western Approaches to the Soviet Union*, ed. Michael Mandelbaum (New York: Council on Foreign Relations, 1988), p. 61.

51. Gianni Bonvicini, "Out-of-Area Issues," in *The Atlantic Alliance and the Middle East*, eds. Joseph I. Coffey and Gianni Bonvicini (Pittsburgh: University of Pittsburgh Press, 1989), p. 10.

52. Michael D. Barnes, "U.S. Policy in Central America: The Challenge of Revolutionary Change," in *Third World Instability: Central America as a European-American Issue*, ed. Andrew J. Pierre (New York: Council on Foreign Relations, 1985), p. 100.

53. Stanley Hoffmann, "The Western Alliance: Drift or Harmony?" *International Security* 6, no. 2 (Fall 1981): 109.

54. A.W. DePorte, *Europe Between the Superpowers: The Enduring Balance* (New Haven, Conn.: Yale University Press, 1979), p. 240.

55. Robert Art, "America's Foreign Policy," in *Foreign Policy in World Politics*, ed. Roy Macridis (Englewood Cliffs, N.J.: Prentice-Hall, 1989), p. 166.

56. Palmer, p. 50.

57. Smouts, p. 166.

58. Richard H. Ullman, "America, Britain, and the Soviet Threat," in *The Special Relationship: Anglo-American Relations Since 1945*, eds. William Roger Louis and Hedley Bull, p. 110.

59. Evan Luard, "Western Europe and the Reagan Doctrine," *International Affairs* 63, no. 4 (Autumn 1987): 567.

60. Luard, p. 567.

61. Stanley R. Sloan, *The Atlantic Alliance and the Third World: Implications of Diverging U.S. and European Approaches* (Washington, D.C.: Congressional Research Service, 1983), p. 17.

62. Sloan, p. 17.

3

The Middle East: The Palestinian-Israeli Conflict

The ongoing, violent Palestinian-Israeli conflict stands in sharp contrast to significant steps toward the peaceful resolution of problems in southern Africa, the peaceful transfer of power by the Sandinistas in Nicaragua, and the growth of democracy in Eastern Europe, Latin America, and elsewhere. The Palestinian-Israeli conflict posed a serious threat to both American and European interests in the Middle East and the Persian Gulf, resulted in increased Palestinian deaths and suffering, and undermined the moral and ethical foundations of Israel. These problems were underscored following Iraq's invasion of Kuwait in 1990. Although it was recognized that the Palestinian issue remained a vibrant force in Middle East politics because it represented a challenge to the Arabs' shared identity and their independence from foreign domination[1] and that Israel's security depended ultimately on eliminating the Palestinian problem from the wider Arab-Israeli conflict, neither the United States nor its West European allies seemed capable of moving the Israelis toward a solution that was acceptable to the Palestinians. A central reason for the stalemate was the unwillingness of many Israelis, after the Palestinian Liberation Organization (PLO) had recognized Israel's right to exist and renounced terrorism in 1988, to accept the demands of Palestinians for a homeland in the West Bank and Gaza, areas illegally occupied by Israeli military forces. It was as though many Israelis believed that to recognize the legitimacy of Palestinian claims would have meant the weakening of their own.[2] But Israel's inability to initiate meaningful policies that would have moved toward resolving the conflict was also linked directly to its serious internal political divisions. Whereas the Palestinians successfully reconciled many of their differences and made a major departure from previous policies, to the dismay of many Israelis their country floundered as its moribund political system was unable to deal effectively with new opportunities presented by changes in the Palestinian position. Saddam Hussein's linkage of the Palestinian-Israeli conflict to his withdrawal from Kuwait further exacerbated Israel's difficulties, especially its relations with the United States. Having forced Iraq to end its occupation of Kuwait, Washington was expected to move more aggressively on resolving the Arab-Israeli conflict.

Although it may be argued that divergent West European and American views on the Palestinian-Israeli issue stem from the fact that "the United States must think strategically, while Europeans, though more dependent on oil than the United States, do not,"[3] differences among the allies emanated from complex historical, economic, political, and cultural factors and not simply from the power differential between Western Europe and the United States. Despite the European allies' inability to alter significantly the status quo in the Middle East without American support, their activities and interests clearly affected U.S. policies in the region. Furthermore, Arab perceptions of West Europeans as being more sensitive than the United States to the Palestinian problem and as more impartial actors in the region undoubtedly strengthened the allies' role as an alternative to both Washington and Moscow. Whereas this did not deprive the United States of its leadership position in relation to the Palestinian-Israeli problem, the Europeans were nonetheless becoming more important players as East-West tensions diminished. But within the alliance tensions about the Middle East were evident from the beginning.

After NATO was formed, the United States and Britain assumed responsibility for preventing Soviet expansion. In 1955 they established the Central Treaty Organization, initially known as the Baghdad Pact Organization, with Iraq and Turkey, and later Iran and Pakistan, to accomplish this objective. The French, however, perceived the Anglo-American effort as a deliberate attempt to undermine their influence in the area. And when the French, British, and Israelis invaded Egypt without consulting Washington after Nasser seized the Suez Canal in 1956, the United States essentially forced them to withdraw, thereby confirming American ascendancy and French and British decline. Thus, having failed to obtain U.S. support, Britain and France were reluctant to acquiesce to U.S. leadership in a region where they had long enjoyed predominant influence. Intra-alliance competition led the Europeans to conclude that Americans were attempting to profit from their misfortunes and were undermining their position in the region to gain favor with the Arabs.[4] Consequently, relations between the United States and Western Europe, and those among the Europeans themselves, in the Middle East were characterized by cooperation, divergence, and sometimes conflict.

Even though the allies agreed that their major interests in the Middle East included access to oil, preventing Soviet expansion, maintaining Israel's security, and resolving the Palestinian-Israeli conflict, there were diverse attitudes among them on developments in the region. Apart from variances in European and American approaches, there were diverse European views, reflecting different historical ties, economic interests, domestic political constraints, and in West Germany's case, the Jewish Holocaust. Yet Washington's preoccupation with the Soviet threat obscured these differences and influenced U.S. policymakers to assume that, because crises in the Middle East threatened Western interests, developing a unified allied position was the appropriate response.[5] Failure to accomplish this united front generated intra-alliance tensions, partly because of divergent European and American views on NATO's responsibilities in conflicts beyond Europe and partly because of varying perceptions of the Soviet threat.

The Europeans' perceptions of the Soviet Union and their historical ties with the Middle East caused them to downplay the Soviet threat. In contrast to the United States, they tended to be concerned primarily with internal sources of instability, the persistent Arab-Israeli confrontation, the dangers posed by radical fundamentalist groups, and the effects of the ongoing Palestinian-Israeli conflict. From Britain's perspective, for example, the United States concentrated too much on building strategic alliances that would alienate the local population, thereby fueling radical opposition movements.

Europeans felt that focusing on the Soviet Union deflected attention from indigenous threats to Western interests.[6] Far more important than Soviet activities as a cause of instability in the Middle East, from the West Europeans' viewpoint, was America's virtually unqualified support of Israel and its general disregard for the Palestinians' legitimate claims. They regarded Israel's policies as dangerously bellicose and insisted that its continued occupation of Arab lands posed a major threat to peace in the region and the world.[7] The central cause of terrorism and violence in the area was seen to be the unresolved Palestinian problem. America's partiality created serious strains in an alliance in which the vast majority of the members were sympathetic to the Palestinian tragedy.

Given the wide range of threats in the broader Middle East and the Persian Gulf region, and the variety of instruments required to deal with them, there was sufficient room for divergent European and American approaches.[8] Furthermore, it could be argued that what appeared to be an unintentional division of labor among the allies was ultimately in the best interest of the West. Nonetheless, deliberate European efforts to distance themselves from American policies toward the Palestinian-Israeli conflict and to develop a distinct European approach by harmonizing their policies created strains that helped undermine the Atlantic partnership. Moreover, competing interests among the Europeans themselves erected obstacles to the realization of a common EC policy, thus engendering more friction among the allies.

Britain's involvement in the Middle East since the First Crusade in 1095 and its historical rivalry with France, Turkey, and Russia for control over what were regarded as strategic assets undoubtedly shaped its perception of its role in the Palestinian-Israeli conflict. Britain's responsibility under the League of Nations for administering the Palestine Mandate and preparing it for eventual independence, and its experiences with Jewish nationalism and terrorism, and the fact that instead of bringing Palestine to independence it actually presided over the demise of the Palestinian state clearly influenced British policy on the Palestinian issue. If the British generally congratulated themselves on their successful transformation of other dependent territories into nominally equal Commonwealth members through negotiations and other nonviolent processes, they were not anxious to draw attention to their failure in Palestine. Complicating Britain's perception of the problem was another reality with which British policymakers grappled, namely Nazi dehumanization of the Jewish people and the Holocaust. Thus Britain was confronted with deciding between two groups of victims and with responding to their legitimate claims. Forced to leave Palestine, partly because of terrorist activities of the Irgun and other Jewish groups, Britain was not completely deprived of credibility with the Arabs. Instead, its problems stemmed primarily from its relationship with the Israelis. Whereas many British policymakers did not overlook the anti-British terrorist activities of Menachem Begin, who became prime minister of Israel in 1977, many Israelis were reluctant to forgive Britain for its policies under the Mandate and its position on the establishment of Israel.[9]

Cognizant of its limited influence on the Israeli government and believing that its long history in the Middle East endowed it with specialized knowledge of the region's politics and cultures, Britain adopted a moderate, even-handed policy on the Palestinian-Israeli confrontation. Its special relationship with the United States, its leadership role within the institution of EPC, its traditional competition with France, and its significant trade with Arab countries meant that its policies were subjected to many cross-pressures. One of these was not influence of ethnic voters. Britain's relatively neutral stance on the broader Arab-Israeli conflict fostered the growth of countervailing Jewish and Arab pressure groups within the Conservative and Labour parties. Yet because the Jewish vote was not particularly homogeneous or concentrated in electoral districts, few members of Parliament worried about losing or gaining seats because of their position on Middle East issues. Furthermore, British Jews, akin to members of Israel's Labor Party, had been dismayed by the belligerent and obdurate policies of Begin and his successors in the Likud party.[10] Similar to the other Europeans, the British viewed the Palestinian-Israeli struggle as a threat to stability throughout the entire region, especially in Gulf states which had a substantial number of Palestinian workers and refugees.[11] Consequently, British policy was shaped by its general support for the United States as its major NATO partner, by competition with France and increasingly with Italy and Germany for markets, its belief that its historical experiences entitled it to a special role in the region, and by the relative lack of domestic constraints. The British government, under both Labour and the Conservatives, pursued a dual-track policy of trying to influence the Arab states to adopt conciliatory attitudes toward Israel and attempting to persuade the United States to pressure Israel to be more sensitive to legitimate Arab concerns.[12]

France adopted a more complex and less consistent policy toward the Palestinian-Israel conflict. Although France supported Israel's right to exist as well as the creation of a Palestinian homeland, it seemed to veer between the two groups, being closer to the Israelis before 1967 and from 1980 to 1982, prior to Israel's invasion of Lebanon, and being generally supportive of the Palestinians from the beginning but more actively in favor of a Palestinian state in the late 1980s.[13] Like Britain, France took a broad view of its interests in the Middle East and tailored its policies accordingly. Although it is relatively easy to dismiss French support for Palestinian rights as a direct consequence of France's overwhelming dependence on Arab oil (estimated at 74 percent), there were diverse motivations for France's position. Consistent with its overall foreign policy objectives, France sought to remove the Arab-Israeli conflict from superpower rivalry by focusing on the indigenous causes of the confrontation and advocating the adoption of measures designed to eradicate them. France also attempted to present itself as an alternative to both superpowers. To further this objective, it initiated dialogue between the Arab states and the EC in mid-1974. France's tendency to view regional conflicts within the North-South, as opposed to the East-West, context was also a factor that shaped its Middle East policy. Even while France under Mitterrand seemed to be aligning itself with the United States in the early 1980s, it continued to proclaim that its actions were expressions of French rather than alliance interests; and France used every opportunity to dissociate itself from American policies.[14]

Whereas Britain and France were confident of their leadership roles in the Middle East, West Germany maintained a much lower profile and preferred to hide behind French and EC foreign policy initiatives. Discredited after World War II and essentially a semi-sovereign state, West Germany was perceived as having a special responsibility for the survivors of the Holocaust specifically and Jews in general. Nazi atrocities narrowed Bonn's maneuverability in the Middle East and influenced the development of a "special relationship" between West Germany and Israel that depended largely on the latter's ability to stand on the moral high ground and the former's sense of guilt for the Holocaust.[15] But the Germans' experiences with divided families in a divided Germany and with the German refugee problem enabled them to understand, to some extent, the plight of the Palestinians. Germans, Israelis, and Palestinians shared the common pain of being victims: in the case of the Germans, of their own actions; in the case of the Israelis and Palestinians, of intolerance and indifference. Yet the victims also became victimizers, thereby muddling the issues of guilt and responsibility.

West Germany's emergence as an economic power, Israel's loss of innocence (which accompanied the growth of its military might), and the acceptance of the reality of Israel's existence by the Palestinians and the Arabs had far-reaching impact on Bonn's Middle East policy in general and its view of the Palestinian-Israeli problem specifically. And as the dreadful events that occurred in Nazi Germany receded from memory, West Germans found it more difficult to accept collective responsibility for the Holocaust.[16] Growing commercial and investment transactions between the Arab states and West Germany, particularly the latter's dependence on oil from the former, created bonds of interdependence between Arabs and Germans that competed with the "special relationship" between Bonn and Tel Aviv.

If the successor generation in Germany modified this relationship, the specific activities of both Arabs and Jews contributed significantly to its erosion. The irony of Israel's stunning success in the Six Day War was that it removed the widely held perception among Germans that Israel needed protection against the Arabs. Equally important, Israel's occupation of Arab territory engendered sympathy for the Palestinians. Furthermore, instead of subscribing to Nasser's rigid ideological position, Anwar Sadat acted against general expectations and visited Israel in 1977, thereby moderating German perception of the Arabs as unrelenting foes of Israel. In the meantime, the Israeli government underwent a radical transformation following the surprise Arab attack against Israel on Yom Kippur in 1973. The extremists within Israel were able to take advantage of Arab aggression, and by 1977 Begin had become prime minister. Despite his conclusion of the Camp David Accords in 1978, Begin's bellicose policies toward the Palestinians robbed Israel of moral authority. Israel was increasingly viewed as an ordinary state. As far as West Germany was concerned, Israel was not interested in peacefully resolving conflicts with relatively weak opponents.[17] Its brutal treatment of Palestinians during the Intifada increased Germany's maneuverability in the Middle East. Bonn's support for the Palestinians put it on the side of human rights, thereby diminishing Israel's moral claim vis-à-vis West Germany and eroding the "special relationship." However, after Iraqi Scud missiles struck Tel Aviv, Germany responded by giving Israel $165 million in humanitarian aid. Sensitive to claims that German firms had helped Iraq acquire chemical weapons, Hans-Dietrich Genscher toured Tel Aviv, and Bonn delivered about $670 million in military assistance to Israel. Included were gas masks, gas-proof vehicles, poison gas antidotes, and Patriot missiles.

America's consistent support of Israel, despite occasional official condemnations of Israel's human rights violations, created a serious dilemma for its European allies whose authority and power in international affairs depended to a large extent on the general observance of human rights and international law. At a more concrete level, Washington's reluctance to employ its substantial leverage with Israel to pressure it to take meaningful steps toward a peaceful resolution of the Palestinian problem was seen by the West European allies as a detriment to their interests in the Middle East and the Gulf.

Similar to West Germany, America's policy toward Israel before the 1990 Gulf crisis was driven not so much by realpolitik calculations as it was by moral and emotional considerations. Arguing that Israel was vulnerable to attack by hostile Arab states, Israel's supporters constantly reminded Americans of their moral obligation to guarantee the survival of the small democratic state.[18] Such appeals to morality had a certain resonance in America, a society which often viewed complex foreign policy issues in moralistic terms. But an unwavering commitment to Israel necessitated ignoring or downgrading the Palestinian component of the Arab-Israeli conflict.[19] In contrast to Western Europe, where Israel was a less emotive issue, the United States was responsive to various pressure groups that lobbied policymakers on Israel's behalf, much to the chagrin of Arab-Americans and the Arab states. Instead of carefully examining indigenous causes of regional conflicts, American foreign policymakers were more comfortable with reducing complex problems to fit the prevailing East-West worldview. Under these circumstances, Israel's importance to America's security was greatly exaggerated. Israel was perceived as "a strong and reliable ally" that offered the United States air, sea, and land bases as well as its considerable military experience.[20]

Although the Arab countries were unwilling to cooperate with the United States to the extent that Israel did (until Iraq invaded Kuwait), they shared America's interest in preventing Soviet expansion in the Middle East. Prior to America's active support of Israel following the 1967 war, when the European allies moved away from Israel and closer to the Arab states, most Middle Eastern governments had viewed the United States as the most friendly and trustworthy Western power. Unlike Britain and France, the United States was unencumbered by a legacy of colonialism or conflict with the Arab people.[21]

It was America's refusal to address the Palestinian problem that alienated even moderate, "pro-Western" Arab countries. Within the context of the Soviet-American rivalry, Middle East experts in the State Department, the CIA, and the Pentagon who believed that the unresolved Palestinian issue was the principal threat to regional stability were generally ignored. For a while, President Carter and his Secretary of State, Cyrus Vance, took a more regional approach to Third World conflicts and initiated a series of efforts to include the PLO in negotiations on the Arab-Israeli confrontation.[22] It was Carter who, less preoccupied with seeing the world from a narrow East-West perspective, advocated the creation of a Palestinian homeland. But the renewal of the Cold War under Reagan once again influenced American policymakers to regard the PLO as a terrorist organization and to dismiss its legitimate grievances against Israel. Ironically, Israel's actions, including its invasion of Lebanon and its brutal response to the Intifada, ultimately triggered American sympathy for the Palestinians and partially influenced Reagan's decision to negotiate with the PLO, much to Israel's dismay.

WEST EUROPEAN ECONOMIC AND MILITARY INTERESTS

Given their historical ties to the Middle East, the Europeans have major economic interests in the region. Extensive commercial interests in the Arab world influenced the West European allies to adopt policies that often contradicted those implemented by the United States. The 1973 OPEC oil embargo against the United States and selected West European countries demonstrated the allies' dependence on the Arab states. As a consequence of the quadrupling of oil prices, the dramatic increase in their financial resources enabled countries like Saudi Arabia, Iran, Iraq, and Kuwait to purchase significant quantities of essential supplies from Western Europe. Europe's dependence on Arab oil and finances helped to shape the West European allies' policies on the Palestinian-Israeli problem and also widened the differences between them and the United States on this issue. Intra-alliance competition also grew out of the sudden transfer of wealth from the industrial countries to OPEC. Unlike Britain, which had significant petroleum reserves in the North Sea, West Germany and France were extremely vulnerable to any interruption in oil imports. France was able to build nuclear power plants to reduce its overwhelming dependence on Middle East oil. However, Germany, for historical reasons, was more constrained by a divisive internal debate on nuclear power plants. Thus, while France imported 70 percent of its petroleum, West Germany relied on external sources for 94 percent of its oil supplies, with approximately 80 percent of the total coming from the Middle East and North Africa.[23] Devoid of oil and major natural resources, Israel was at a disadvantage, a reality that was reflected by major alterations in the West European allies' policies in the Middle East.

Israel's relatively small population limited its commercial value to the Europeans in comparison with the Arab countries. Between 1983 and 1987, for example, France's exports to Israel amounted to less than 0.4 percent of its total exports, whereas the Arab countries' share fluctuated between 8 and 11 percent. French imports from Israel during the same period remained around 0.3 percent of its total imports, compared to approximately 10 percent from the Arab states.[24] Middle East trade within the EC as a whole was also significant. In 1988 the Middle East sent 2 percent of its exports to Africa, 16 percent to Asia (excluding Japan), 12 percent to the

United States, 18 percent to Japan, and 27 percent to the European Community. Similarly, the Middle East took 1 percent of its imports from Africa, 11 percent from Asia (excluding Japan), 11 percent from the United States, 9 percent from Japan, and 29 percent from the EC.[25] Western Europe's emphasis on economic growth made its economic relations with the Arab states even more significant. And as the Single European Market was becoming a reality members of the EC met with their counterparts from the Arab states to establish a more permanent framework for ongoing economic and political issues. The Arabs' principal objective was establishing cooperation in order to facilitate exports of agricultural products and petroleum to Europe.[26]

But Israel's "special relationship" with West Germany and Western Europe's support for Israel's right to exist as an independent state also engendered economic ties between Israel and the EC. Both Holland and Germany, due largely to their experiences, advocated preferential treatment for Israeli exports to the EC. Despite French opposition to Israel's application for preferential status, partly because of the 1967 war, a compromise was eventually reached and the Preferential Trade Agreement was concluded with Israel in 1970. It provided substantial trade advantages for Israel, especially when compared to a similar trade agreement signed in 1964.[27] Although Israel benefited from various EC trade provisions, many Israelis were concerned about the size of their country's trade deficit with Western Europe, which increased by roughly 300 percent between 1980 and 1988. They were also troubled that they were exporting primarily agricultural products, textiles, chemicals, and diamonds. Advanced technology products accounted for only 10 percent of their exports, partly due to EC rules of origin that did not permit Israeli products to be competitive with West European products.[28] But while the Israelis wanted the Europeans to remove barriers to their exports, they did not demonstrate a similar concern for Palestinian exports.

When the EC decided in 1986 to reduce import duties by as much as 80 percent on produce from the Occupied Territories in order to provide Palestinian farmers with an alternative market to Israel, where their goods were subject to discriminatory taxes and other unfair trade practices, the Israeli authorities used various measures to obstruct Palestinian exports. Only when the EC threatened to revoke Israel's own preferential trade agreements did Israel allow Palestinians to be their own shipping agents.[29] Yet the Israelis arbitrarily prevented the free flow of trade by (1) levying exorbitant taxes on Palestinian produce that was shipped across the Allenby Bridge to Jordan; (2) banning the sale of Palestinian products within Israel, even as it sent Israeli goods into the Occupied Territories; (3) destroying vegetables intended for export to Europe by "accidentally" storing them at very high temperatures; and (4) subjecting Palestinian produce to security checks, during which boxes were torn open and their contents damaged. In light of these violations, the European Commission admonished Israel about possible EC sanctions.[30]

Another factor influencing the allies' policies toward the Palestinian-Israeli conflict was America's financial support for Israel. Although West Germany initially provided foreign assistance to Israel under a reparations and restitution agreement, an integral component of the relationship between the two countries was the large aid transfers from Bonn to Tel Aviv. Similar to West Germany, the United States believed that it should provide financial assistance to ensure Israel's survival. According to the U.S. State Department, between 1948 and 1989 the United States provided over $43 billion in assistance to Israel, and approximately $3 billion in fiscal year 1990.[31] In sharp contrast to the allocations for Israel, the United States gave Palestinians in the West Bank and Gaza roughly $98 million in direct assistance between 1975 and 1989. For fiscal year 1990, the State Department requested a total of $12 million to fund projects to improve health, water, and sanitation; to develop agricultural credit and private sector activities; and to construct schools and roads.[32] Given the restrictions imposed by the Israeli government on the West Bank and Gaza during the Intifada and the Persian Gulf crisis, it was extremely unlikely that these funds would actually benefit the Palestinians to the degree intended. As former President Carter observed, "it is a matter of consternation and condemnation among Arab leaders, and even in some European nations, that the U.S. government budgets more than $7 million each day for the Israelis in economic and military aid and this level of financial assistance is seldom seriously questioned when the annual budget is prepared in Washington."[33] But Senator Robert Dole challenged this by questioning aid allocations to traditional allies and suggesting that, in light of major developments in world politics, foreign aid should be reviewed. Israel's decision not to respond to Iraqi attacks during Operation Desert Storm, despite significant damage and direct threats to its security, strengthened its bargaining position in relation to obtaining aid from the United States.

In addition to trade and foreign assistance, the Western allies, to differing degrees, are major suppliers of advanced military technology in the Middle East. Unencumbered by military obligations to Israel, the West European allies, with the exception of Germany, often took advantage of America's inability to complete military sales to Saudi Arabia and other Middle East countries—due primarily to domestic political pressure from Israel's supporters. For example, when Congress blocked the sale of forty-eight F-15 fighter planes to Saudi Arabia in 1986, the Saudis turned to the British to buy an estimated $17 billion package consisting of seventy-two Tornado combat aircraft, forty-eight strike aircraft, and twenty-four interceptors, as well as training craft, parts, and munitions.[34] In September 1989 the Bush administration informed Israel that the United States intended to sell Saudi Arabia three hundred tanks and that it would address Israel's security concerns if Israel did not actively oppose the sale or encourage its allies in Congress to block it.[35] Inadvertently, Israel and its Arab neighbors undermined their own security by increasing military expenditures instead of addressing the Palestinian problem, the underlying determinant of Arab-Israeli tensions.

For analytical purposes, the Palestinian-Israeli problem will be divided into four periods. The first discusses early Western European involvement in Palestine, developments leading to the establishment of the state of Israel, the demise of the Palestinian state, and European and American attempts to reconcile two irreconcilable claims to the same territory. The second period begins with the Six Day War in 1967 and evaluates the European and American responses to Israel's military power vis-à-vis its Arab neighbors. The third period, which starts with the Arab attack on Israel on Yom Kippur 1973, discusses the impact of energy politics on the Western alliance and American diplomacy following the war, and ends with the Venice Declaration, initiated by the West European allies in 1980. The fourth period coincides with the advent of the Reagan administration and the Reagan initiative of 1982, Israel's invasion of Lebanon, the Intifada, Reagan's decision to commence negotiations with the PLO in 1988, and President Bush's efforts to reach a negotiated settlement.

THE CREATION OF ISRAEL AND THE PALESTINIAN PROBLEM

Although the creation of Israel is closely connected to rampant anti-Semitism throughout most of Europe that culminated in the Holocaust in Nazi Germany, Jewish interest in a homeland cannot be divorced from the destruction of Jerusalem by the Romans. But the tragic circumstances experienced by Jews living in many European countries and the Holocaust led ultimately to a double tragedy. In a very real sense, both Jews and Palestinians became victims of Hitler's hatred of the Jews. And it was religious intolerance and economic competition that prompted the Europeans to participate in the Crusades from the eleventh through the fourteenth centuries against Moslems who had dominated the Holy Land and had persecuted Christian inhabitants.

Always an integral part of the Christian Crusades, trade dominated European concerns when religious issues subsided. Commercial competition between France and Britain eventually turned the Middle East into a cockpit of rivalry among the major Western European states. By the seventeenth century Britain had established itself as a major trading nation in the region, and the Levant Company, the Turkey Merchants, and the East India Company were given the responsibility for administering British trade relations with the Middle East.[36] But France and Russia were hardly complaisant. Under a treaty of Friendship and Commerce signed in 1535 between Sulayman of the Ottoman Empire and Francis of France, the French obtained the right to trade in Ottoman ports and an exemption from the jurisdiction of local courts in the Levant (now Syria and Lebanon). Anglo-French competition and success in the Middle East inevitably led to Spain's, Holland's and Austria's involvement in the struggle for influence within the Ottoman Empire.[37]

British interests in India, French engineering abilities, and declining Ottoman power culminated in the consolidation of West European influence in Egypt, in particular, and the region in general. Having gained joint ownership of the Suez Canal, Britain and France not only had to increase their activities in Egypt but also had to make trade-offs. The formation of an alliance between Russia and France, during the period that Britain was preoccupied with an impending war with the Boers in South Africa, forced Britain to give France a free hand in Morocco in exchange for the same for itself in Egypt. And in 1907 Britain and Russia agreed to divide Persia (now Iran) into separate spheres of influence.[38] In the meantime, Zionism had emerged as an important force in Europe. Clearly dependent on the European countries for territory for a Jewish homeland, many Zionists approached Britain as well as Portugal in order to gain access to land in the Middle East or in Africa. Taking advantage of the colonization fervor in Western Europe, Theodor Herzl sought the support of European governments in establishing a Jewish state. "To European leaders he argued that Zionism would serve their interests in the Middle East."[39]

Arab revolts against the Ottoman Empire in 1916, the capture of Jerusalem in 1917, and subsequent British control over Palestine under the League of Nations mandate system paved the way for the establishment of a Jewish homeland in Palestine. As a Class A mandate, Palestine was technically already an independent state under British supervision. Syria and Lebanon became French mandates, partly as a result of the Sykes-Picot agreement in 1916 between Britain and France. The United States played a minor role in the critical events that became the roots of the Palestinian-Israeli conflict. Nevertheless, President Woodrow Wilson endorsed the Balfour Declaration issued by British Foreign Secretary Lord Balfour in a letter to Lord Rothschild.[40] Endorsing the Balfour Declaration did not deny the existence of a Palestinian state because the declaration called for a Jewish homeland in Palestine that would not replace the Palestinian state. But British actions as well as clarifications of the Balfour Declaration added to the confusion and angst of Arabs and Jews. The Churchill White Paper, designed to clarify the Balfour Declaration, reaffirmed that Palestine was not to be converted into a "Jewish National Home," only that such a home should be founded in Palestine. It further emphasized that the British government would not contemplate the disappearance or subordination of the Arab population, language, or culture in Palestine.[41] Compounding the misunderstandings and feelings of betrayal among Arabs was the rapidly increasing Jewish immigration to Palestine between 1922 and 1939. The horrifying events in Germany and many countries' refusal to admit Jewish refugees from the impending Holocaust transformed Palestine and set the stage for the Palestinian-Israeli struggle.

Confronted with the terrifying realities of the Holocaust on the one hand and the desire to protect British national interests on the other, foreign policymakers in London, principally Ernest Bevin and Winston Churchill, were at odds on how to resolve the issues of Jewish immigration and a Jewish homeland in Palestine. Although Winston Churchill, as Colonial Secretary in 1922, had attempted to clarify the Balfour Declaration, his sympathy toward Zionist aspirations and the experiences of World War II influenced him to favor partitioning Palestine. His determination to preserve the Anglo-American alliance led him to subordinate the Arab-Jewish conflict to more important strategic interests. But Bevin, while not necessarily anti-Zionist, was more sympathetic to the Arab viewpoint. Believing that problems emanating from the Holocaust should be solved in Europe, specifically by integrating Jews into European societies instead of permitting Jewish immigration into Palestine, Bevin "refused to countenance the creation of a Jewish State because of its disruptive impact on the Arab world and, in turn, the British Empire."[42] Yet Bevin favored a binational or federated Arab-Israeli state in Palestine. Despite their conflicting views, neither Churchill nor Bevin believed that Palestine could absorb Europe's Jewish population.

Frustrated by their inability to move London more decisively toward the establishment of a Jewish state in Palestine, Zionists shifted their lobbying efforts to Washington. They organized the Biltmore Conference in New York in May 1942 to articulate their objectives and to pressure the United States to persuade Britain to act. Consequently, the Palestinian issue became entangled in domestic American politics and resulted in serious strains in the Anglo-American alliance. But strategic considerations during the war forced President Roosevelt to balance his sympathies toward the Zionist claims against Allied military strategy. With German forces in North Africa and the eastern Mediterranean, the United States had concluded that Arab support was essential to the defense of the Middle East.[43] Furthermore, there were considerable American economic interests in the Arab world that had to be taken into account.

Yet American as well as Soviet opposition to British imperial designs in the Third World in general and in the Middle East specifically led to a tacit alliance between Moscow and Washington in favor of the Jews at the end of World War II.[44] Weakened by the war, Britain was undoubtedly more vulnerable to American pressure, and U.S. sympathy for displaced Jews as well as its own reluctance to alter its immigration laws to facilitate an influx of Jews ultimately influenced Britain to relinquish control of Palestine.

Having turned the Palestinian problem over to the United Nations, Britain decided to withdraw from Palestine in May 1948 after refusing to implement the UN partition plan. And while the United States supported the UN vote on the creation of Israel and recognized the new state literally minutes after it came into existence on May 14, 1948, Britain abstained on the UN vote and did not recognize Israel until a year later. By so doing, Britain was not only demonstrating its differences with the United States on Palestine but was also ensuring its continued influence in the Arab world. On the American side, there was much disagreement about the wisdom of backing the creation of a Jewish state in the Arab world. Even American support for Israel was tenuous. As Rubinstein put it, "For Washington, Israel was more of an embarrassment than a commitment. Had Stalin not permitted arms and immigrants to flow from Eastern Europe, it would not have survived the first Arab-Israeli war of 1948–1949."[45] The United States had embargoed arms to the Middle East in 1947.

Escalating tensions between the United States and the Soviet Union at the beginning of the Cold War influenced Americans to concentrate to an even greater extent on the Arab world. The Arab-Israeli conflict was obviously detrimental to broader Western objectives. In addition to monitoring arms supplies to the region under the Tripartite Declaration in 1950, Britain, France, and the United States focused on political and economic solutions to the growing Arab-Israeli confrontation. Although the Europeans favored a political solution, they generally acquiesced to America's preference for the equivalent of a Marshall Plan for the Middle East.

Robert McGhee of the U.S. State Department advocated Western assistance to countries affected by the war in Palestine as a means of achieving a high standard of living and stability in the area, thereby protecting it from Russian infiltration.[46] However, part of the U.S. plan called for the return of Palestinian refugees to their homeland, an idea that was dismissed by the fledgling Israeli state out of fear that the Palestinians would pose a security risk. Moreover, the Irgun rejected any compromise with the Palestinians, including the UN partition resolution. Arguing that partition of the "homeland" was illegal, the Irgun and its leader, Menachem Begin, refused to recognize the UN decision. Instead they insisted that "Jerusalem was and will for ever be our capital. Eretz (greater) Israel will be restored to the people of Israel. All of it. And for ever."[47] This promise was aggressively implemented when Begin became prime minister in 1977 and was continued throughout the 1980s and early 1990s by the Likud Party, which refused to compromise with its coalition partner, the Labor Party, on a Palestinian homeland.

But Israel's policies directly conflicted with America's new global responsibilities and its efforts to prevent Communist expansion in the Middle East. Alienating the Arab states from the West was contrary to America's strategy of containment, articulated by President Truman. The objective was to establish a strategic connection between NATO and a related network of alignments in the Middle East, one that included the Arab countries.[48] Clearly, then, the Arab-Israeli conflict was not in America's interest, and subsequent U.S. administrations until 1967 endorsed President Eisenhower's idea of impartial friendship and neutrality in the conflict. Many Arab states, however, did not embrace U.S. strategic aims in the region, and decided to remain neutral in the Cold War. Unlike the United States, France moved closer to Israel, cooperated with it on several scientific projects, and became its primary arms supplier until the Six Day War in 1967, after which America assumed that role. Ironically, it was French and British collaboration with Israel during the attack on Egypt in 1956 that demonstrated to the allies that the United States was opposed to their imperial designs in the Middle East and that it would remain neutral in the Arab-Israeli conflict.

Britain, France, and Israel attempted to achieve their own specific objectives which, from the U.S. perspective, undermined efforts to keep the Soviets out of the Middle East. Israel participated in the 1956 invasion to neutralize the Fedayeen who had been attacking it and to reopen the Straits of Aqaba. France's goal was to overthrow Nasser because he supported the Algerian liberation movement. Britain was concerned about the possible closure of the Suez Canal to British oil shipments and was unwilling to accept passively Nasser's seizure of the Canal.[49] Forced to withdraw by the United States, Britain and France were disabused of any illusions of great power status they may have had. While the allies were humiliated, the U.S. reputation among the Arab states improved. But America's success in this crisis would later become an obstacle to its efforts to persuade the allies to get involved in Third World conflicts. Recognizing the limits of their power, the West Europeans defined their interests narrowly and concentrated on rebuilding Europe.

Germany's involvement in the Arab-Israeli conflict was delayed not only by the devastation it suffered during the war but also by conditions imposed on it by the United States, Britain, the Soviet Union, and France. Yet growing Soviet activities in Egypt following the Suez crisis paved the way for a greater German role. In fact, it was the Cold War that enabled Bonn to adopt a more active foreign policy and to become a member of NATO. Communist influence in Egypt and the Soviet Union's decision to supply arms to Egypt, Syria, and Iraq prompted Washington to include Bonn in its Middle East strategy. Unwilling to jeopardize its relations with the Arabs, but apprehensive about the destabilizing impact an arms imbalance would have on the region, the United States secretly encouraged West Germany to supply arms to Israel in 1961.[50]

However, Germany was also reluctant to risk damaging its relations with the Arabs, despite its "special relationship" with Israel, and therefore tried to maintain a careful balance between the two sides. When German Chancellor Konrad Adenauer took office in 1949, he made reconciliation with the Jewish people a principal foreign policy goal, and met with Israel's Prime

Minister David Ben-Gurion in April 1960 in New York.[51] The German
Foreign Office made overtures to Israel by opening a visa office there in
1956, but diplomatic recognition was postponed until 1965, twelve years
after Germany signed the Reparation Agreement. Had it not been for American pressure and Egypt's miscalculations on recognizing East Germany,
West Germany might have waited even longer to establish diplomatic relations with Israel. Thus, even if the "special relationship" was initially
mutually beneficial, Bonn had fewer compelling reasons to maintain it as
West Germany was increasingly accepted into the family of nations while,
simultaneously, Israel was being ostracized.

Although France had supplied Israel with sophisticated weapons until
1967, the relationship between the two countries was complex. France's
historical ties to the Middle East made it reluctant to recognize Israel. At
the same time, Israel's socialist ideology appealed to French socialists, and
the growing Soviet presence in Egypt and Syria facilitated improvements in
the Franco-Israeli relationship. The subsequent war in Algeria further
strengthened French-Israeli ties as France was increasingly isolated in the
Arab world. However, growing French dependence on Middle East oil and
a change in policy in Algeria eroded the relationship between Israel and
France. Although de Gaulle's policy of "parallelism" in the Middle East
was generally accepted by both Israel and the Arab states, by the early 1960s
France had tilted away from Israel. France believed that reconciliation with
Algeria would not only result in greater French access to Algerian oil but
would also enable France to establish anticolonial credentials in Third World
conflicts. France's approach to the Middle East was now consistent with its
foreign policy objective of being a Third Force, an alternative to the superpowers for developing countries. [52] By 1967 the foundation had been
firmly established for France's decisive pro-Arab shift. But if the Six Day
War prompted the European allies to distance themselves from Israel, it had
the opposite effect on the United States.

THE AFTERMATH OF THE SIX DAY WAR: 1967–73

Israel's defeat of the Arabs in the 1967 war created serious problems as
well as opportunities for those countries involved in the Middle East conflict.
The United States found itself more closely aligned with Israel but increasingly at odds with its West European allies. If the Six Day War widened
the differences between the United States and its NATO partners, it also
brought the Middle East conflict into the broader U.S.-Soviet rivalry, triggered the growth of a religious fundamentalism within Israel, contributed
to increased Palestinian nationalism and terrorist acts by the PLO, isolated
Israel in the international community, focused attention on the Palestinian
problem, and weakened Israel's political and moral foundations. The 1967
war was not only a watershed in alliance relations, but also served as the

catalyst for international recognition of a Palestinian national identity separate from that of Jordan.

Central to the Palestinian-Israeli problem was Israel's expansion into Arab territory during the 1967 war. The lands seized included Gaza and the West Bank, an area that contained the city of Jerusalem and other holy places of great significance to Jews, Arabs, and Christians. In addition, Israel regarded the captured territories as a strategic asset which could be used as a bargaining chip in negotiations with the Arabs.[53] Although a large majority of Israel's leaders may have been willing to trade land for peace, the dynamics unleashed by the war had complicated the situation for both hawks and doves. The Soviet Union's decision to sever diplomatic relations with Israel, growing internal political divisions on the question of the Occupied Territories, European condemnation of Israel's policies in the Occupied Territories, and expanded American support for Israel heightened Israel's security as well as its insecurity. On the one hand, world Jewry and the United States were motivated to defend Israel against its Arab enemies; on the other hand, American support was clearly ambiguous, not only because of the United States' preoccupation with the Vietnam War but also because of its concern that a new Middle East crisis would be advantageous to the Soviet Union's efforts in the Arab world. Further complicating any external attempts to resolve the Palestinian-Israeli problem was the rekindled interest of Jewish fundamentalists in controlling all of what they regarded as historical Israel and the subsequent political emergence of one of the strongest proponents of greater Israel, Menachem Begin.[54] Such extreme views helped to fuel PLO terrorist activities against Israel.

Although the PLO was strengthened by increased Palestinian and Arab nationalism after the Six Day War, it faced major obstacles in the various Middle East countries, and perhaps more importantly, internally. Despite their support for the Palestinians, Arab states were generally apprehensive about having an independent, divisive national liberation movement operating within their boundaries. Conflict among the different factions of the PLO could trigger internal instability in politically fragile Arab countries.

It was largely due to these concerns that the Egyptians called an Arab summit in 1964 to formally recognize the PLO as the manifestation of the Palestinian demand for national self-determination.[55] By 1967 the PLO had achieved a greater measure of unity. A Palestinian National Council (PNC) or parliament was formed, followed by the creation of a Central Committee and an Executive Committee to administer areas such as health, education, welfare, information, and the guerrilla forces. Under Yasir Arafat's leadership in 1969, more radical PLO factions were somewhat constrained, and greater emphasis was placed on obtaining international support for the Palestinians. The PLO established diplomatic missions in over one hundred countries and used its observer status in the UN to influence international public opinion.[56] Furthermore, conflict between the Jordanian army and

Palestinian guerrillas in 1970 ultimately resulted in a wave of Palestinian refugees from Jordan into Lebanon. Political chaos weakened Lebanon sufficiently to enable the PLO to establish an independent political and military organization there, and to pose a direct threat to Israel's security.

Strongly influenced by Israel's victory over Arab forces to which it had provided military assistance, the Soviet Union moved quickly to regain its lost credibility with the Arabs. Members of the Warsaw Pact alliance, with the exception of Romania, terminated diplomatic relations with Israel. As Touval observed, by 1967 the Middle East conflict had become intertwined with the East-West struggle; the U.S.-Soviet and the Arab-Israeli conflicts had become interdependent.[57] Between 1969 and 1974, the Soviet Union recognized the PLO as a national liberation movement and the Palestinians as a separate and distinct people, provided for the indirect supply of arms and equipment to the PLO initially and direct transfers later, and officially declared support of a Palestinian state.[58] Well-orchestrated, violent terrorist acts by the PLO against innocent Israeli citizens eroded any sympathy Americans may have had toward the PLO. But the Western allies moved closer to the Arabs in light of Israel's violation of international law on military occupation, which had emanated from Europe's own experiences.[59]

Among the West European states, France reacted most sharply to Israel's involvement in the Six Day War. Israel's most reliable arms supplier prior to 1967, France swung toward the Arab countries after the war, condemned Israel as the aggressor, and terminated military aid to Israel, thereby paving the way for America to become Israel's most important ally. But France's reaction to the war was greatly influenced by de Gaulle's vision of that country's role in the world and, paradoxically, by its inability to more decisively shape developments in the Middle East. Israel had acted successfully against de Gaulle's admonition. More important, the 1967 conflict vividly showed de Gaulle that the realization of his foreign policy objectives faced major, if not insurmountable, obstacles. As De Porte put it, what was lost was his dream of reducing the dependence of the Middle East states on the superpowers. War brought the United States and the Soviet Union into direct collaboration to end the conflict,[60] thereby undermining France's goal of serving as an alternative to the superpowers in the Third World.

Nevertheless, France continued to try to persuade Israel to settle for secure and recognized borders, the stated objective of the war, in exchange for Arab lands taken during the conflict. By developing closer ties with the Arab countries and attempting to demonstrate the effectiveness of its diplomacy, France aimed at preventing the superpowers from resolving the Palestinian question without French participation.[61] As the PLO gained international prominence following the war, France adopted a policy that recognized the national rights of Palestinians. Unlike the United States and Britain, France established official contacts with the PLO as early as 1974, when France's

Minister of Foreign Affairs Jean Sauvagnargues met with Arafat. In exchange for more active French support for the Palestinians, France asked the PLO to suspend terrorist activities against Israel and to recognize that state's right to exist within its pre–1967 borders.[62] France's position was generally supported by the other European allies, including West Germany.

The Arab-Israeli war coincided with West Germany's growing economic and political power, its success in improving relations with the Soviet Union, and its growing integration into the EC and the international community. As Feldman pointed out, "Germany gradually became critical of Israel as its need for Israeli approval declined. Germany was, once recognized diplomatically by its former victims, a member of the family of nations, free to speak out as any other nation."[63] On relatively controversial issues, Bonn could always hide behind EC policy statements.

While Britain was critical of Israel's actions, unlike France, it did not radically alter its position on Israel. Instead, it increasingly served to bridge European and American differences on the Palestinian-Israeli conflict. Compared to France and West Germany, Britain was confronted with more complex choices, partly because of its historical responsibilities in Palestine, its significant economic and military interests in the Middle East, its perception of its own "special relationship" with the United States, and the Arabs' perception of Britain's role in the conflict. Whereas France completely ended arms supplies to Israel, Britain imposed an embargo that was conditioned on the willingness of all other arms-supplying countries to refrain from sending arms to the region. When it was apparent that the Soviet Union was not adhering to the embargo, Britain ended its embargo against Israel two days after imposing it.[64] Britain's refusal to abandon Israel in the face of escalating Soviet involvement in the war resulted in strong anti-British feelings and actions in the Arab countries. Based on Cairo Radio broadcasts that British and American air forces had participated in the fighting on Israel's side, Arab leaders implemented a series of punitive measures against Britain. The Egyptian government closed the Suez Canal to all traffic, which greatly affected British shipping; Iraq, Syria, and the Sudan terminated diplomatic relations; Iraq, Kuwait, Algeria, Syria, and Lebanon "took steps that interfered" with oil supplies primarily to the United States and Britain; and British embassies, consulates, and other offices were damaged in many Arab cities.[65]

Steps had to be taken to provide for the safety and evacuation, if necessary, of British subjects. Britain chartered ships and aircraft to supplement commercial sailings and flights. Equally important, Britain had to consider withdrawing its troops from the Middle East and to liquidate its bases in the region, especially on Aden.[66] Realizing that its commitments in the Middle East could not be abandoned suddenly, Britain stressed diplomatic solutions to the Arab-Israeli conflict. As a middle power with limited military resources, Britain emphasized that "the primary responsibility for finding a lasting settlement in the Middle East, rested upon the international community acting through the UN."[67]

Britain was instrumental in obtaining UN Security Council agreement on appropriate peace terms, and Lord Caradon, leader of the British delegation to the UN, was responsible for drawing up Resolution 242, which was passed unanimously and became a milestone in the history of the broader Arab-Israeli conflict.[68] Resolution 242 was also the pivotal landmark in the narrower Palestinian-Israeli confrontation, one that laid the foundation for the proclamation of a Palestinian state in 1988. Resolution 242 addressed the Palestinian problem within the prevailing geopolitical circumstances in the Middle East, that is, as a refugee problem, and did not focus on a Palestinian state because the Occupied Territories were regarded as belonging to the Arab states that controlled them before 1967. However, by 1969 serious attention was given to the plight of the Palestinian people and their aspiration for a homeland in the West Bank and Gaza.[69] Thus, inadvertently, Britain initiated movement toward a Palestinian state.

While Britain viewed the Soviet Union as a threat to Western interests in the Middle East, it tended to focus on indigenous problems that would facilitate Communist infiltration in the region. Maintaining a military balance between Israel and its neighbors was a primary objective of British policy. Another crushing defeat for the Arabs was, in Britain's view, advantageous to the Soviet Union. As Secretary of State for Foreign Affairs Douglas-Home observed, "the only thing which enabled the Russians to be champions of the Arab cause was the existence of the Arab-Israeli war. That, and that alone, is why they are able to pose today as the champions of the Arabs, because Arab instincts are antagonistic to communism."[70] Britain endeavored to convince the Arab states that seeking to annihilate Israel was "futile and wrong and that there must be a negotiated peace with guarantees for Israel's security and theirs."[71]

France's decision to cut off arms supplies to Israel when the Soviet Union was providing more weapons to Egypt and Syria posed a serious challenge for the American policy of controlling the arms race in the Middle East. To preserve the balance between Israel and the Arab states, the United States became Israel's primary arms supplier after 1967. But Britain's decision to withdraw its military forces from the region, at the height of America's involvement in Vietnam, inevitably led to an increased U.S. role in efforts to resolve the Middle East conflict.

From President Lyndon Johnson's viewpoint, the Arab-Israeli confrontation could ultimately lead to war between the Soviet Union and the NATO allies.[72] Therefore, despite its preoccupation with Vietnam, America tried to persuade Israel to exchange land for peace, and worked with the Soviet Union, to the chagrin of France, to secure peace in the Middle East. However, the necessary ambiguity of Resolution 242, which was consistent with

American policies, provided the Arabs and Israelis convenient loopholes which each side used to its advantage. Believing that occupation of the conquered territories enhanced their bargaining power, the Israelis were reluctant to withdraw. Instead, for security as well as religious and political reasons, Israel was determined to redraw the boundaries. Compounding the problem on one hand was Israel's fear that indirect talks would lead to mediation and that in such a triangular negotiating situation its bargaining power would be diminished; on the other was Egypt's and Jordan's view that engaging in direct negotiations was tantamount to recognizing Israel.[73] In an effort to downplay its serious disagreement with Israel on the Occupied Territories, the United States "focused on trying to dilute the unified Arab position by encouraging Egyptian and Jordanian interest in separate settlements involving minor territorial alterations."[74]

With the onset of détente, it was widely believed that Washington and Moscow could ensure stability in the Middle East.[75] But the Soviet Union, reluctant to act inconsistently with Egypt's perceived interests, refused to endorse America's suggestion for the development of a common U.S.-Soviet statement on principles for settling the Arab-Israeli dispute. U.S. views, embodied in the Rogers Plan, were also rejected by Egypt and Israel.[76] Failure to make progress on Israel's withdrawal from the Occupied Territories and Arab refusal to recognize Israel's right to exist contributed to the outbreak of war on Yom Kippur in 1973.

FROM THE YOM KIPPUR WAR TO THE VENICE DECLARATION: 1973–80

The period between 1973 and 1980 was characterized by widening European and American approaches to the Palestinian-Israeli problem as well as serious strains within the alliance over NATO's role in out-of-area conflicts, especially in relation to assisting U.S. efforts to transport military supplies to Israel during the 1973 Yom Kippur War. Similarly, the allies disagreed on how to respond to the Arab oil embargo, partly because the Arab states divided the members of the alliance by focusing on their dependence on Middle East oil supplies. European determination to distinguish its policies in the Middle East from those of the United States by working through the institution of European Political Cooperation helped the Arabs achieve their objectives. Yet the policies advocated by President Carter were closer to the European approach, and contributed to diminishing tensions within the alliance. At the same time, however, the implementation of Euro-Arab dialogue and growing European support for a Palestinian homeland continued to create intra-alliance frictions. Perhaps the major catalyst for both divergent and common U.S. approaches to the Palestinian-Israeli dispute was the rise of the Likud Party and the reinvigoration of Jewish fundamentalism. Overall, the period was characterized by advances and retreats, by bold foreign policy actions and strenuous denials by foreign policy officials.

When Egypt and Syria launched a surprise attack against Israel on Yom Kippur in 1973, the United States responded by organizing a massive airlift of military supplies to Israel and by engaging in unprecedented diplomatic efforts to end hostilities. But various American actions were strongly opposed by the European allies as well as by Israel. Only Portugal among the European allies, partly because of its own interests in obtaining NATO support in Angola, allowed U.S. planes to refuel on its territory. Undoubtedly worried about Arab threats to impose an oil embargo, the allies carefully distanced themselves from American activities and reiterated their view that Israel should withdraw from Arab territories.

From Israel's perspective, however, occupation of the territories was a complex issue. On the one hand, failure to resolve this issue was clearly a factor in the Arabs' decision to attack Israel, and additional territories did not significantly improve Israel's security. On the other hand, without the additional territory, it was argued, Israel would have certainly suffered a major defeat and its very existence would have been threatened.[77] This view was seriously challenged by Iraqi Scud missile attacks on Israel during Operation Desert Storm. Yet Israel's view of security principally in terms of military might was inconsistent with that of the United States, Israel's most dependable ally. From America's perspective, it was essential for each side to achieve a victory. U.S. Secretary of State Kissinger utilized his diplomatic skills to accomplish the objective of a "double victory and no defeat." But by preventing Israel from achieving a decisive victory over the trapped Egyptian Third Army, the United States engendered serious tensions with Israel.[78] However, such disagreements were almost inevitable, primarily because Israel's narrow security interests could not be easily reconciled with the broader complex interests of the United States, a superpower with global responsibilities.

The 1973 war also created conflicts within NATO as well as within individual members of the alliance. Similar to the other West European allies, Britain refused to grant American cargo planes landing rights at bases in Britain and Cyprus. However, unlike France and West Germany, Britain had to contend with significant internal opposition to that policy. Although it may be argued that Britain's decision to refuse American planes with supplies for Israel permission to use its bases was a logical outgrowth of its arms embargo following the outbreak of hostilities, the decision to impose the embargo itself was severely criticized. Sensitive to the charge that Britain's policy of supplying military weapons to both the Arabs and the Israelis had contributed to the war, Secretary of State for Foreign and Commonwealth Affairs Douglas-Home noted that when the war began Britain allowed only those arms that were already en route to Egypt, Israel, and Jordan to reach their destination. Furthermore, since the Arab states had ordered a significantly larger number of weapons than Israel, the embargo was far more detrimental to the former than to the latter.[79] But David Owen, an opposition member of Parliament, argued that Britain's embargo undermined the relationship of trust, friendship, and equality between Europe and the United States, and that it had detrimental consequences for the NATO alliance. He directly challenged the government's approach by asserting that "one cannot conduct a policy that was evenhanded that exposed the United States alone to be the sole defender of Israel in time of need and put the U.S. in a position of supplying ammunition for tanks we supplied to Israel."[80] From Britain's perspective, the only constructive approach was to put itself in a position to reconcile the belligerents and to prevent future wars between them. British foreign policymakers pointed out that this strategy was consistent with those of virtually all of the West European countries.[81] Nevertheless, Britain was viewed as being more concerned about alienating French opinion and promoting European solidarity than with preserving the European-American alliance that was essential for safeguarding West European security and economic prosperity.[82]

If the 1973 oil embargo, which resulted from the war, prompted the United States to search more actively for peaceful solutions to the Arab-Israeli conflict, it also exposed tensions within the Western alliance. France, for example, ardently opposed American plans to unite major consumer countries to counterbalance OPEC's power and refused to participate in the International Energy Agency that was created to demonstrate NATO's solidarity during the oil crisis. France believed the United States was using the energy crisis to reassert its leadership over disintegrating alliance affairs. [83] Even though France joined the allies at the Washington Energy Conference in 1974, it concluded bilateral petroleum agreements with Saudi Arabia, Kuwait, and Libya that guaranteed it ample supplies of oil in exchange for increased shipments of French weapons and technology.[84]

The OPEC oil embargo created divisions among the Western Europeans because individual countries were treated according to the Arab perception of their commitment to the Palestinian cause. While France and Britain were accorded friendly status, the Netherlands and the United States were denied petroleum because of their support for Israel. By punishing the United States, Arab countries also succeeded, inadvertently, in creating economic and political havoc in Europe precisely when the West European allies were emerging as an alternative to the superpowers in the Middle East.[85] Cognizant of their newly acquired power and recognizing the need to repair relations with Europe, the Arabs influenced the EC to begin dialogue with them. France was instrumental in convincing the European allies to agree to dialogue with the twenty-one member-states of the Arab League. From the outset the Europeans and the Arabs had both convergent and conflicting objectives for Euro-Arab dialogue, although their goals would eventually merge. Whereas the Europeans were motivated principally by economic considerations to engage in this dialogue, the Arabs emphasized political factors, particularly the Palestinian issue. The dialogue was also a way for the Europeans to demonstrate their independent role in an area in which the United States and the Soviet Union had begun to dominate diplomatic efforts.[86]

Joint European foreign policy-making also facilitated West Germany's formulation and implementation of a Middle East policy that was less constrained by its "special relationship" with Israel. Chancellor Willy Brandt visited Algeria and Egypt in early 1974 to promote Euro-Arab dialogue. Bonn's support of the Palestinians, though still somewhat hidden behind French initiatives and European Political Cooperation, had become more apparent.[87]

American policy was also changing as it became evident that Israel was not prepared to cooperate in the negotiation process. Under President Ford, U.S. policy toward Israel was more restrained and increasingly emphasized the importance of the Palestinian issue. In early 1976 the Ford administration proposed a reduction in military aid to Israel to show America's dissatisfaction with Israel's slow movement on the peace initiative. In addition, William Scranton, who had advocated an evenhanded U.S. policy in the Middle East, was appointed ambassador to the UN. In his first UN speech Scranton criticized Israel for altering Jerusalem's status and for establishing settlements in the Occupied Territories.[88] However, as part of the negotiations that resulted in Israel's partial withdrawal from the Sinai, Henry Kissinger consented to Israel's request that Washington not negotiate with the PLO until that organization recognized Israel's right to exist. Nevertheless, contacts between the PLO and the United States continued, even though UN Ambassador Andrew Young resigned in 1979 due to controversy concerning his discussions with a PLO official. John Gunther Dean, who was the U.S. ambassador in Lebanon between 1978 and 1981, held approximately thirty-five meetings with PLO officials in Beirut with authorization from Secretary of State Vance.[89] Given Carter's views on the Palestinian-Israeli problem, such meetings, whatever the official justification for them, were consistent with changing American policy.

Unlike previous American presidents, Carter called for Palestinian self-determination based on his belief that the solution to the problem required a homeland for the Palestinians.[90] This marked a significant departure from the traditional American view of the Palestinians as refugees and brought U.S. policy closer to that of its West European allies. Yet Begin's election, the political strength of the New Zionists in Israel, the Camp David Accords between Israel and Egypt that were brokered by the United States, America's preoccupation with the 1980 elections, and American hostages in Iran contributed to both intra-alliance friction and European leadership on the Palestinian-Israeli issue.

The Arab attack on Israel in 1973 contributed to the formal establishment of Gush Emunim in 1974, an organization that embodied the ideology of the New Zionism. And by weakening the Labor Party, the war also helped Begin to become prime minister. These two developments represented a watershed in Israeli history and the Palestinian-Israeli conflict. Begin's Likud coalition government, strongly supported by Sephardic Jews and Gush Emunim, was dedicated to "the realization of historical Palestine in its entirety, uncontaminated by talk of any partition. Menachem Begin and his Likud supporters legitimized the strategy of annexation not only in the name of security, but in the name of religious messianism."[91] These groups' ideologies eschewed compromise and embraced violence as a policy instrument. Unlike traditional Zionism, the New Zionism downgraded the importance of normal relations with other countries and viewed isolation from the international community in religious terms. As Seliktar put it, "Israel's new belief system has generated a bleak, basically Hobbesian view of world politics. This view leaves little room for justice and morality."[92]

Yet Begin's tendency to view all actions against Israel in terms of the Holocaust and to hold other countries to a higher level of morality in relation to Israel gave rise to sharp disagreements between Israel and the West European allies. This was particularly true of West German-Israeli relations. Having opposed the normalization of ties between the two countries in the 1950s and 1960s, Begin evinced his personal distaste for Germany and for Chancellor Helmut Schmidt.[93] Instead of being intimidated by Begin, West Germany adopted a more balanced Middle East policy, became more active in the Palestinian issue, and was partly responsible for initiating European policies designed to strengthen the Palestinians and to influence the Israelis to make territorial concessions.[94]

When Begin signed the Camp David Accords in 1979 and agreed to return Egyptian territory, it was generally believed that Israel and Egypt would implement provisions in the treaty for Palestinian autonomy. But Israel saw the peace agreement with Egypt as a way of diminishing Arab threats to its security by neutralizing Egypt's military might in the Arab-Israeli conflict. Having eliminated Egypt as an immediate threat, and aware of Egypt's isolation in the Arab world, Begin was relatively unencumbered in pursuing his goal of "fortifying and settling the occupied territories and removing perceived threats by preemptive military strikes against some of the neighbors."[95] But if Carter realized that Begin's strategy was inconsistent with America's foreign policy objectives only after Camp David, the European allies, particularly France, did not enthusiastically embrace the agreement from the beginning, partly because they were excluded from the process.

America's failure to persuade Israel and Egypt to agree on negotiations concerning Palestinian autonomy by the May 26, 1980, deadline, and its preoccupation with presidential elections and the hostages held by Iran created an opportunity for the West European allies to assume responsibility for maintaining the peace process. Determined to exercise political influence commensurate with its growing economic might, the EC under British and French leadership, enacted the Venice Declaration in June 1980. While reiterating support for Israel, the Venice Declaration advocated a comprehensive peace settlement in which the Palestinian people, represented by the PLO, would actively participate.[96] Widely viewed as recognizing the PLO, the Venice Declaration was strongly opposed by both Israel and the United States. Nevertheless, it remained the policy of the EC throughout the 1980s, and an irritant in alliance relations until President Reagan agreed to talk with the PLO in late 1988 after it renounced terrorism and recognized Israel's right to exist.

THE PREDOMINANCE OF THE PALESTINIAN ISSUE AND WEST EUROPEAN RESPONSES: 1980–91

The Soviet invasion of Afghanistan, the Iranian revolution, and the Iran-Iraq War refocused America's efforts on its strategic interests in the Middle East and refueled the Cold War between Moscow and Washington. The Palestinian-Israeli conflict was largely subordinated to these broader regional concerns, a shift that was implemented by Carter and continued by Reagan. Reagan's anticommunism crusade prompted him to assume that strategic arrangements involving moderate Arab states and Israel, to prevent Soviet expansionism, could be divorced from the Palestinian-Israeli problem. But Saudi Arabia, the most important American Arab ally, concentrated on formulating a peace plan similar to the Venice Declaration. Developed by Prince Fahd, the plan called for (1) Israel's withdrawal from territory occupied during the 1967 war; (2) the establishment of a Palestinian state in the West Bank and Gaza, with East Jerusalem as its capital; (3) recognition of the right of Palestinians to return to their homeland; (4) the removal of Israeli settlements from the Occupied Territories; and (5) freedom of worship in the Holy Land for all religions.[97] Saudi objectives clashed with America's strategic plans and created divisions within the Reagan administration itself. Endorsing the Saudi initiative would have contradicted Kissinger's agreement with Israel on nonrecognition of the PLO until certain conditions were met and would have undermined the Camp David Accords as the framework for a peaceful settlement. The Reagan administration's failure to reconcile its strategic vision with the Saudi plan resulted in the derailment of both,[98] and engendered intra-alliance tensions as the British and others supported the Saudi proposals.

The election of conservative governments in Britain and West Germany and the Socialists' rise to power in France under Mitterrand initially narrowed some of the differences between the United States and its West European allies. Mitterrand, who had promised to reverse the pro-Arab positions of his predecessors, was supported by French Jews, was widely regarded as pro-Israel, and had close ties with Israel's Labor party. Within a week of Mitterrand's election, Arab investors withdrew over $8 billion from French banks, followed by another $15 billion over the next three months.[99] To reverse this outflow of money and to prevent the possible loss of arms sales to and petroleum imports from the Middle East, Mitterrand quickly adopted many of the policies he had criticized. He supported the Fahd Plan, immediately dispatched high-level officials to the Middle East, appointed Michèl Jobert, a strong advocate of Palestinian rights, as Trade Minister, visited the region within six months after his election, and, contrary to Israeli expectations, called for the creation of a sovereign Palestinian state.[100] The June 1981 Israeli raid on the French-built Iraqi nuclear reactor, which killed a French technician, and Israel's invasion of Lebanon, a former French protectorate with close ties to France, severely damaged French-Israeli relations. But these events also forced the United States to address the Palestinian-Israeli dispute. Ironically, a major goal of Operation Desert Storm and the UN resolution that formally ended the war on April 11, 1991, was the destruction of Iraq's nuclear capability.

A major factor influencing Israel's decision to invade Lebanon was the constant Palestinian rocket attacks and terrorist raids on northern Israel. Although the Israelis justified their actions in terms of national security, their principal objective was to destroy the PLO and thereby eliminate the problem of Palestinian nationalism in the Occupied Territories.[101] Israel's actions were clearly inconsistent with U.S. interests in the Middle East, and were immediately condemned by the United States and its West European allies. Britain's Secretary of State for Foreign and Commonwealth Affairs, Francis Pym, articulated the perspective of most Europeans. Refusing to accept Israel's stated justification for the invasion, Pym noted that Israel's professed objective of establishing a twenty-five-mile security zone in Lebanon had been exceeded as its troops moved into Beirut. Akin to Operation Desert Storm, the scale of the invasion was also viewed as disproportionate to the objective of achieving security from Palestinian terrorist attacks. Furthermore, from Britain's viewpoint, by destroying the PLO leadership in Beirut, which had attempted to lead a disparate movement toward a diplomatic solution of Palestinian grievances, Israel had inadvertently assisted the extremists. As Pym put it, "clearly, Israel cannot destroy the entire Palestinian people. The PLO enjoys widespread support among the Palestinians throughout the Middle East. The destruction of the PLO's political structure will lead to frustration and despair—the very conditions in which extremists have always flourished."[102]

The West Europeans and Americans collaborated to end the fighting in Beirut, but convergence and conflict in American and European policies remained. Reagan sent Special Envoy Philip Habib to Lebanon to negotiate a ceasefire between the PLO, through Saudi intermediaries, and the Israelis. While France supported the overall American ceasefire efforts, it was critical of U.S. attempts to focus on the narrow issue of Israel's military presence in Lebanon instead of the broader Palestinian-Israeli conflict. When approximately fourteen hundred Palestinians were massacred in the Sabra and Shatila refugee camps, in the part of Beirut controlled by Israeli soldiers, the United States and its allies condemned the massacre. The EC called for measures to ensure the safety of civilians and demanded the immediate withdrawal of Israeli forces from Beirut, noting that Israel had violated the Habib Plan relating to the ceasefire. The Europeans also emphasized that peace could be achieved only through a comprehensive settlement that included the PLO.[103] But while the Europeans stationed troops associated with the U.S. multilateral force in Lebanon subsequent to the massacres, their objectives diverged from America's. Whereas American troops were perceived as being primarily concerned with the broader issues of helping Amin Gemayel's government restore order in Lebanon, and thus involved in a more political endeavor, the British, French, and Italian troops were regarded as playing a humanitarian role—to prevent additional massacres.[104] The French, by stationing their contingent in the Sabra and Shatila camps, underlined the centrality of the Palestinian issue in any Arab-Israeli peace negotiations.

The shortsightedness of Israel's invasion was demonstrated not only by the moral dilemmas it raised and the widespread protests it ignited within Israel but also by the fact that Palestinian nationalism was not destroyed. Apart from the Intifada on the West Bank and in Gaza, which began in 1987 and continued into 1991, Israel was confronted by even more PLO guerrillas in Lebanon in 1990 than were there in 1982 during the invasion.[105] Moreover, the Lebanese government, weakened even more by the invasion, was largely incapable of preventing the Palestinians from rebuilding their organization. However, by 1991, Lebanon was under greater Syrian control, and the Lebanese army had succeeded in disarming the PLO in July of that year. Israel's invasion also influenced the development of the Reagan initiative in September 1982.

Essentially reaffirming the American position on the Camp David Accords and UN Resolution 242, President Reagan's Middle East policy opposed Israeli settlements in the Occupied Territories and viewed them as obstacles to the Camp David process. In the President's view, Resolution 242 required Israel to withdraw to its pre–1967 borders in exchange for peace with its neighbors. Reagan opposed Israeli control of the West Bank and Gaza as well as the creation of a Palestinian state. Instead, he proposed self-government for the Palestinians in association with Jordan.[106] Although the Reagan initiative was relatively moderate, compared to the Venice Declaration, Britain decided to support it. France and the other European allies were less enthusiastic, and both the Israelis and the Palestinian rejected it.

Between 1983 and 1987, when the NATO allies paid comparatively little attention to the Palestinian-Israeli conflict, Israel consolidated its control of the Occupied Territories. Israel acquired Palestinian lands by direct purchase, through seizure, and by legal manipulation of ancient laws and customs. Regardless of the method, most Palestinians resented being deprived of their ancestral lands; however, since the area was governed by the military, there were few meaningful legal avenues available to protest Israel's arbitrary laws and actions.[107] Furthermore, Israeli authorities could simply deport anyone from the Occupied Territories, a practice condemned by the West European allies and the United States. On instructions from the EC, the West German ambassador in Israel expressed the EC's view that Israel was violating the Geneva Convention of 1949 on the protection of civilians in time of war by its actions in the West Bank and Gaza.[108] Similarly, the United States issued a statement at the UN indicating that Israel's deportations violated Article 49 of the Fourth Geneva Convention, and pointed out that "such harsh measures are unnecessary to maintain order. They also serve to increase tension rather than contribute to the creation of a political atmosphere conducive to reconciliation and negotiation."[109] Widespread violations of Palestinian rights during twenty years of occupation and a sense of hopelessness, emanating in part from the moribund peace process, ultimately triggered the Intifada in December 1987.

Willing to die for an improvement in their situation and a homeland, the Palestinians defied the Israeli army and held mass demonstrations. Their demands included (1) repatriation of deportees, (2) release of political prisoners, (3) withdrawal of the Israeli army from residential areas, (4) termination of Israeli settlements in the West Bank and Gaza, (5) an end to the government's confiscation of Arab land, (6) no taxation of Palestinians in the Occupied Territories, and (7) removal of restrictions on Palestinians in the areas of employment, trade, and agriculture.[110]

The Intifada demonstrated in the most obvious way that the Palestinian issue was at the crux of the Arab-Israeli problem. It focused international attention on Israeli rule in the Occupied Territories and reinvigorated the peace process. The Palestinianization of the conflict was facilitated when various Palestinian groups united under the umbrella of the PLO during the meeting of the PNC in early 1987 and by significant financial contributions from Saudi Arabia and other countries. But the momentum was generated both by a new sense of empowerment and the brutal measures used by Israeli soldiers to crush the uprising. [111]

While indicating that many Palestinians were killed by other Palestinians, the United States criticized Israel for violating human rights in the Occupied Territories and for causing avoidable deaths and injuries. The State Department condemned such Israeli practices as demolishing homes for "security reasons," inhumane beatings, the destruction of property, and arbitrary arrests.[112] The European allies' responses were consistent with the United States'. A delegation of the Parliamentary Assembly for Euro-Arab Cooperation visited the Occupied Territories and expressed concern about the "extent of the violation of the most elementary rights of the Palestinian population." Asserting that the uprising reflected the "wholly understandable frustration and resentment at the length of the occupation and the iron fist policy," the EC concluded that the "level of force employed by the authorities had, in any case and by any standard, been excessive."[113] The British criticized Israel for having a double standard on human rights. William Waldegrave, Secretary of State in the Foreign and Commonwealth Office, noted it was "ironic that the Israelis should campaign, with our full support, for the human rights of Soviet Jews. Israel must apply the same criteria to its treatment of the Palestinians."[114]

But increased Jewish immigration from the Soviet Union and U.S. restrictions on the number of Jews it would accept influenced Israel to offer incentives to Jews to settle in Israel (including the Occupied Territories) from late 1989 through 1991. Israel continued to build housing for the new immigrants in the Occupied Territories even as Baker was trying to initiate dialogue between Israel and the Arabs in 1991. In addition to the Likud's firmly-held belief that all of Palestine belongs to Israel, many Israelis worried about the implications of a relatively fast-growing Palestinian population. The West Bank Data Base Project estimated that, given the population growth rates in the mid-1980s for Jews and Palestinians, the proportion of the Jewish population in the area of Mandatory Palestine would decrease from 64 percent in 1984 to 57–59 percent in the year 2000, and under 55 percent by 2005.[115] Thus, when Prime Minister Yitzhak Shamir declared in 1990 that "for a big immigration, we need a big and strong state,"[116] it was clear that, despite later semantic maneuvering in response to international disapproval of Israel's role in helping Soviet Jews settle on the West Bank, the Likud government was unlikely to recognize Palestinians' claims to an independent homeland.

Although the Palestinian National Council had passed resolutions in 1974 and 1977 regarding the creation of a Palestinian state alongside Israel, ongoing PLO terrorist activities and the Palestinians' inability to surmount numerous obstacles to their attempts to communicate this change in policy obscured the movement toward moderation and the acceptance of a two-state solution to the Palestinian-Israeli problem. While the United States and Israel continued to be wedded to a solution involving Jordan, the Palestinians had moved toward an independent state under their control. Therefore, when Jordan severed all legal and political responsibilities for the West Bank in mid–1988, it was complying with Palestinian policy. Furthermore, it disabused Israel and the United States of their belief that the Palestinians were peripheral participants in the Palestinian-Israeli conflict. More important than the demise of the "Jordanian option" was the realpolitik assessment of the situation by the PNC and their decision in November 1988 to accept Israel's right to exist, to renounce PLO terrorism, and to embrace a negotiated settlement to the Palestinian-Israeli dispute.[117] By so doing, the Palestinians strengthened the momentum they had gained from the Intifada and radically changed the game in their favor. However, their support for

Iraq during the 1990–91 Gulf crisis resulted in serious political setbacks and economic costs.

Israel, naturally concerned about the security risks a Palestinian state would pose, reacted clumsily. Serious divisions within Israel surfaced at a time when extremists in the Likud and small religious political parties had succeeded in alienating some American Jews by their renewed efforts to determine Jewishness using very narrow criteria. American Jews were increasingly divided over events in Israel and the issue of a Palestinian state. Many had played a critical but controversial role in getting the Palestinians to deal constructively with Israel.[118] Despite the fact that Jews were concerned about the implication of a Palestinian state for Israel's security, more liberal factions seemed to support Heller's conclusion that "the actual consequences of such a settlement are more a function of the probable dynamics of the environment after peace and the character of the Palestinian state than the mere fact of its existence."[119] But if moderate Israelis found this assessment acceptable, Gush Emunim and the New Zionists were rigid and uncompromising.

Having stated their commitment to establishing a Palestinian state as part of a comprehensive negotiated settlement in the Venice Declaration and subsequent statements, the West European allies evinced a far more enthusiastic response than the United States to the PNC's policy, although the European and American positions had converged to an unprecedented degree.[120] West Germany, alluding to its consistent and unequivocal support for Israel's right to exist as well as the right of the Palestinian people to self-determination, viewed the PNC's actions as important steps toward a durable and just peace in the Middle East.[121] But if the Europeans felt that these developments were constructive, Israelis strenuously disagreed with their positive statements. The Foreign Ministry declared that while the Europeans presented the PNC's decision as a breakthrough, their analysis was not corroborated by facts. Secretary-General of the Arab League Klibi also expressed disappointment with the Europeans, albeit for different reasons, asserting that they had avoided forcing Israel into a corner and that they gave the impression that Palestinians could do even more than accepting the relevant UN resolutions and condemning terrorism.[122] Nonetheless, the Palestinians had to rely on the Europeans to pressure the United States to recognize the PLO's significant policy shift.

Strongly influenced by Israel's supporters in Congress and elsewhere, the Reagan administration, prior to the PNC's decision in Algiers, decided to close the Palestinian Information Office in order to demonstrate concern over terrorism, even as the United States claimed to fully support the legitimate rights of the Palestinian people. The United States also acknowledged that it was important for Palestinian representatives to participate in all stages of negotiations and that "the rights of the Palestinians in a just and peaceful resolution of the Arab-Israeli conflict are no less important than the right of Israel to live in peace with its neighbors."[123] That such fence-straddling strategies underscored the susceptibility of American foreign policy to unreasonable interest group demands was demonstrated by the later United States decision not to grant Arafat a visa to enter the country to address the UN. Citing Arafat's association with terrorism in general and the murder of an American citizen, Leon Klinghoffer, in particular, American officials argued that Congress had conditioned U.S. entry into the UN headquarters agreement on the retention of authority by the U.S. government to bar entry to aliens in order to safeguard American security.[124] The apparent weakness of this argument, and its inconsistency with previous U.S. policy that allowed Arafat to address the UN in New York in 1974, prompted the Europeans to strongly criticize their ally, especially in light of the moderation exhibited by the PNC's decision in late 1988. West Germany, France, the Netherlands, Italy, and to a lesser extent, Britain, saw the U.S. State Department's action as inimical to the peace process it claimed to encourage.[125] Whatever the underlying U.S. strategy may have been, the State Department succeeded in isolating Israel and the United States from the world community and influenced the European allies and others to move the UN meeting from New York to Geneva where Arafat could get a hearing.

The Europeans played a significant behind-the-scenes role in Geneva to convince Arafat to say precisely what the United States required as conditions for opening dialogue with the PLO. Americans, in official as well as private capacities, also urged Arafat to unequivocally denounce terrorism and to recognize Israel's right to exist. The British in particular consistently and quietly pressured Washington to talk with the PLO. Noting that the PLO had met American conditions, President Reagan "authorized the State Department to enter into substantive dialogue with PLO representatives."[126]

Following this watershed change in U.S. policy toward the Palestinian-Israeli conflict, Arafat was invited to hold official talks with the EC in January 1989. The Europeans underscored their support for a comprehensive international conference to solve the dispute, but stopped short of diplomatic recognition of the PLO's proclaimed state, largely because the PLO did not control any territory. France, however, decided to elevate the PLO Liaison and Information Office in Paris to the status of General Delegation for Palestine without giving it diplomatic status or privileges, although it benefited from increased protection. But Mitterrand, during his meeting with Arafat, expressed his concern about maintaining the PLO Charter of 1964, which he viewed as contrary to the November 1988 PNC policy shift.[127] Similar to France, Britain, while waiting for the Bush administration to articulate its policy on the Palestinian-Israeli conflict in light of Reagan's statement, declared its support for the PLO's new position and urged revitalized negotiations under U.S. leadership. In the meantime, William Waldegrave, Britain's Secretary of State in the Foreign and Commonwealth Office, met with Arafat in Tunisia in January 1989. Both Prime

Minister Thatcher and Waldegrave admonished the Israelis about refusing to talk with the PLO. They urged Israel to explicitly state, as Arafat did at Geneva, that all proposals and ideas were subject to discussion, and observed that the Palestinians had offered important concessions so that dialogue could be started while Israel had offered nothing.[128] Responding to the European initiatives, representatives from the Likud compared the PLO to the Nazis. Ariel Sharon, for example, asserted that the Europeans were making a tragic mistake in talking with Arafat. As he put it, "this capitulation by the European democracies before the man who has more Jewish blood on his hands since the Nazis, is exposing Israel to danger, is delaying peace, and increasing violence."[129]

In contrast to the Labor members of Israel's coalition government, who were willing to talk with the PLO and exchange land for peace, the Likud adamantly opposed any compromise with the PLO and believed that it could dictate the terms for negotiations as well as who would represent the Palestinians. Obviously designed to terminate momentum toward a comprehensive negotiated settlement, those unrealistic expectations ultimately resulted in the demise of the Labor-Likud coalition and led eventually to a coalition government in mid–1990 composed of Likud and extreme right religious parties. All efforts to reconcile Palestinians and Israelis, including the Mubarak peace initiative (which sought direct talks between Israel and the Palestinians as well as Israel's acceptance of a set of proposals on how elections could be conducted on the West Bank and Gaza), were either directly rejected or rendered meaningless by Likud.[130]

Both the West European allies and the United States urged Israel to change its policy. In a speech before the American-Israeli Public Affairs Committee (AIPAC), one of Israel's most ardent supporters, U.S. Secretary of State James Baker stated that the United States supported neither annexation nor permanent Israeli control of the West Bank and Gaza, nor an independent Palestinian state. In this uncharacteristically straightforward speech, Baker called on Israel to "lay aside, once and for all, the unrealistic vision of a greater Israel. Forswear annexation. Stop settlement activity. Allow schools to reopen. Reach out to the Palestinians as neighbors who deserve political rights."[131] Although surprised by America's new assertiveness on the Palestinian-Israeli conflict, Israeli leaders continued their practices.

But various factions within the PLO also ignored Baker's advice to renounce violence and reach out to the Israelis and convince them of their peaceful intentions. Instead, PLO members such as George Habash, leader of the Popular Front for the Liberation of Palestine, mobilized opposition against moderate PLO efforts toward a negotiated settlement and advocated continued guerrilla warfare against Israel.[132] These unrealistic attitudes strengthened Likud's argument that Israel should not negotiate with the PLO because of its terrorist activities. Every terrorist attack against Israel, including one by PLO dissident Abdul Abbas on May 30, 1990, was presented to the United States as evidence of PLO duplicity and lack of commitment to peaceful conflict resolution. No effort was made by Likud to humanize the other side or to recognize their problem.

Largely due to Israel's lack of movement on the peace process, Washington in mid-1990 initially rejected calls from Shamir and others to end dialogue with the PLO because of terrorist activities.[133] Concerned about renewed terrorism by PLO factions competing with Arafat, Baker pressed Arafat to disavow the May attack. However, Israel's intransigence and Shamir's scuttling of the peace process also drew a sharp public rebuke from the United States. Frustrated by the commitment of the right-wing coalition government, formed in June 1990 under Shamir's leadership, to strengthen and expand Jewish settlements in the Occupied Territories and to use more violence to crush the Intifada, Baker offered the Israelis the White House telephone number and urged them to "call us when you are serious about peace."[134] Shortly thereafter President Bush reluctantly ended U.S. dialogue with the PLO because Arafat refused to disavow the May attack.

Despite differences between the United States and its West European allies, by 1991 their policies had converged to an unprecedented degree. In an attempt to consolidate the international alliance against Saddam Hussein, the United States supported UN resolutions condemning Israel's violence against the Palestinians and calling for an international peace conference to settle the Palestinian issue. But Iraqi Scud attacks on Israel during the war engendered cooperation between Israel and America. Nevertheless, the Gulf crisis further underscored the Arab states' importance to Western interests, and the end of the Cold War and the opening of an Israeli consulate in Moscow in early 1991 diminished Israel's strategic significance to the United States.

Unprecedented Arab cooperation with the United States during the Gulf crisis and the strong position taken by the international community against Iraq's occupation of Kuwait influenced Washington to reinvigorate diplomatic efforts to solve the Arab-Israeli conflict in general and the Palestinian-Israeli problem in particular. Whereas the European allies, especially France, favored a greater role for the UN Security Council in settling the Arab-Israeli dispute, the United States proposed convening regional peace talks, co-sponsored by Washington and Moscow. This regional meeting was viewed as a step toward direct talks between Israel and the Arab states and between Israel and the Palestinians.[135] While the Israelis agreed to attend the meeting, there was little evidence to suggest that the difficult issues in the Palestinian-Israeli conflict would be quickly resolved. The Arabs as well as the European allies favored an international peace conference under UN auspices, an approach which Israel adamantly opposed.

NOTES

1. Aaron David Miller, *The Arab States and the Palestinian Question* (New York: Praeger, 1986), p. 11.

2. Jimmy Carter, *The Blood of Abraham* (Boston: Houghton Mifflin, 1985), p. 113.

3. Adam M. Garfinkle, "America and Europe in the Middle East: Problems for U.S. Policy," in *The Middle East and the Western Alliance*, ed. Steven Spiegel (London: Allen and Unwin, 1982), p. 10.

4. William B. Quandt, "The Western Alliance in the Middle East: Problems for U.S. Policy," in *The Middle East and the Western Alliance*, ed. Steven Spiegel (London: Allen and Unwin, 1982), p. 10.

5. Garfinkle, p. 9.

6. Rosemary Hollis, "Great Britain," in *The Powers in the Middle East*, ed. Bernard Reich (New York: Praeger, 1987), p. 68.

7. John Palmer, *Europe Without America? The Crisis in Atlantic Relations* (New York: Oxford University Press, 1987), p. 68.

8. Shahram Chubin, "West European Perceptions of Europe's Stake in Persian Gulf-Indian Ocean Security," in *The Great Game: Rivalry in The Persian Gulf and South Asia*, ed. Alvin Rubinstein (New York: Praeger, 1983), p. 133.

9. Geoffrey Edwards, "Britain," in *European Foreign Policymaking and the Arab-Israeli Conflict*, eds. D. Allen and A. Pijpers (The Hague: Martinus Nijhoff, 1984), p. 53.

10. Edwards, p. 51.

11. Edward Heath, "A Strategic Way Around the Quagmire," *The Times* (London), December 2, 1980, p. 12.

12. Edwards, p. 49.

13. Roy C. Macridis, "French Foreign Policy: The Quest For Rank," in *Foreign Policy in World Politics*, ed. Roy C. Macridis (Englewood Cliffs, N.J.: Prentice-Hall, 1985), p. 67.

14. Macridis, p. 67.

15. Lilly Gardener Feldman, *The Special Relationship Between West Germany and Israel* (Boston: Allen and Unwin, 1984), pp. 1–5.

16. Udo Steinbach, "German Policy on the Middle East and the Gulf," *Aussenpolitik* 32, no. 4 (1981): 318.

17. Steinbach, p. 319.

18. Gerald M. Steinberg and Steven L. Spiegel, "Israel and the Security of the West," in *The Middle East in Global Strategy*, ed. Aurel Braun (Boulder, Colo.: Westview Press, 1987), p. 27.

19. Everett Mendelsohn, *A Compassionate Peace: A Future for Israel, Palestine, and the Middle East*, (New York: Hill and Wang, 1989), p. 216.

20. Nitza Nachmias, *Transfer of Arms, Leverage, and Peace in the Middle East* (Westport, Conn.: Greenwood Press, 1988), p. 6; and Michael Handel, "Israel's Contribution to U.S. Interests in the Middle East," in *Israel, The Middle East, and U.S. Interests*, eds. Harry S. Allen and Ivan Volgyes (New York: Praeger, 1983), pp. 82–83.

21. Walid Khalidi, "Toward Peace in the Holy Land," *Foreign Affairs* 66, no. 4 (Spring 1988): 777.

22. Martin Indyk, "Faulty Assumptions, Failed Policy," in *Superpower Involvement in the Middle East*, eds. Paul Marantz and Blema S. Steinberg (Boulder, Colo.: Westview Press, 1985), p. 200.

23. Feldman, p. 205; and Stephen J. Artner, "The Middle East: A Chance for Europe?" *International Affairs* 56, no. 3 (Summer 1980): 421.

24. Marcus Wright, "France and the Middle East," *Middle East Economic Digest* 31 (September 26, 1987): 39.

25. "Survey: The Arab World," *The Economist*, May 12, 1990, p. 20.

26. Youssef M. Ibrahim, "Western Europe Seeks Arab Economic Ties," *The New York Times*, December 20, 1989, p. A6.

27. Feldman, pp. 114–15.

28. "EEC/Israel," *Europe: Agence Internationale D'Information Pour La Presse*, (cited as *Europe*), May 24, 1989, p. 5.

29. "Trade Wars the Middle East Way," *The Economist*, April 14, 1990, p. 73.

30. "Trade Wars"; and Khalil Touma, "Gaza Citrus Producers, EC Upset at Sabotage of Products at Seaport," *Al Fajr-Jerusalem Palestinian Weekly*, November 27, 1989, p. 1.

31. Deputy Assistant Secretary Edward S. Walker, "FY1990 Assistance Request for the Middle East," *Department of State Bulletin*, May 1989, p. 61.

32. Walker, p. 62.

33. Carter, p. 54.

34. Mendelsohn, p. 148.

35. Thomas L. Friedman, "U.S. Tells Israel It Plans to Sell Saudis Three Hundred Tanks," *The New York Times*, September 29, 1989, p. A1.

36. Hollis, p. 179.

37. Timothy J. Piro, "France," in *The Powers in the Middle East*, ed. Bernard Reich (New York: Praeger, 1987), p. 227.

38. Hollis, p. 181.

39. John Quigley, *Palestine and Israel: A Challenge to Justice* (Durham, N.C.: Duke University Press, 1990), p. 6.

40. Gershon R. Kieval and Bernard Reich, "The United States," in *The Powers in the Middle East*, ed. Bernard Reich (New York: Praeger, 1987), p. 56.

41. Hollis, p. 186.

42. William Roger Louis, *The British Empire in the Middle East, 1945–1951* (Oxford: Clarendon Press, 1985), p. 384.

43. Dan Tschirgi, *The American Search for Mideast Peace* (New York: Praeger, 1989), p. 2.

44. Louis, p. 395.

45. Alvin Z. Rubinstein, "Editors Preface," in Bernard Reich, *The United States and Israel: Influence in the Special Relationship* (New York: Praeger, 1984), p. v.

46. Ilan Pappé, *Britain and the Arab-Israeli Conflict, 1948–1951* (New York: St. Martin's Press, 1988), p. 124.

47. Menachem Begin, *The Revolt* (London: W. H. Allen, 1951), p. 335.

48. Tareq Y. Ismael, *International Relations of the Contemporary Middle East* (Syracuse, N.Y.: Syracuse University Press, 1986), p. 144.

49. Charles A. Kupchan, *The Persian Gulf and the West: Dilemmas of Security* (Boston: Allen and Unwin, 1987), p. 165.

50. Tschirgi, p. 7.

51. Helmut Kohl, "Our Liability Continues," in *Twenty Years of Diplomatic Relations Between the Federal Republic of Germany and Israel*, eds. Otto R. Romberg and Georg Schwinghammer (Frankfurt: Tribune-Verlag, 1985), p. 10.

52. Piro, p. 238; and Thankmar Frhr von Munchhausen, "France's Relations with the Arab World," *Aussenpolitik* 32, no. 4 (1981): 360.

53. Carter, p. 38.

54. Ian S. Lustick, *For the Land and the Lord: Jewish Fundamentalism in Israel* (New York: Council on Foreign Relations, 1988), p. 42.

55. Tschirgi, p. 24.

56. Carter, p. 111.

57. Saadia Touval, *The Peace Brokers: Mediators in the Arab-Israeli Conflict, 1948–1979* (Princeton, N.J.: Princeton University Press, 1982), p. 135.

58. Galia Golan, "The Soviet Union and the Palestine Liberation Organization," in *The Soviet Union and the Middle East in the 1980s: Opportunities, Constraints, and Dilemmas*, eds. Mark V. Kauppi and R. Craig Nation (Lexington, Mass.: Lexington Books, 1983), p. 190.

59. Artner, p. 421; and Connie de Boer, *West European Public Opinion and the Palestine Question* (Washington, D.C.: International Center for Research and Public Policy, 1986), p. 23.

60. A. W. DePorte, *Europe Between the Superpowers: The Enduring Balance* (New Haven, Conn.: Yale University Press, 1979), p. 240.

61. Philippe Rondol, "France and Palestine: From Charles de Gaulle to François Mitterrand," *Journal of Palestinian Studies* 16, no. 3, (Spring 1987): 89.

62. Rondol, p. 92.

63. Feldman, p. 163.

64. *Parliamentary Debates* (Commons), 5th ser., vol. 861, 16–25 October (1973), col. 431.

65. George Brown, Secretary of State for Foreign Affairs, "Statement," *Parliamentary Debates* (Commons), 5th ser., vol. 747, 31 May–9 June (1967), col. 1068.

66. Prime Minister Harold Wilson, "Statement," *Parliamentary Debates* (Commons), 5th ser., vol. 748, 12–23 June (1967), col. 62(w).

67. *Parliamentary Debates* (Commons), 5th ser., vol. 750, 10–21 July (1967), col. 151.

68. Hollis, p. 193.

69. Cyrus Vance, *Hard Choices: Critical Years in American Foreign Policy* (New York: Simon and Schuster, 1983), p. 160.

70. *Parliamentary Debates* (Commons), 5th ser., vol. 861, 16–25 October (1973), col. 537.

71. *Parliamentary Debates* (Commons), 5th ser., vol. 861, 16–25 October (1973), col. 537.

72. Lyndon B. Johnson, *The Vantage Point* (New York: Holt, Rinehart and Winston, 1971), pp. 287–88.

73. Touval, p. 144.

74. Tschirgi, p. 23.

75. William B. Quandt, *Camp David: Peacemaking and Politics* (Washington, D.C.: The Brookings Institution, 1986), p. 17.

76. Quandt, p. 17.

77. Gershon R. Kieval, *Party Politics in Israel and the Occupied Territories* (Westport, Conn.: Greenwood Press, 1983), p. 91.

78. Reich, *The United States and Israel*, p. 30.

79. *Parliamentary Debates* (Commons), 5th ser., vol. 861, 16–25 October (1973), col. 422.

80. *Parliamentary Debates* (Commons), 5th ser., vol. 863, 30 October–9 November (1973), col. 221.

81. *Parliamentary Debates* (Commons), 5th ser., vol. 863, 16–25 October (1973), col. 421.

82. *Parliamentary Debates* (Commons), 5th ser., vol. 863, 30 October–9 November (1973), col. 226.

83. Werner J. Feld, "West European Foreign Policies: The Impact of the Oil Crisis," *Orbis* 22, no. 1 (Spring 1978): 71.

84. Feld, p. 70.

85. David Allen, "Political Cooperation and the Euro-Arab Dialogue," in *National Foreign Policies and European Political Cooperation*, ed. Christopher Hill (London: Allen and Unwin, 1983), p. 70.

86. Robert J. Lieber, "The European Community and the Middle East," in *Crisis and Conflicts in the Middle East*, ed. Colin Legum (New York: Holmes and Meier, 1981), p. 93; and Roy H. Ginsberg, *Foreign Policy Actions of the European Community* (Boulder, Colo.: Lynne Rienner, 1989), p. 167.

87. Ilan Greilsammer and Joseph Weiler, *Europe's Middle East Dilemma: The Quest for a Unified Stance* (Boulder, Colo.: Westview Press, 1987), p. 35.

88. Ismael, p. 152.

89. Lally Weymouth, "Andrew Young Wasn't the Only One," *The Washington Post National Weekly Edition*, June 12–18, 1989, p. 23.

90. *Weekly Compilation of Presidential Documents*, March 21, 1977, p. 361.

91. Amos Perlmutter, "Israel's Security Option," *Foreign Affairs* 64, no. 1 (Fall 1985): 144. See David Newman, "Introduction: Gush Emunim in Society and Space," in *The Impact of Gush Emunim: Politics and Settlement in the West Bank*, ed. David Newman (New York: St. Martin's Press, 1985), pp. 1–2.

92. Ofira Seliktar, "Israel: The New Zionism," *Foreign Policy*, no. 51 (Summer 1983): 132.

93. Greilsammer and Weiler, p. 36.

94. Michael Wolffsohn, *West Germany's Foreign Policy in the Era of Brandt and Schmidt 1969–1982* (Frankfurt: Verlag Peter Lang, 1986) p. 34; and "West Germany and the Middle East: Chancellor Addresses Bundestag," *Europe*, May 8, 1981, p. 4.

95. Carter, p. 45.

96. "Venice Declaration: EC Statement on the Middle East, June 13, 1980," *Bulletin of the European Communities* 13, no. 6 (1980): 10–11. See "According to Israel, European Initiative Is Bound to Fail," *Europe*, April 17, 1981, p. 3.

97. Anthony H. Cordesman, *The Gulf and the West: Strategic Relations and Military Realities* (Boulder, Colo.: Westview Press, 1988), p. 36.

98. Roger D. Hansen, "The Reagan Doctrine and Global Containment," *SAIS Review* 7, no. 1 (Winter-Spring 1987): 50.

99. Piro, p. 252.

100. Thomas Carothers, "Mitterrand and the Middle East," *The World Today* 38, no. 10 (October 1982): 382.

101. Harold H. Saunders, "The Arab-Israeli Conflict in Global Perspective," in *Restructuring American Foreign Policy*, ed. John D. Steinbruner (Washington, D.C.: The Brookings Institution, 1989), p. 223.

102. *Parliamentary Debates* (Commons), 6th ser., vol. 19, 1–12 March (1982), col. 212.

103. "Statement of the Foreign Ministers on the Middle East Situation," *Bulletin of the European Communities* 15, no. 9 (1982): 53.

104. Stanley Hoffmann, "The U.S. and Western Europe" *Foreign Affairs* 63, no. 3 (1985): 461.

105. Ihsan A. Hijazi, "PLO Completes Buildup in Lebanon," *The New York Times*, April 2, 1990, p. A3.

106. Alan J. Kreczko, "Support the Reagan Initiative," *Foreign Policy*, no. 49 (Winter 1982–83): 140–44.

107. Mendelsohn, pp. 47–49; and Carter, p. 122.

108. *Bulletin of the European Communities* 21, no. 1 (1988): p. 49; see *Parliamentary Debates* (Commons) 6th ser., vol. 144, 11 January (1989), col. 825; and "Statement of the Ministers of Foreign Affairs on the Situation in the Occupied Territories," *Bulletin of the European Communities* 21, no. 2 (1988): 78–79.

109. "Statement by Herbert S. Okun, U.S. Deputy Permanent Rep. to the UN, on January 5, 1988, before the Security Council on Israeli Deportations," *Department of State Bulletin*, March 1988, p. 82.

110. Ann Mosely Lesch, "Anatomy of an Uprising: The Palestinian Intifadah," in *Palestinians Under Occupation: Prospects for the Future*, eds. Peter F. Krogh and Mary C. McDavid (Washington, D.C.: Center for Contemporary Arab Studies, 1989), p. 110.

111. See Jamal R. Nassar and Roger Heacock, "The Revolutionary Transformation of Palestinians Under Occupation," in *Intifada: Palestine at the Crossroads*, eds. Jamal R. Nassar and Roger Heacock (New York: Praeger, 1990), pp. 91–206.

112. "State Department Says Israel Still Violates Arab Rights," *The New York Times*, February 21, 1990, p. A4.

113. "Middle East: Visit of a Delegation of the Parliamentary Assembly for Euro-Arab Cooperation to the Occupied Territories," *Europe*, March 7, 1989, p. 4; and Grigoris Papadopoulos, *Statement on Behalf of the Twelve Member States of the European Community* (New York: UN Special Political Committee, 1988), p. 2.

114. *Parliamentary Debates* (Commons), 6th ser., vol. 138, 24 October–4 November (1988), col. 808.

115. Meron Benvenisti, *Demographic, Economic, Legal, Social, and Political Developments in the West Bank: 1986 Report* (Jerusalem: The West Bank Data Base Project, 1986), p. 4.

116. Joel Brinkley, "Meant for Home Audience, Comments on Soviet Jews Draw World Criticism," *The New York Times*, February 5, 1990, p. A9.

117. Philip Mattar, "The Critical Moment for Peace," *Foreign Policy*, no. 76 (Fall 1989): 142–43.

118. See Robert Pear, "U.S. Jews Organize to Urge Israel-PLO Talks," *The New York Times*, July 23, 1989, p. A17; and Norman Podhoretz, "Israel Isn't Suicidal," *The New York Times*, October 22, 1989, p. E3.

119. Mark A. Heller, *A Palestinian State: The Implications for Israel* (Cambridge, Mass.: Harvard University Press, 1983), p. 132.

120. Karolos Papoulias, Minister for Foreign Affairs of Greece, *Statement on Behalf of European Community and Its Twelve Member States, December 13, 1988* (Geneva: UN General Assembly, 1988), p. 3.

121. Foreign Office, "Genscher Hails Recognition of UN Resolution by PLO" (Bonn: Federal Republic of Germany, 1988), p. 1.

122. "Reactions to the Twelve's Declaration," *Europe*, November 24, 1988, p. 4.

123. U.S. Department of State, "U.S. Orders Closure of Palestine Information Office," *Department of State Bulletin*, November 1987, p. 43.

124. U.S. Department of State, "U.S. Denies Visa to PLO Leader Arafat," *Department of State Bulletin*, February 1989, p. 53.

125. "Declaration of the Twelve Concerning the Refusal of the U.S. to Grant Arafat a Visa," *Bulletin of the European Communities* 21, no. 11 (1988): 89; "Disappointment and Questions Concerning Arafat Visa Denial," *Europe*, November 28, 1988, p. 3; and "Spokesman Criticized U.S. Decision on Arafat," *FBIS-WEU*, November 29, 1988, p. 6.

126. "President Reagan's Statement on U.S. Opens Dialogue with PLO, December 14, 1988," *Department of State Bulletin*, February, 1989, p. 51.

127. "Mitterrand Asks Arafat to See That the PLO Clarifies Matters in Its Charter," *Europe*, May 3, 1989, p. 3; and "Mitterrand Has Announced That the Paris Office Will Become a General Delegation for Palestine," *Europe*, January 7, 1989, p. 4.

128. "Waldegrave Interviewed on Mideast, Lebanon," *FBIS-WEU*, June 22, 1989, p. 2; "Thatcher Urges Israel to Talk to PLO," *FBIS-WEU*, March 28, 1989, p. 9; and *Parliamentary Debates* (Commons), 6th ser., vol. 145, 17 January (1989), col. 156.

129. "Contacts With the PLO Are a Tragic Mistake, Said Sharon," *Europe*, February 3, 1989, p. 3.

130. Bernard Weinraub, "Mubarak Sees Bush and Cautions Israel," *The New York Times*, October 3, 1989, p. A6; Stephen Cohen, "Mideast Peace: Bridge vs. Wedge," *The New York Times*, October 3, 1989, p. A25; and Mary Curtius, "Israeli Debate on PLO Talks Getting Sharper," *Boston Globe*, February 4, 1989, p. 1.

131. Secretary of State Baker, "Principles and Pragmatism: American Policy Toward the Arab-Israeli Conflict," *Department of State Bulletin*, July 1989, p. 27.

132. Ihsan Hijazi, "Habash Opposing Arafat on Talks," *The New York Times*, March 9, 1990, p. A7.

133. Thomas L. Friedman, "PLO Not Engaged in Terror, U.S. Official Asserts in Congress," *The New York Times*, May 25, 1990, p. A3.

134. Tom Masland, "When You're Serious, Call Us: A Challenge to Israel," *Newsweek*, June 25, 1990, p. 37.

135. Thomas L. Friedman, "Israel Backs Plan for Single Session on Mideast Peace," *The New York Times*, April 10, 1991, p. A1.

4

The Gulf: The Iran-Iraq War and Operation Desert Storm

Compared to the other regional conflicts, the Iran-Iraq War and Iraq's occupation of Kuwait stood out as examples of Third World crises in which there was a significant degree of West European and U.S. cooperation. But to conclude that the Gulf conflict, especially prior to Iraq's invasion of Kuwait, represented a case of Western collaboration in the Third World under the auspices of NATO would be misleading. Although the allies worked together during the Iran-Iraq War, they were separated along national lines. If America wanted to demonstrate Western solidarity in defense of Western interests, the Europeans opted for distance from the United States to achieve the same objective. Even European navies, which operated under WEU, were not coordinated. Despite their attempts to harmonize their policies through the institution of EPC, the West European allies themselves supported a division of labor within the alliance partly because of their different interests and relations with countries participating directly in the conflict. France, for example, had been closely identified with the Arab countries, but West Germany had significant economic ties with both the Iranians and the Arabs. Britain, on the other hand, believed that its deep historical ties with the region and its consistent policy of evenhandedness positioned it to be impartial, even though it became the major arms supplier to the Saudi Arabians, principal backers of the Iraqis in their struggle with the Iranians. Nonetheless, the Europeans shared similar perceptions of the Soviet threat, endeavored to insulate the Gulf problems from détente with Moscow, and focused on domestic and regional causes of instability in the Gulf, thereby downplaying the East-West dimension of the conflict.

The complex nature of the Iran-Iraq War militated against simplistic Communist-anti-Communist perceptions of reality. In fact, the United

States and the Soviet Union both wanted to improve relations with Iran, the pivotal country in the region, but Iran was generally disinterested and expressed its equal hatred of Soviets and Americans in unequivocal terms. The Soviet Union and the United States had more common than divergent interests in this confrontation. Both saw continued fighting as detrimental to their objectives; both worried about the inimical aspects of Islamic fundamentalism; both sought to achieve a negotiated settlement through the UN; both supported Iraq militarily to maintain an equilibrium, even as they made overtures to Iran that included weapon sales; and both escorted Kuwaiti tankers during Iraq's war against shipping. The overarching non-ideological principle under which the Europeans, Americans, and Soviets operated in the Gulf was freedom of navigation, a generally accepted norm of international law that facilitated cooperation among the five permanent members of the UN Security Council in efforts to impose a ceasefire between Iran and Iraq. However, despite their common interests, Moscow and Washington had competing objectives, including the diminution of the other's influence in the area. Yet the complexity of the Iran-Iraq War reduced the superpowers' ability to significantly alter the outcome to their advantage.

Concerned about escalating violence and its impact on their countries' stability, Gulf leaders attempted to diffuse tension by working together through the Gulf Cooperation Council and turning to the European allies as an alternative to the superpowers. But internal problems and various territorial claims by many of these states against each other hampered their collaboration, a reality underscored by Iraq's subsequent invasion of Kuwait. Furthermore, they were confronted with the fact that the United States alone among the NATO allies had sufficient military power to safeguard their interests against Iran, even though close association with Washington could engender domestic opposition. The perceived American indifference to Arab claims in the Palestinian-Israeli conflict also argued against strategic cooperation with the United States, especially in states with large numbers of Palestinians, until the Arabs themselves were threatened by Iraq's occupation of Kuwait.

The discovery of secret American arms deals with Iran further undermined the Arabs' willingness to collaborate with the United States, but American duplicity was matched by that of the Soviet Union, West Germany, France, and other countries. The French and Germans allegedly sold arms to Iran as well as Iraq; Israel supplied Iran with much-needed weapons and spare parts and influenced Washington to do the same to win the hostages' release from Lebanon; and Israel's traditional enemies, Syria and Libya, also supported Iran.

Problems in the Gulf were inextricably linked to the Palestinian-Israeli dispute, the dynamics of the Iranian revolution, the Soviet invasion of Afghanistan, and the general East-West conflict. Despite (or because of) the fact that the West European allies had greater stakes than the United States in the outcome of the Gulf confrontation, the allies adopted a far more cautious approach and eschewed close cooperation with America as NATO allies. Even during the unprecedented international cooperation against Iraq following its invasion of Kuwait, the allies stressed that their participation in the coalition against Iraq was under the auspices of the UN. The allies' historical involvement, especially Britain's, in the Gulf, their different perceptions of the Soviet threat and commitment to divisible détente for Europe, and their preoccupation with economic power (in light of their military decline) contributed to their complex and nuanced relationship with the United States in the Persian Gulf crisis.

WESTERN EUROPE'S HISTORICAL TIES WITH THE PERSIAN GULF

Britain, the first Western European country to become deeply involved in the Gulf, was primarily concerned about protecting its lucrative trade with India against pirates based in the Gulf's estuaries. Although the British had concluded a treaty with the Sultan of Muscat in 1798, it was not until 1820 that Britain began to prepare more comprehensive treaties to be signed with Gulf leaders. In an effort to eradicate the pirates, British authorities in India launched an expeditionary force to the Gulf in 1819 that burned pirate vessels, demolished the forts of local sheikhs connected with the pirates, and chased the residents into the hills.[1] To protect their interests, the British moved quickly to formalize the new rules by concluding a General Treaty of Peace in 1820 with local rulers. The treaty, whereby the Arabs agreed to "a cessation of plunder and piracy on land and sea forever," was formulated by British Captain T. Perronet Thompson. Under the agreement the Arabs surrendered their vessels, towers, and guns in return for the restoration of their pearling industry and fishing boats. Arab leaders also promised to punish tribes that continued to engage in piracy, and the British government agreed to take notice of any attack on the vessels of friendly Arabs flying the appropriate flag. These boats were permitted to enter British ports to engage in commerce.[2] Subsequent agreements, such as the Treaty of Peace in Perpetuity of 1853 with the Trucial Sheikhs, as they were later called, allowed the British navy to directly enforce the provisions. Between 1880 and 1916, more extensive protective arrangements were negotiated with the Trucial Sheikhdoms, entitling Britain to conduct their foreign relations, to handle their security problems, and to maintain order in the region.[3] The shift in British policy from noninvolvement in the Gulf's internal affairs to protectionism stemmed from the discovery of oil in the region and Britain's determination to exclude its rivals. Britain, through extensive agreements, essentially monopolized control over the Gulf Kingdoms in exchange for protecting them from external threats.

Although other countries successfully challenged British power in the Gulf, none managed to replace it. Even the United States deferred to Britain until 1971, when the latter ended its historical role of protector. The United States routinely reviewed developments in the area with the British, and was willing to allow Britain to exercise responsibility for the Gulf.[4] America's growing support for Israel following the 1967 war further eroded its position with countries such as Iraq, but Britain's historical ties with the region and its generally impartial policy toward the Palestinian-Israeli conflict enhanced its relations with many Gulf states, despite its devolution of power. At the same time, however, Britain's tendency to cooperate with the United States, even when the two countries did not entirely agree, provided protection for American interests in particular and those of the alliance in general. West Germany, on the other hand, viewed Gulf problems from a narrower national perspective and, unlike Britain, was more apprehensive about conflicts in the Gulf and their consequences for Europe. With little historical involvement in the Gulf, Bonn saw America's commitment to the region in terms of a subtraction from Germany's own security.[5]

Unlike the Gulf countries, neither Afghanistan nor Iran willingly allowed the British to exercise extensive control over them. Britain's imperial expansion and competition with the Soviet Union in Asia brought it into direct contact with Iran. Both Russia and Britain, which maintained Afghanistan's neutrality for much of the nineteenth and twentieth centuries, dominated Iran from the early nineteenth century until 1918, when internal consolidation of the Bolshevik revolution removed Russia as a rival. The British proceeded to monopolize Iranian oil until 1951, when the Iranians nationalized their petroleum industry. While there were Iranians who viewed imperial power positively and even solicited British involvement in the country, many Iranians bitterly resented external interference. With their own imperial past, many Iranians were reluctant to accept what they regarded as British arrogance.[6] Yet internal divisions assured continued British influence in Iranian affairs. Compared to Britain, France was not perceived as a threat to Iran. Germany had only brief but largely infamous relations with Iran, a development that encouraged British, Soviet, and American activities in Iran.

Between 1930 and 1941 Iran's leader, Reza Khan, had developed close ties with Nazi Germany, and many Germans lived in Iran. When Britain and the Soviet Union requested that the Germans be expelled in 1941, the Shah refused. British and Soviet troops invaded Iran, forced the Shah to abdicate, and appointed his son, Mohammed Reza Pahlavi, as the new Shah. The United States, whose interests in Iran were mainly in the hands of missionaries and businessmen, became increasingly involved in Iran as it assumed global responsibilities in the wake of Soviet expansionism.

Having stationed troops in Iran in collaboration with the Soviet Union and Britain, the United States soon found itself confronting its wartime ally, the Soviet Union. Believing that the Soviets had assisted the Communist Tudeh Party of Iran in overthrowing the central government in the Azerbaijan and Kurdistan regions of Iran, the U.S. military advisers in the country helped the Shah to crush the Communist uprising. This was the beginning of America's alliance with the Shah,[7] which lasted until the Iranian revolution in 1979. Direct American participation in the 1953 coup that returned the Shah to power after Mohammed Mossadegh assumed control in 1952 had long-range implications for U.S.-Iranian relations. Iran's strategic location in the Cold War environment substantially enhanced its value to American foreign policymakers. Anti-Communist-influenced geo-strategic calculations prompted Washington to perceive the Gulf states, primarily Saudi Arabia, as part of its "twin-pillars" policy for the protection of western interests. But for the former British dependencies on the Arab side of the Persian Gulf, it was hardly reassuring to be now informed that their security rested in the hands of Iran, for most of them had long-standing territorial disputes with their more powerful eastern neighbor.[8] Weakened militarily by World War II, the West European powers largely avoided similar dilemmas by concentrating primarily on economic arrangements with the Gulf.

THE WEST EUROPEAN ALLIES' ECONOMIC AND MILITARY LINKS WITH THE GULF

Western Europe's geographic proximity to and its dependence on petroleum from the Gulf contributed to economic interdependence between the two regions. The Gulf countries, which controlled more than half of the world's known oil reserves in 1991, imported manufactured products from Western Europe and Asia. As economic and political issues became increasingly intertwined, the West Europeans—who were perceived by the Arabs as being more sympathetic to their views, respectful of their culture, and less threatening than either of the superpowers—were regarded as preferred trading partners. The economic dynamism of the Single European Market, and Arab fears of being shut out, heightened the need for economic cooperation between Western Europe and the Gulf. Furthermore, Europe's successful economic integration appealed to many in the Gulf who saw their own regional cooperative efforts as a viable solution to their growing political and economic challenges. Consequently, in June 1988 the EC and the Cooperation Council for the Gulf Arab States signed a Cooperation Agreement that augmented previous collaborative arrangements in the areas of industry, agriculture, fisheries, trade, energy, science and technology, environmental issues, training, and investment. In the trade sector they accorded each other most-favored-nation treatment.[9] Given the vast reserves of oil, natural gas, and coal in the Gulf, and Europe's demand for these resources, relations between the two regions were likely to be strengthened. France, Germany, and Italy were extremely dependent on petroleum from the Gulf.[10]

Most of the revenues derived from oil exports were recycled as the Gulf states purchased industrial materials from Europe and contracted with European firms to construct various projects. Thirty-five percent of all Arab exports in 1986 (estimated at $84 billion) went to the EC, compared to 8 percent for the United States, about 43 percent of all Arab imports (estimated at $93 billion) came from the EC, compared to 11 percent from the United States. The major threat to Western Europe's market share came not from the United States but from Asia, particularly Japan. Japanese cars dominated the markets of the Arabian peninsula, while civil engineering companies from South Korea and Taiwan were awarded major construction contracts.[11] And there were wide discrepancies among the West European countries in terms of their trade with the Gulf. French and West German companies were assisted by their governments, whereas British firms were less likely to receive similar treatment.

Consistent with its postwar policy of promoting economic development at home and encouraging German companies to export manufactured products, Bonn collaborated with the private insurance company Hermes Kreditversicherunas, to provide export credit insurance for companies exporting to the Gulf and elsewhere. Despite the Iran-Iraq War during the 1980s, the West German Economic Affairs Ministry, which administered the Hermes program, provided protection for companies operating in Egypt, Iran, Saudi Arabia, and Turkey—West Germany's main customers in the Middle East.[12] By avoiding controversial political issues and concentrating on trade, West Germany emerged as Iran's major trading partner following the Iranian revolution. German technology was widely used in Iran and Iranian workers were trained in West German factories. All of the West European allies had significant trade with the other Gulf states, especially with Saudi Arabia[13] (see Table 1).

Even though these economic links influenced West European policies on the Iran-Iraq War, especially West Germany's toward Iran, the realities of economic interdependence eventually convinced both Iraq and Iran to improve relations with Western Europe. For example, Iran signed several agreements with French companies in 1990 to rebuild or complete projects that were destroyed by Iraqi planes and missiles, which were probably supplied by France. The French building group GTM Entrepose signed a $45 million contract to repair Iran's Nasr platform, and Technip, an engineering group controlled by French public sector companies, was awarded the management contract to complete the Gulf's largest petrochemical complex, the Bandar Khomeini project, abandoned by the Japanese firm Mitsui after it was repeatedly bombed by Iraq.[14] During the war, France supported Iraq, although it also allegedly provided weapons to Iran.

For France, Britain, and, to a lesser extent, West Germany, arms sales were an important part of their trade with the Gulf. And competition among NATO allies for the vast arms market in the Gulf was likely to continue,

Table 1
OECD Exports to Gulf States

	U.S. $ Million			Percentage of OECD Exports		
	1984	1985	1986	1984	1985	1986
Bahrain:						
Canada	38	36	34	3.3	3.6	3.6
FR Germany	112	95	130	9.6	9.4	13.8
Italy	156	82	57	13.3	8.1	6.0
Japan	273	193	122	23.3	19.2	12.9
USA	145	107	122	12.4	10.6	20.6
UK	185	209	192	15.8	20.8	20.3
Total OECD	1,172	1,006	046			
United Arab Emirates:						
France	282	373	330	6.0	7.8	7.4
FR Germany	419	418	488	8.9	8.8	11.0
Italy	585	456	372	12.6	9.6	8.4
Japan	1,122	1,174	1,043	23.8	24.6	23.5
USA	695	596	493	14.7	12.5	11.1
UK	724	805	853	15.4	16.90	19.20
Total OECD	4,713	4,770	4,445			
Iran:						
France	181	158	98	1.9	2.1	1.6
FR Germany	2,308	1,647	1,499	23.9	22.1	24.1
Italy	950	607	653	9.8	8.2	10.5
Japan	1,672	1,360	1,154	17.3	18.3	18.6
USA	162	74	34	1.7	1.0	0.5
UK	940	681	585	9.7	9.2	9.4
Total OECD	9,646	7,445	6,214			
Iraq:						
France	685	683	491	10.7	10.2	8.7
FR Germany	860	842	650	13.5	12.6	11.6
Italy	626	686	565	9.8	10.2	10.1
Japan	805	1,318	1,224	12.6	19.7	21.8
USA	664	427	527	10.4	6.4	9.4
UK	459	577	651	7.2	8.6	11.6
Total OECD	6,374	6,693	5,618			
Saudi Arabia:						
France	2,282	1,220	1,197	9.2	6.5	7.4
FR Germany	2,198	1,759	1,541	8.9	9.3	9.5
Italy	2,385	1,836	1,463	9.7	9.7	9.0
Japan	5,596	3,922	2,786	22.7	20.8	17.2
USA	5,564	4,474	3,449	22.6	23.7	21.3
UK	1,854	1,628	2,209	7.5	8.6	13.7
Total OECD	24,674	18,873	16,176			
Kuwait:						
France	716.20	253.34	291.89	13.9	5.7	7.0
FR Germany	596.03	480.46	466.12	11.5	10.8	11.2
Italy	526.06	426.07	338.08	10.2	9.5	8.1
Japan	1,425	1,548	1,231	27.6	34.7	29.6
USA	635.48	550.61	656.63	12.3	12.3	15.8
UK	402.92	451.01	440.62	7.8	10.1	10.6
Total OECD	5,167	4,467	4,153			
Total Gulf (Excl. Oman):	4,285	2,833	2,520	8.1	6.4	6.6
France	6,581	5,346	4,861	12.5	12.1	12.7
FR Germany	5,283	4,155	3,502	10.0	9.4	9.1
Italy	11,067	9,680	7,709	21.0	12.9	20.0
Japan	7,950	6,293	5,418	15.1	14.3	14.1
USA	4,743	4,536	5,095	9.0	10.3	13.3
UK	52,581	44,111	38,309			
Total OECD						

Source: Foreign Affairs Committee, House of Commons, *The Iran/Iraq Conflict: Minutes of Evidence*, April 20, 1988 (London: HMSO, 1988), p. 122.

especially in light of reductions in European military forces, and ongoing conflicts in the Middle East and the resolution of conflicts in other regions of the world. In the late 1980s Oman, for example, spent 40 percent of its budget on defense, while Saudi Arabia allocated about $2,700 per capita for its military. With less than 3 percent of the world's population, Saudi Arabia made over 8 percent of the world's military expenditures.[15]

Following Iraq's invasion of Kuwait, Saudi Arabia allocated over $15 billion to acquire weapons from the United States. However, the Arabs' perception of Europeans as more evenhanded in their policies toward the Palestinian-Israeli conflict and America's limited maneuverability due to pressures from pro-Israeli lobbies in Washington combined to give the West European allies an advantage over the United States in the competition for weapons sales to the Gulf, especially prior to Operation Desert Storm. Strong Congressional opposition to American arms sales to Saudi Arabia repeatedly forced the White House to cancel proposals to sell Saudi Arabia weapons regarded as essential for its own security as well as for the protection of American interests. Sensitive to Israel's legitimate security concerns, successive U.S. administrations attempted to reassure Congress that proposed sales posed no threat to Israel and would not change the overall military balance in the region.[16] The West European allies, often in competition with each other, capitalized on America's problems, a situation which suited the Arabs who wanted to demonstrate their independence in the global arms market. After the United States was pressured in 1985 not to sell Saudi Arabia advanced tactical aircraft, Britain was awarded the unprecedented contract involving more than $18 billion. Similar contracts between Saudi Arabia and Britain were concluded in 1988.

Although Britain and its consortium partners, West Germany and Italy, became the leading arms merchants in the Gulf in the mid–1980s, France had long been the major supplier of arms to the Middle East and the Gulf. Several factors propelled France's aggressive and sometimes indiscriminate weapons sales abroad. These included (1) France's commitment to its own autonomous defense policy and independence within NATO, (2) its belief that countries have the sovereign right to defend themselves, (3) its desire to reduce Third World countries' reliance on the superpowers and enhance its own influence in developing areas, (4) efforts to lower development and production costs per unit by increasing volume, and (5) providing employment for over one hundred thousand French citizens whose jobs were directly connected to exports and for another two hundred thousand in the arms industry.[17]

Beginning with its radical policy change after the Six Day War, when it stopped selling arms to Israel, France became the major supplier of weapons to the Arab states, particularly Saudi Arabia and Iraq—two countries on which it relied for most of the 80 percent of its petroleum imports from the Middle East. Thus, weapons sales were instrumental in offsetting the cost of oil imports. Approximately 79 percent of all French arms exports went to the Middle East, compared to 7.4 percent to Western Europe and North America, 7 percent to Latin America, and 2.8 percent to sub-Saharan Africa.[18] Throughout the Iran-Iraq War France sold Iraq a wide variety of weapons systems, including fighter jets, missiles, and sophisticated radar systems to defend military and civilian airfields and the oil-producing regions of the country. France continued to sell weapons, allegedly to both Iraq and Iran, despite the EC's decision to embargo sales of weapons to the combatants during the war. Iraq's possession of such sophisticated weapons later complicated international efforts to force Iraq to end its occupation of Kuwait.

Britain's historical ties to the Gulf and its impartiality on the Palestinian-Israeli conflict facilitated its unprecedented arms sales contracts with Saudi Arabia between 1985 and 1990. With about twenty-seven thousand British citizens in Saudi Arabia alone and tens of thousands living elsewhere in the Gulf, and given its long military dominance over as well as cooperation with the region, Britain was well-placed to take advantage of America's refusal to sell Saudi Arabia certain types of advanced fighter jets.[19] Unlike France, Britain was not determined to have a large, autonomous, arms-manufacturing capability, partly because of its close political and military partnership with the United States within the NATO alliance and its extensive collaboration with West Germany and Italy in defense research and weapons production. Furthermore, the British appeared to be more sensitive than the French to moral and political issues surrounding questionable arms sales. Even though Britain shared with France the widely accepted view that every nation has the right to legitimate self-defense, it was more concerned about checking applications for specific purchases, and generally took into consideration political, strategic, security, and humane factors when deciding to sell weapons abroad.[20] But Britain's dependence on arms sales to the Gulf was even greater than France's in the late 1980s. Almost half of Britain's exports went to the Gulf, and approximately six hundred thousand jobs in Britain were directly linked to arms sales after the 1985–90 contracts with Saudi Arabia were signed.[21]

The Iran-Iraq War undoubtedly contributed to increased British weapons sales to Kuwait, Oman, the United Arab Emirates, and Saudi Arabia. As the leading member of a British-West German-Italian consortium that produced technologically advanced Tornado fighter jets, Britain was granted the Al-Yamamah contract, which included not only unprecedented transfers of military aircraft but also provided for greater cooperation between Britain and Saudi Arabia in economic, technical, scientific, academic, and cultural fields. The first contract under the Al-Yamamah program provided primarily for the transfer of seventy-two Tornado jets in exchange for Saudi oil. Estimated at $15 billion, this contract was followed by other agreements for additional Tornado warplanes, minesweepers, Blackhawk helicopters, and other weapons. In addition British companies were involved in the construction of two military aircraft bases. The 1985 and 1988 contracts alone totaled over $20 billion.[22] But Britain, with an eye on postwar relations with Iran, refused to sell arms to Iraq and Iran, although it continued commercial transactions with Iran and sold that country an early warning radar system, hospital equipment, and rough terrain vehicles on the grounds that they would be used for peaceful purposes.

Compared with France and Britain, West Germany was far more constrained by its recent past, the Holocaust, and its "special relationship" with Israel. Nevertheless, as Israel lost the moral high ground and Germany gained acceptance into the community of nations, an integral component of its changed policy toward the Palestinian-Israeli conflict was the limited sale of military equipment to the Middle East and the Gulf. Israel, understandably concerned about arms sales to Saudi Arabia in the early 1980s, appealed to Bonn to "listen to the voice of historical conscience and to shelve this shameful deal."[23] West Germany eventually reviewed military technology transfers to Saudi Arabia and concluded that certain companies' plans to build a factory in Saudi Arabia to produce artillery and tank ammunition were contrary to its stringent controls on arms exports. But among those who advocated that the embargo be reconsidered was Franz Josef Strauss, who argued that Germany should sell arms to the Saudis because the United States, Israel's staunchest ally, also sold weapons to them. [24] Despite Germany's refusal to permit the transfer of technology by German firms, its participation with Britain and Italy in the consortium that signed the Yamamah contracts with Saudi Arabia enabled Germany to accomplish its objectives by other means.

THE WEST EUROPEAN ALLIES AND
THE GULF CONFLICT

Before Iraq invaded Kuwait, Europe's growing political assertiveness and economic renewal, combined with the Gulf states' apprehensions involving the United States as a close ally in the region, reinforced the Europeans' view that they were an effective alternative to both superpowers. The West Europeans viewed America's uncritical support of Israel and its tendency to view regional problems in terms of East-West confrontation as rendering it largely incapable of impartial and objective analysis of the region's problems. As Douglas Hurd, Secretary of State in the Foreign and Commonwealth Office stated, "they are not anxious to call for American help, partly because of U.S. support for Israel, and partly because they do not want to transform their problem into what they do not believe it to be at present— a confrontation between East and West."[25]

Determined to remain nonaligned and having to confront a reinvigorated Islamic movement directed against westernization that was most often associated with the United States, the Gulf states tended to regard Western Europe as a reliable alternative to America. Even the allies' relative weakness was perceived as a positive factor by Gulf leaders who argued that cooperation with Western Europe was easier and less threatening than with either superpower precisely because Europe could no longer dominate the area.[26] The Gulf states also realized that the West European allies, who themselves depended on American military protection, could not replace the United States in the region, a reality underscored by the large American force in Saudi Arabia after Iraq's occupation of Kuwait, but they believed the Europeans could counterbalance the Americans. The West European allies' response to the Iranian crisis and the Soviet invasion of Afghanistan indicated how they would approach the Iran-Iraq War within the context of the NATO alliance.

The revolution in Iran and the seizure of American diplomats in Tehran induced President Carter to abandon his regional policy approach for the more traditional, postwar global confrontation with the Soviet Union. Whereas the European allies expressed sympathy and called for release of the hostages, they were reluctant to subscribe to America's policy of confrontation with Iran because they viewed the U.S. approach as counterproductive and beneficial to Moscow. From America's perspective, however, the failure of the West to unite against Iran would only encourage further radicalization of the revolution. But the Europeans concluded that both superpowers had to be restrained, and adopted a more impartial approach that did not significantly differentiate between the superpowers.[27]

Despite their general opposition toward using economic sanctions as coercive instruments of foreign policy, the Europeans were sufficiently worried about U.S. threats to take military action against an increasingly intransigent Iran that they agreed to actively support U.S. diplomatic and economic measures against Iran. Yet the agony of daily humiliation, assisted in part by Carter's decision to focus principally on obtaining the hostages' release and the media's willingness to broadcast nightly the drama in Tehran, eventually prompted Carter to attempt to rescue the hostages in late April 1980. But instead of solving the hostage problem, the failed rescue effort exacerbated an already dangerous situation in Iran and influenced the European allies to distance themselves from the United States. Believing that they should have been consulted in advance about the rescue operation, the allies not only felt deceived but viewed Americans as inept and unreliable partners.[28]

Underlying tensions within NATO emanated from other sources as well. Personal feelings, especially Chancellor Helmut Schmidt's dislike of President Carter, undoubtedly had an impact on alliance relations. But more important were significant economic links between Iran and the West Europeans, particularly West Germany. For despite their participation in America's sanctions against Iran, the Europeans were extremely careful not to seriously impair their commercial relations. Immediately after the hostages were released, the Europeans not only removed sanctions but also stressed that they had always "fully respected Iran's independence and the Iranian people's right to determine its future itself," and that they hoped the way was open for normal relations.[29] It was this emphasis on trade that helped to shape the allies', especially West Germany's, response to the Iran-Iraq war. Similar considerations influenced the allies' response to the Soviet invasion of Afghanistan, the prelude to America's preoccupation with Soviet involvement in the Gulf.

Perceiving Soviet aggression in Afghanistan as a direct threat to American interests in the Persian Gulf and neighboring countries, the Carter administration, pressured in part by election politics, reacted strongly. Despite their shared concerns about Soviet involvement in Afghanistan, the allies disagreed sharply on how to respond. The crisis highlighted long-standing fundamental differences between the United States and Western Europe on East-West issues. Divergent perspectives on the threat, different perceptions of national interests, and diverse internal political dynamics combined to create serious tensions within NATO. America's general indifference to developments in Afghanistan prior to the Soviet invasion and the low priority U.S. foreign policymakers accorded Afghanistan contrasted sharply with the extreme sense of urgency the United States exhibited after the invasion. From the Europeans' viewpoint, the Soviets' historical links to and their growing presence in Afghanistan throughout the 1970s should have moderated Washington's response.

Whereas the United States considered the invasion as a major threat to the East-West geo-strategic configuration of power, most of the allies saw Afghanistan as largely peripheral. And while American officials were confident that the Soviets knew exactly what they were doing and did not miscalculate in Afghanistan, many West Europeans were reluctant to accept the worst-case scenario and were more likely to view the invasion as an example of Soviet misjudgment.[30] America's resumption of its ideological crusade in 1980 against communism had effectively stifled the less-popular assessment that the Soviet Union had underestimated the resilience of Afghan resistance. Thus, when Soviet Foreign Minister Eduard Shevardnadze admitted ten years later that his country's military aggression against Afghanistan was a mistake,[31] Americans were surprised not only by this unprecedented openness but also by the fact that many Soviets had realized from the beginning that sending Soviet troops into a neighboring state was shortsighted and would be costly. Clearly, the Afghan resistance movement's use of American-supplied Stinger missiles had a bearing on the Soviets' conclusion. Nevertheless, most Europeans refused to share America's anxiety over Soviet involvement in Afghanistan, despite their rhetoric to the contrary.

During their EPC meeting on January 15, 1980, the West Europeans issued a declaration emphasizing their opposition to Soviet actions in Afghanistan. Essentially endorsing America's position, they rejected Moscow's justification for military intervention and stressed that the invasion constituted a flagrant violation of the sovereignty of a nonaligned Islamic country. Furthermore, they noted that Soviet aggression threatened peace and stability in the Indian subcontinent, the Middle East, and the Arab world. Pointing out that the EC had devoted continuous efforts to preserving détente, which they regarded to be in the interest of the international community, the allies declared that they were convinced that détente was indivisible and had a global dimension.[32]

However, the Europeans' behavior contradicted their declared policy. West Germany, to a much greater extent than Britain, viewed détente as divisible and Schmidt was determined not to allow Afghanistan to undermine Bonn's broader foreign policy objectives. European détente was indeed separate from what remained of global détente. Believing that confrontation with Moscow was detrimental to their interests, the allies maintained normal relations with the Soviet Union. Work on the natural gas pipeline from Siberia to Western Europe continued despite Washington's attempts to stop it, and no meaningful sanctions were implemented. Instead, the French Creusott Loire steel group negotiated a contract to build a $300-million steel mill at Novolipetsk that closely resembled one canceled by the American firm, Armco. Likewise, the West German Klickner-Werke Company agreed to construct a $311-million aluminum plant in Siberia, a project originally negotiated with Alcoa.[33]

Despite their general agreement that Afghanistan was not as crucial to overall East-West relations as the United States thought it was, the Europeans adopted different approaches, with Britain implementing policies that were closer to America's position. In contrast to West Germany and France, which had more to gain from preserving détente with the Soviet Union, Britain did not view détente as divisible. Wary about détente even prior to Afghanistan and more determined to maintain strong links with the United States within the context of the NATO alliance, Prime Minister Thatcher evinced a greater preference for "getting tough with the Russians" than for preserving EC solidarity. But if Thatcher supported American policy on Afghanistan, Britain's Foreign Secretary Lord Carrington was far more reserved.[34] Carrington endeavored to bridge differences between Western Europe and the United States and to assume the role of an honest broker between the West and the Soviet Union. As president of the European Council of Ministers, Carrington had to balance his country's concerns with those of the EC. Carrington went to Moscow in July 1981 to attempt to break the deadlock over Afghanistan and to find a compromise that would have enabled Moscow to gracefully extricate itself from its self-imposed quagmire. However, this unsuccessful European effort was greeted with suspicion in Washington,[35] since independent European foreign policy initiatives were perceived as challenges to America's leadership of the alliance. France had also effectively sabotaged an earlier European initiative that called for a neutral, nonaligned Afghanistan. Endorsed by the EC, the proposal was to be the basis for a more detailed European policy. But France's decision to conduct bilateral negotiations with Moscow on Afghanistan forced the EC to abandon its initiative.[36]

Britain, akin to France and West Germany, continued to pursue its own independent policy despite its commitment to harmonizing Western Europe's foreign policies. While the government did not convince the British Olympic Committee to join the U.S. boycott of the Olympics and did not interfere with British trade with Afghanistan, an effort was made to assist the Afghan resistance. Although the government declined to address the question of British Blowpipe missiles in Afghanistan, consistent with the established practice of not answering such questions in the House of Commons, there was sufficient evidence to indicate that Britain, like the United States, had supplied sophisticated missiles. In early July 1987 the Soviet Union lodged a protest with Britain, claiming it had provided the "newest weapons, including the Blowpipe anti-aircraft systems, to Afghan groups fighting against the legitimate government of the Democratic Republic of Afghanistan."[37] Yet, given Britain's secrecy laws, it was difficult to ascertain the extent of British military assistance to the resistance.

While Britain was primarily concerned with keeping NATO together on the Afghanistan issue, West Germany's main objective appeared to be maintaining bridges between East and West in order to alleviate Cold War tensions. Furthermore, Germany's geographic proximity to the Soviet Union and the possible domestic political implications of Bonn's policy on the issue complicated its position on Afghanistan. Taking a strong position on Afghanistan while making conciliatory gestures toward Moscow underscored the Bonn dilemma. If West Germany had vigorously opposed the Soviet Union, it would have risked détente and trade but could have weakened the opposition Green Party. Yet being closely identified with the American position could have resulted in a dangerous groundswell of opposition to American policy if that was seen to be creating unnecessary risks and tensions. Under these circumstances it was politically astute for the government to formulate a policy that could be identified as European and not merely a product of Bonn's relationship with Washington.[38]

West German leaders continued to meet with the Soviets and signed an economic cooperation agreement with Moscow, even as they advocated a division of labor among the allies that would allow the European allies to provide economic assistance to Turkey, Pakistan, and the Gulf states. Even though West Germany's Foreign Minister Hans-Dietrich Genscher may have been correct when he asserted that it was an illusion for anyone in Moscow to assume that the invasion of Afghanistan could be used to separate Europeans from Americans,[39] the reality was that the Europeans themselves had decided to distance their policies from those of the United States.

France's position on Afghanistan was similar to Germany's. While condemning Soviet military intervention, the French did not subscribe to America's view that Afghanistan was a stepping stone to the Persian Gulf. Having received assurances from Leonid Brezhnev that the invasion had been forced on him by hard-liners in the Kremlin and a plea for help to reinforce his position and lessen international tensions, French leader Giscard d'Estaing traveled to Warsaw in May 1980 to meet with Brezhnev, apparently believing that he alone among Western leaders could resolve the crisis in Afghanistan.[40] This occurred when the NATO allies were attempting to implement a common policy against Moscow. Instead of reducing economic transactions with the Soviet Union, France actually increased them. Less than a year after the invasion French trade with the Soviet Union rose by 33 percent over the previous year. The French signed a ten-year contract to supply an estimated $8 billion worth of agricultural products, oil rigs, a steel mill, and other French technologies to the Soviet Union in exchange for oil and other raw materials. And shortly after the invasion, France had begun importing Soviet gas.[41] Far from uniting the allies, the crisis in Afghanistan widened the distance between the West Europeans and the United States. And despite cooperation among the allies during the Iran-Iraq War, the Europeans insisted on not being identified with the United States, a strategy which was probably the most effective given the complexities of the Gulf.

THE IRAN-IRAQ WAR AND THE ALLIES' RESPONSES

Cooperation between the United States and its West European allies in the Gulf conflict was more apparent than real. Several complex factors combined not only to facilitate allied collaboration but also to prevent a united Western approach under the aegis of the NATO alliance. Even though the United States and its European allies had many common interests in the Gulf, their perceptions of the Soviet threat and approaches to the conflict often diverged. The Europeans' dependence on petroleum from and their significant economic and military links with the region actually meant that America was defending European interests to a much greater extent than it was protecting its own. Yet the allies generally saw U.S. actions as jeopardizing those interests and viewed America's close relationship with Israel as an impediment to their diplomatic efforts in the Gulf. Further complicating European-American cooperation were the views and interests of the Gulf states themselves. Generally inclined to regard the Europeans as a counterbalance to the Americans, Gulf leaders did not share the U.S. preoccupation with superpower rivalry—from their perspective Iran presented the greater threat. Neither did they subscribe to U.S. strategic plans that compartmentalized developments in the Gulf from the broader Arab-Israeli issue. Finally, the fact that the superpowers had more parallel than conflicting interests and objectives, and that the Gulf states were determined to avoid a superpower rivalry in the region, allowed the European allies to pursue more independent policies without engendering serious strains within the alliance.

American interests in the Gulf were clearly defined. The renewal of the Cold War in late 1979 and early 1980, partly in response to U.S. election politics, influenced Carter and his National Security Adviser Zbigniew Brzezinski to perceive problems in the Gulf—generated by the incipient Iran-Iraq war, the Soviet invasion of Afghanistan, and the emergence of Islamic fundamentalism in Iran—within the context of East-West confrontation. American policymakers were concerned about having continued access to oil from the Persian Gulf, both for the United States and the West European allies. They wanted to prevent the Soviet Union from achieving its long-standing objective of gaining access to a warm water port and its more recent goal of an increased naval and political presence in the Indian Ocean. Another U.S. objective was to develop closer relationships with moderate Arab states and to provide them with the necessary military weapons and assistance to guarantee their stability. But the U.S.-Soviet rivalry dominated all other foreign policy considerations. As Zbigniew Brzezinski put it, "it was with this superpower context in mind that the Carter administration began the complex process of putting together a long-term U.S. foreign policy for the Gulf and the Indian Ocean region. The result was what came to be known as the Carter Doctrine."[42] As the Iran-Iraq War progressed U.S. policymakers were faced with an additional set of issues. Having concluded that the war was detrimental to United States and Western European interests, American policymakers tried to (1) ensure that neither Iran nor Iraq won a decisive victory, (2) prevent the Soviet Union from benefiting from the war, (3) limit escalation of the conflict by preventing weapons from reaching the belligerents, and (4) retain U.S. credibility as a reliable partner of the Arab states, especially Saudi Arabia.[43] Growing U.S.-Iran antagonism over the hostage issue, American economic sanctions against Tehran, and the U.S. position on the Palestinian-Israeli confrontation rendered it extremely difficult for the United States to balance these objectives. Yet Washington's preoccupation with the Soviet threat militated against any serious effort to achieve a balanced policy in the Gulf.

Accused of being "soft on communism" during a presidential election year, Carter attempted to demonstrate firmness and resolve. The inherent danger of responding to ideological demands was the tendency to project American views of reality onto what was essentially a regional conflict. Consequently, efforts were made to build a Rapid Deployment Force, to increase joint military exercises with Oman and Egypt, to stockpile military weapons in the area, and to increase naval and air deployments in the region.[44] Underlying these policies was the assumption that the Soviet Union had the ability to mobilize its forces for deployment in the Gulf relatively quickly. Direct Soviet military involvement was viewed as inimical to Western interests. Ironically, in 1990, the United States found itself in an unprecedented postwar alliance with the Soviet Union to counteract Iraq's threat to the region.

Although the European allies agreed with the United States that a preponderant Soviet presence in the Gulf would jeopardize Western interests, they objected to America's preoccupation with the Soviet threat and its emphasis on addressing the threat militarily. Europeans generally argued that the Soviet Union, realizing its miscalculation in Afghanistan, had little intention of employing military force in the Gulf. Defining the Gulf problem in terms of East-West confrontation was seen by the Europeans as fostering internal instability in Saudi Arabia, Kuwait, and elsewhere, thereby increasing the threat to Western oil supplies.[45] The Europeans preferred to use diplomatic and economic instruments of foreign policy and to focus on indigenous sources of conflict and instability. While the allies were more willing than the United States to live with political upheavals, fragmentation, and secession in the Third World, they wanted to find solutions to regional conflicts.[46] The Europeans' strategies for dealing with these problems reflected their complex relationships with the Third World and their own capabilities and national interests. The allies had realized, much sooner than the United States, that the complex political dynamics of the Gulf also posed serious challenges for the Soviet Union.

Historically sensitive to perceived threats from neighboring countries, the Russians had long tried to gain security through expansion. Iran's 1,250-mile border with Russia inevitably made it a target of Russian aggression. But Britain was also interested in expanding its own empire, which brought the Russians and the British into situations of conflict as well as cooperation. In Afghanistan, Iran, and elsewhere, competing imperialistic designs clashed and problems had to be resolved. In Iran's case, Russia and Britain agreed in 1907 to divide the country into two spheres of influence. Although the new government of the Soviet Union renounced the agreement, by 1921 a Soviet-Iranian treaty was signed which entitled the Soviets to intervene militarily if forces threatening the Soviet Union entered Iran.[47] And in 1941 the British and the Soviets, responding to the Nazi threat, divided Iran. The Soviets left in 1946 only after being pressured to do so by the United States. Escalation of the Cold War only heightened Soviet interest in Iran, as the United States had persuaded Iran to join the Baghdad Pact in 1955 to contain Soviet expansion. It was clearly Moscow's objective to weaken U.S. influence on its border by driving a wedge between Iran and the West.

Similarly, the Soviets attempted to establish a foothold in Iraq. Twelve

years after gaining its independence from Britain in 1932, Iraq established
diplomatic relations with the Soviet Union. However, when Iraq joined Iran,
Turkey, and Pakistan as a member of the Baghdad Pact in 1955, diplomatic
ties with Moscow were severed. But Iraq's close identification with the West
during the height of Arab nationalism, inspired in part by Egypt's President
Gamal Nasser, led to the downfall of the British-installed Hashemite mon-
archy in a coup d'etat in 1958. Iraq's pro-Western orientation was terminated when its new leaders withdrew from the Baghdad Pact, canceled an
Anglo-Iraqi agreement, and ousted all British soldiers.[48] The consolidation
of Iraq's relationship with Moscow was facilitated by U.S. support of Israel
during the 1967 and 1973 wars and by America's close alliance with the
Shah of Iran, whose assistance to Kurdish forces enhanced their ability to
oppose Baghdad's authority. Iraq's reliance on the Soviet Union for weapons
and advice intensified as the Kurds escalated their armed struggle against
the government. However, when petroleum prices quadrupled following
OPEC's oil embargo in the mid–1970s, Iraq reduced its dependence on
Moscow and improved commercial relations with Western Europe.[49] The
Soviet Union's historical ties with Iran and Iraq as well as its desire to
maintain or restore good relations with both, partly to diminish America's
opportunities in the region, paradoxically brought Soviet and American
interests closer in the Iran-Iraq War, a reality which enabled the European
allies to more easily cooperate with the United States to end the conflict.

Soviet foreign policy objectives in the Gulf, from America's perspective,
included countering U.S. influence in the region, establishing more durable
links with the Gulf states, maintaining ties with both Iran and Iraq, and
emerging as the major extra-regional power in the postwar period.[50] From
the U.S. viewpoint, the Iran-Iraq War helped to advance Soviet policies. But
if the Soviets saw the war as providing opportunities for them to threaten
Western oil supplies and reduce U.S. influence, they were also convinced
that instability in the Gulf would have serious political consequences for
the Soviet Union. From the Soviets' perspective, the United States in particular and the West in general stood to gain from the weakening of Iran
and Iraq. Regional instability was seen as enabling the United States to
escalate its involvement in the Gulf on behalf of pro-Western regimes such
as Saudi Arabia, a view confirmed in 1990 after Iraq invaded Kuwait. The
Soviet Union had little to gain from either Iran's or Iraq's defeat. Even
though Iran under Khomeini was not pro-Moscow, it was at least anti-
Washington. But a new government in Iran could have been pro-Western.[51]

It soon became apparent, however, that neither the United States nor the
Soviet Union would gain from the Gulf war and that both had common
interests which could be advanced by ending the conflict. Neither superpower wanted Iran to be able to spread Islamic fundamentalism beyond its
own borders. Both wanted to prevent the war from spreading to other
countries. Moreover, the Arab states had managed to remove the conflict

from East-West confrontation to some extent by not siding with one superpower or the other. Despite their differences, both Washington and Moscow ultimately concluded that working for a negotiated settlement through the UN was in both countries' interests.[52]

Determined to remain independent of both superpowers, the Gulf states adopted policies that were inconsistent with America's globalist view of problems in the region. They did not agree with the U.S. assertion that Moscow wanted to intervene militarily in the Gulf, and they took measures to reduce the probability of superpower confrontation in the area. Assured of Washington's support, many countries attempted to build closer ties with Moscow. Kuwait, which established diplomatic relations with the Soviet Union in 1963, asked both Washington and Moscow to protect its ships in the Gulf. Although many leaders in the Gulf believed that superpower involvement in the region was potentially more dangerous than the Iranian threat, they nonetheless endeavored to draw the United States and the Soviet Union into the conflict in order to expedite ending the war.[53] (They hoped that the West European allies would persuade the United States to moderate its more militaristic approach.)

Equally important, the Gulf leaders were convinced that Washington was unable to reduce internal threats to their countries' stability. On the contrary, they believed that close association with the West in general and the United States especially would foster the growth of domestic radical groups with links to the Islamic fundamentalist movement in Iran. Relations between the Gulf states and the United States were affected by the refusal of many in Congress to objectively assess Israel's security needs and the dangers posed by selling arms to neighboring countries. Due to its failure to question Israel's routine objections to American military transfers to Saudi Arabia, Kuwait, and elsewhere, Congress undermined U.S. efforts at collaborative defense arrangements with the Gulf. But more than any other issue, America's fear of offending Israel by implementing a policy that would actually safeguard Palestinian rights, instead of simply reiterating well-worn policy statements which were largely ignored by Israel, strained relations between the United States and the Gulf states.

The centrality of religion to these countries' domestic and foreign affairs made Israel's occupation of Jerusalem and other holy places an extremely important political issue, especially for Saudi Arabia.[54] In addition to being the self-appointed guardian of the holy places of Islam, Saudi Arabia, along with the smaller Gulf states, had significant numbers of Palestinian refugees who were in high-ranking political and commercial positions.

Also, Ayatollah Khomeini's desire to radically alter existing political arrangements in the Islamic world and to decrease the influence of extra-regional forces in the Gulf had direct implications for Saudi Arabia and other countries that were perceived as allies of the superpowers. For example, in September 1989, Saudi Arabia, faced with growing terrorist activities by Shiite Muslims sponsored by the Iranian government, decided to execute sixteen Kuwaiti Shiites accused of collaborating with Iran.[55] These executions followed several terrorist attacks against Saudi Arabia by Iran-supported groups. The possible dangers to internal stability emanating from a combination of Palestinian nationalism and Islamic fundamentalism undoubtedly prompted many Gulf leaders to avoid an overly close alliance with Washington prior to the 1990 Gulf crisis.

From the onset of the Iran-Iraq War the Gulf states attempted to strengthen their collective security by forming the Gulf Cooperation Council (GCC) in mid-1981. By sharing intelligence to counter internal subversion and by establishing a framework for economic cooperation, the Gulf states were also attempting to demonstrate their independence from the superpowers and to underscore the regional nature of the Iran-Iraq conflict.[56]

Tensions emerging from territorial disputes, religious cleavages, ethnic dissension, and ideological contests had long characterized relations among the Gulf states.[57] The Iran-Iraq War, which began in 1980 when Saddam Hussein invaded Iran, demonstrated the inability of the region's leaders to resolve these underlying problems. Although Iran's Shah Reza Pahlavi and Iraq's Saddam Hussein had reduced tensions between their countries by concluding the Reconciliation Agreement in Algiers in 1975, boundary disputes were not eliminated. For more than three hundred years relations between Iran and Iraq had been influenced by conflicting territorial claims along their 730-mile border. More than any other issue, Iraq's determination to maintain access to the Shatt al Arab waterway generated serious confrontation with Iran. But if Iraq was concerned about Iran's claims to its commercial link to the Gulf, Kuwait was equally nervous about Iraq's interest in acquiring two islands, Bubiyan and Warba, that were part of Kuwait. In fact, Iraq had not disavowed an earlier claim to all of Kuwait, based on previous Ottoman sovereignty over the latter.[58] Consequently, the Iran-Iraq war renewed Kuwait's fears (well founded, as Iraq's invasion of Kuwait in 1990 tragically demonstrated) and complicated its stance toward the belligerents. Yet Iran's new militancy, evidenced by Khomeini's policy of spreading his Islamic fundamentalist revolution to neighboring states where Sunni Muslims dominated, influenced the Gulf states, including Kuwait, to support Iraq even as they attempted to terminate the conflict diplomatically.

Relatively powerless to persuade either Iran or Iraq to find a peaceful solution to the conflict, due in part to America's lack of diplomatic relations with both countries, the Carter administration responded to the war by adopting a neutral position, sending Saudi Arabia the four AWACS reconnaissance planes it had requested, and by encouraging the West European allies to increase their naval presence in the Arabian Sea and the Indian Ocean. Both Britain and France sent additional ships to the region.[59] Although Carter's policy of neutrality was adopted by the Reagan administration, there was an unmistakable preference for Iraq. When Israel bombed the French-built nuclear reactor near Baghdad in June 1981, the United States condemned the action and, in a relatively rare occurrence, voted for a UN resolution against Israel. By 1990, however, U.S. officials were emphasizing Iraq's potential nuclear capability as a justification for war against it. And while the United States implemented an arms embargo against Iran, albeit largely ineffective, Iraq faced no such restrictions; on the contrary, U.S. allies, particularly France, were encouraged to supply Iraq with military equipment. However, Iraq's acquisition of French anti-ship Exocet missiles and Super Etendard jets prompted Reagan to initiate the ceasefire resolution that passed the UN Security Council in October 1983.[60] Yet Iran's rejection of the ceasefire with Iraq further eroded America's neutrality. Many of America's own allies, principally Israel, continued to sell arms to Iran.[61] Soviet efforts to maintain good relations with both Iran and Iraq further complicated American policy but simultaneously lessened overt superpower rivalry and enhanced the West European allies' role in ending the war and protecting Western interests.

When the Iraqi government denounced the Reconciliation Agreement and attacked military targets in Iran on September 22, 1980, the West European allies stressed the bilateral nature of the conflict, emphasized the need to avoid actions that could lead to escalation, and called upon the superpowers to show restraint. They also endorsed the appeal of the Secretary-General of the Islamic Conference for an immediate ceasefire and declared their willingness to support any international initiative that would have facilitated a political settlement. Above all, they underscored the importance of respecting international law on navigation in the Gulf for the entire international community.[62] Britain, West Germany, France, Italy, Japan, and the United States, all of whom had major interests in the Gulf region, agreed to discuss issues such as navigation through the Straits of Hormuz and the status of international oil supplies, and concluded that there was no immediate threat to international shipping in the Gulf.[63] Initially Iran looked to the EC for support against what it regarded as Iraqi aggression. Iran's ambassador in Bonn, Behdi Nabab, later viewed the nonpartisan position adopted by the European allies as tantamount to favoring Iraq's invasion of his country.[64]

Despite their efforts at foreign policy coordination through EPC, the allies had divergent and sometimes conflicting approaches to the crisis. West Germany, for constitutional as well as historical reasons, was not militarily involved in the Gulf. Its trade interests in Iran and its growing arms trade with Saudi Arabia prompted it to take a neutral position. However, Germany viewed Iraq as the aggressor and attempted to maintain cordial relations with Iran in order to protect its interests and to diminish that country's isolation from the West. West German Foreign Minister Hans-Dietrich Genscher visited Iran in mid-1984, the first West European foreign minister to have done so since the Iranian revolution.[65] Britain, on the other hand, supported America's neutrality as well as its decision to improve facilities on Diego Garcia and to develop the Rapid Deployment Force. But Britain, determined to maintain its commercial relations with the Iranians and the Arabs, did not officially support arms sales to either Iran or Iraq. When France initiated an effort to condemn Iranian actions in the UN Security Council, Britain obstructed it, partly because France had unabashedly helped Iraq.[66]

From Britain's viewpoint, French sales of Super Etendard jets and Exocet missiles to Iraq had enabled the latter to attack neutral shipping in the Gulf with impunity and to conduct horrendous air raids against Iran. Thus, French actions had directly threatened Western interests in the Gulf. But from France's perspective, Iran, with a population almost three times Iraq's, could have eventually overwhelmed its adversary by sending "human waves" to attack it. Furthermore, rapprochement with Iraq protected French interests in the Arab world, fostered greater French contacts with a country that wanted to decrease its dependence on Moscow, and helped to prevent an Iranian victory and its destabilizing consequences for the Gulf states. Therefore France, by not allowing Iraq to collapse, was also protecting Western interests.[67] French support of Iraq was consolidated by Iran's role in hostage-taking in Lebanon, by a number of political disputes between France and Iran, and by Iranian attacks on French ships in the Gulf. Yet alliances in the Iran-Iraq war were extremely complex and muddled, a reality that ultimately undermined U.S. policy in the region.

Ideologically driven, American foreign policy under the Reagan administration was replete with paradox and contradiction, a fact that became more obvious after Reagan left office. Reagan's obsession with undermining the Sandinista regime in Nicaragua, his compassion for the families of American hostages in Lebanon, and his tendency to view complicated matters in simplistic terms influenced him to involve the U.S. government in the Iran-Contra scandal. In 1983 the United States launched an effort to diminish the flow of weapons to Iran and, to a much lesser extent, to Iraq in order to end hostilities in the Gulf. Known as Operation Staunch, the American initiative focused on bilateral consultations with allies in Western Europe and elsewhere to find ways to deprive Iran of access to weapons.

The policy seemed to succeed, and the Reagan administration pointed out that in 1984 twenty-three Western nations had sold arms worth more than $1 billion to Iran, but by 1987 only four Western countries were detected shipping arms with a total value of less than $200 million.[68] The United States had also succeeded in restoring full diplomatic relations with Iraq, and American officials were very reluctant to condemn Iraq's actions, especially its widespread and barbaric use of chemical weapons against Iranian civilians. Yet between 1984 and 1987, the U.S. government itself violated its own policy by secretly shipping arms to Iran. European as well as Arab allies were very surprised by America's overtures to Iran.

Several factors influenced President Reagan's decision to transfer weapons to Iran. A major consideration was continuing military assistance to the Nicaraguan Contras following the passage of the Boland Amendment, which effectively prevented direct transfusions of U.S. aid to the rebel movement.[69] A second factor was the President's administrative style, which favored delegation of authority to subordinates without adequate oversight. Consequently, there appeared to be a loss of presidential control over major foreign policy matters. A third factor related to the release of American hostages held in Lebanon by groups believed to be directed from Iran. With his administration divided on the issue of opening contacts with Iran, partly because of domestic political considerations, the President allowed his sympathy for the hostages' families and the news of William Buckley's death in captivity to influence his decision. A fourth factor, related to the third, was Israeli pressure on U.S. officials to open dialogue with Iran. Israel, which had been shipping U.S. arms to Iran in violation of U.S. law relating to arms transfers to third countries, had its own reasons for persuading Washington to trade arms for hostages. Israel, surrounded by hostile Arab states, had created constructive relations with Iran, a non-Arab country. When Jews were being persecuted in Iraq, Israel's request that Iran serve as a transit point for the refugees was granted. Believing that Islamic fundamentalism was a temporary phenomenon that would not outlast Khomeini, Israeli officials wanted to maintain contacts with Iranian moderates. More importantly, an Arab world preoccupied with the Iran-Iraq war was not a threat to Israel. Furthermore, divisions within the Arab world because of the war were undoubtedly viewed to be a positive development. If prolonging the war was not in the interests of the Western allies, sapping Iraq's and Iran's military strength was perceived to be beneficial to Israel.[70]

U.S. arms transfers were viewed as essential in gaining the release of the American hostages, opening dialogue with Iran, foreclosing Soviet access to and influence in Iran, and ensuring the flow of oil from the Gulf to Western Europe, Japan, and the United States.[71] However, spare parts supplied by the United States for Iran's Hawk missiles could have also been seen as an attempt to counter French arms sales to Iraq. The Hawk missiles were primarily used to protect Iran's oil facilities from missiles and planes France had transferred to Iraq. To some, the Western allies were perceived as working at cross-purposes. Yet it could also be argued that there was a division of labor within the alliance that ultimately helped the West by preserving its access to both sides. President Reagan's address to the nation on November 13, 1986, though replete with erroneous information, confirmed that U.S. officials wanted to maintain contacts with both Iraq and

Iran. According to the President, he authorized the transfer of small amounts of defensive weapons and spare parts for defensive systems to Iran. "My purpose was to convince Tehran that our negotiators were acting with my authority, to send a signal that the U.S. was prepared to replace the animosity between us in a new relationship."[72] Despite good intentions, American actions contradicted early policy objectives, particularly Operation Staunch. Contrary to the president's claim that the modest deliveries of U.S. weapons could easily fit into a single cargo plane, later evidence indicated that enough weapons were transferred to affect developments in the war.[73] In fact, U.S. arms transfers may have contributed to the war's escalation and the increased attacks by both belligerents on neutral shipping.

Regardless of the perceived potential benefits, selling arms to Iran had a disastrous impact on America's relations with its allies in the Persian Gulf and Western Europe. It was already obvious to U.S. policymakers that Saudi Arabia, Kuwait, Oman, and other countries were extremely worried about the implications for their stability of an Iranian victory. From the very beginning Kuwait and Saudi Arabia had allocated billions of dollars to assist Iraq against Iran. Given the Gulf states' dependence on U.S. protection, despite their ambivalence, U.S. arms transfers to Iran raised serious questions about America's reliability and commitment to their security.[74] The West European allies, generally reluctant to concede U.S. leadership in foreign affairs, were uncomfortably reassured that U.S. officials lacked the wisdom to conduct an effective foreign policy. From the Europeans' perspective the Iran-Contra scandal demonstrated U.S. duplicity and incompetence. The scandal also contributed to the further erosion of U.S. leadership in the NATO alliance.

But the West European allies were not entirely innocent, either. Although the evidence was not as conclusive or as embarrassing as in America's case, there were serious allegations that France, West Germany, Spain, and, to a much lesser degree, Britain had also sold arms to Iran after Operation Staunch was launched. The most serious charge against Britain was the presence of an Iranian arms procurement office in London. The British government contended that this office was "kept under the closest possible scrutiny."[75] According to El Pais, the Spanish government knew about weapons transfers to Iran and had authorized the sale of $250 million worth of Spanish arms to Iran. Libya was used as a trans-shipment point until 1986, when Spain complied with the U.S. embargo against that country. Many of the weapons allegedly came from state-owned military industries and were shipped to Libya and Indonesia.[76]

France and West Germany appeared to have supplied military weapons to both Iran and Iraq. In the late 1980s there was serious tension in American-West German relations because it was widely believed, and later confirmed, that West German firms had helped various countries, including Libya, to acquire chemical and other types of weapons. The West German state-owned Fritz Werner industrial equipment company had delivered weapons to Iran and Iraq throughout the war. Richard Pohl, managing director of the firm, confirmed that his enterprise had delivered arms to Iran in accordance with German law, and emphasized that his company had been examined by the Darmstadt Regional Finance Office on behalf of the West German government.[77] Similarly, French firms and the French government itself were involved in arms sales to Iran, despite strong French support for Iraq.

French arms were smuggled to Iran between 1984 and 1986, and even though end-user certificates indicated that the weapons were destined for Brazil, Thailand, Yugoslavia, Ecuador, and Peru, the French government was aware that Iran was in fact the recipient. President Mitterrand and his defense minister, Charles Hernu, were briefed in 1984 about the trade. Conservative French Prime Minister Jacques Chirac raised the issue in late 1987, but refused to seek formal legal questioning of Mitterrand because of the Gulf's volatility. Despite political confrontation between Iran and France, or because of it, two Air France cargo planes loaded with missile guiding systems and radar equipment from the French Matra arms factory landed at the Mehrabad military airport in Iran in 1987.[78] The nature of the West German and French systems of government militated against an investigation similar to the one conducted in the United States on the Iran-Contra scandal. Nevertheless, available evidence suggested that the flow of arms to Iran was sufficient to enable that country to inflict serious damage on the Iraqi air force during its bombing raids on Iranian shipping. Essentially, American as well as European arms sales to Iran ultimately contributed to Reagan's decision to significantly increase U.S. military involvement in the Gulf in 1987 and to call upon the allies for assistance.

Although Iran's aggressive use of small, armed speedboats to attack neutral ships in the Gulf and its laying of crude but effective mines to destroy oil tankers were factors that prompted a major Western presence in the Gulf, there were two main reasons for the turn of events in 1987. First, the Soviet Union, taking advantage of America's loss of credibility after the Iran-Contra scandal and determined to play a role in the Gulf commensurate with its superpower status, had sent warships into the Gulf for the first time in late 1986. This action was precipitated by Iran's decision to board and search a Soviet ship suspected of carrying arms. America's determination to prevent the Soviet Union from enhancing its influence in the region prompted Reagan to act. As Richard L. Armitage, Assistant Secretary for International Security Affairs in the Department of Defense, put it, "we have under eight successive presidents tried to limit or keep out the Soviets from the Persian Gulf and we felt to give them a leg up would be unconscionable."[79] Second, but more important, once American secret arms sales to Iran became public, the Reagan administration was under tremendous pressure to repair its credibility with its allies and at home. Richard W.

Murphy, Assistant Secretary of State, noted that "in light of the Iran-Contra revelations, we had found that the leaders of the Gulf states were questioning the coherence and seriousness of U.S. policy along with our reliability and staying power. We wanted to be sure the countries with which we have friendly relations—Iraq and the GCC states—as well as the Soviet Union and Iran understood the firmness of our commitments." [80] Reagan endorsed Operation Staunch, called upon China to stop delivering Silkworm missiles to Iran, and eagerly agreed to reflag Kuwaiti tankers. Contrary to superpower rivalry in the Gulf, Kuwait decided to enlist both Soviet and U.S. protection for its tankers, which had become primary targets of increased Iranian attacks. By involving both superpowers Kuwait clearly intended to minimize its dependence on one or the other. Furthermore, this action would simultaneously signal Iran that it was alienated from the international community and force the superpowers to find a negotiated settlement to the war. But if Kuwait and the GCC wanted international protection of Gulf shipping, the Reagan administration, apprehensive of Soviet activities in the area and perceiving the Iran-Iraq War in terms of a zero-sum game in relation to the Soviet Union, moved quickly to accept Kuwait's request and to emphasize American support for the Gulf states. U.S. competition with the Soviet Union on the reflagging issue seemed inconsistent with the nature of the war.[81] It was as though American policymakers were oblivious to the reality that neither the Soviet Union nor the United States could gain significantly from superpower competition.

Most West European allies, by contrast, preferred to maintain a low profile and to favor international cooperation, particularly through the UN Security Council, to allow neutral shipping to operate freely in the Gulf. Britain, for example, did not follow the United States on the reflagging issue. When pressed by opposition Labour Party leader Neil Kinnock on Britain's involvement in reflagging Gulf ships, Prime Minister Thatcher pointed out that "if other ships apply for British registration, the ordinary conditions apply, and we consider each of them separately."[82] The Europeans' maneuverability was limited, however, when U.S. Navy frigate *USS Stark* was hit by two missiles fired from an Iraqi F-1 Mirage aircraft about seventy miles northeast of Bahrain, and thirty-seven Americans were killed. While the Reagan administration largely excused Iraq's action, Congress was less reluctant to criticize Iraq and to debate whether the War Powers Act should be applied in the Gulf. Comparing American actions in the Gulf to those in Lebanon in 1983 that had resulted in the tragic loss of American lives, Congressional critics questioned the need for American ships in the Gulf. Moreover, neither the Europeans nor the Japanese, who depended on oil from the Gulf to a much greater extent than the United States, were actively involved in protecting Gulf shipping. Given Iran's increased mine-laying activities and attacks on neutral shipping as well as the growing consensus in Congress that the allies should protect their own interests, Reagan moved more aggressively to enlist the West Europeans' cooperation.

Initially reluctant to participate in American strategic designs for the Gulf, the European allies eventually expanded their activities in the region in order to protect interests they held in common with the United States. Their decision to deploy their naval forces and to send minesweepers to the Gulf marked an unprecedented degree of cooperation with the United States in the Third World. Yet American and European collaboration was not a coordinated NATO response. While the United States had attempted to get the allies to work through NATO in various Third World conflicts, the Europeans had consistently resisted, preferring either separate national actions or a European approach. Each country perceived its interests differently, despite the overall common interests of preserving freedom of navigation and access to petroleum supplies. Thus, even though the allies all favored cooperation, they resisted abdicating their autonomy. More important, the Europeans committed their forces not only to protect their oil supplies, which they did not believe were seriously threatened, but also to restrain the United States. As Stein astutely observed, "it was largely because Europeans feared the consequences of unilateral military action in an area of vital interest that they committed forces for joint-out-of-area action."[83] However, this paradox of cooperation and autonomy ultimately safeguarded the allies' individual as well as collective interests without either further impairing NATO or European foreign policy coordination.

Lacking the prestige of more expensive and technologically sophisticated weapons systems, minehunters and minesweepers had assumed a low priority in the U.S. Navy. Ironically, the Iranians were able to frustrate the most advanced navy in the world with relatively crude mines simply because American strategic planners had once again overlooked the obvious: no provisions had been made for mine forces. The United States had relied on its European allies since the early 1970s for most mine warfare missions.[84] Consequently, America turned to its allies for minesweepers. Initially, the Netherlands, West Germany, and Britain rejected U.S. requests. The Netherlands, confronted with domestic political opposition to deploying forces outside Europe, was more comfortable with operating under the auspices of WEU or sending the minesweepers directly to Kuwait. West Germany argued that sending minesweepers to the Gulf was incompatible not only with its constitution but also with its responsibilities within NATO. From Bonn's perspective, apart from the fact that German forces were prohibited by the basic law from operating outside the NATO alliance area, U.S. efforts in the Gulf were largely irrelevant to NATO. Nonetheless, Defense Minister Manfred Woerner agreed to discuss possible additional tasks for the German navy to relieve the United States of certain responsibilities within the NATO area.[85] Essentially, Bonn endeavored to remain neutral in a conflict in which both combatants were its leading trade partners in the Gulf.

Britain, given its historically close relationship with the United States and its commitment to NATO, was in a more difficult position than the Netherlands and West Germany. Britain had already committed approximately one-fifth of its navy to the Gulf and had been actively, though quietly, escorting its ships through the Gulf. While rejecting America's request for minesweepers, Britain promised to keep the situation under review and indicated that its position was subject to change, depending upon the circumstances. Yet the decision was consistent with the main thrust of Britain's policy of maintaining a low-profile, nonprovocative presence in the Gulf. British policymakers were concerned that providing protection for the minesweepers would inevitably increase the number of British ships in the region, and feared that additional ships could have inadvertently escalated tension and undermined British diplomatic efforts to terminate the war.[86] The Iranian Deputy Foreign Minister M. Larijani had specifically requested that the Europeans not collaborate with the United States. But developments in the Gulf eventually prompted the allies to increase their naval presence in the region. However, they also obtained a commitment from the United States to work through the UN Security Council to end the war.

Unlike West Germany and Britain, France did not believe that its involvement in the Gulf would exacerbate the situation. Its relations with Iran had sharply deteriorated, partly because of its overt support for Iraq. Following an attack on a French oil tanker in mid-1987, France decided to provide a naval escort for its ships. France prepared its Toulon air-sea force for action in the Gulf.[87] It had already abandoned its nominal neutrality by selling arms to Iraq and by allowing French pilots to fly on board five Super Etendard jets, which carried air-to-sea Exocet missiles Baghdad had purchased to destroy Iranian oil tankers. France also modified about forty Mirage F-1s so that they could be armed with Exocet missiles.[88] France's activities undoubtedly contributed to its readiness to support an expanded American naval commitment in the Gulf. But France, like the other European countries, carefully avoided close association with the United States, preferring instead to coordinate its activities with the Europeans under WEU's auspices.

Once France and Britain decided to send minesweepers to the Gulf, Britain criticized Italy and the Netherlands for not doing likewise. After a meeting of WEU experts at The Hague in mid-August 1987, the Netherlands agreed to send minesweepers as part of a concerted intervention by WEU to ensure freedom of navigation in the Gulf. Alfred Cahen, Secretary-General of WEU, had encouraged all members of the EC to participate and noted that by deciding on a joint presence in the Gulf "the countries of WEU had taken a first European act in external security matters."[89] Underscoring their neutrality and emphasizing their adherence to international law regarding freedom of navigation, the French, Dutch, Belgian, Italian, and British navies exchanged information routinely and developed greater cooperation, even as they safeguarded their autonomy and denied WEU operational control over them. Mine counter measures (MCM) ships from Western Europe and the United States cleared several mined areas and checked hundred of miles of shipping lanes. The British gave Dutch and Belgian ships logistic support as well as protection, and in July 1988 the three countries decided to create an integrated MCM force called CALENDAR (named after the joint Anglo-Dutch-Belgian operation that cleared the Scheldt Estuary of mines in 1944).

By October 1988, CALENDAR and the MCM forces of the remaining WEU states combined to conduct Operation Cleansweep, a coordinated check of a shipping lane 2,000 yards wide and 300 miles into the Gulf from the Strait of Hormuz.[90] France and Britain, given their naval capabilities, assumed much of the European responsibility for patrolling the Gulf. West Germany made an indirect contribution to Western efforts by sending its naval vessels to areas from which NATO ships were withdrawn for operations in the Gulf.[91] France and Italy routinely exchanged information about risks and implemented operational coordination of their navies. But the French and Italians maintained that no common response had been considered in case ships were attacked. Italy's Foreign Minister M. Andreotti believed that a more thorough coordinated effort could have caused serious political problems for the Gulf countries if the actions of individual Western states had been perceived as an allied approach.[92]

The British Royal Navy's Armilla Patrol had been in the Gulf and Indian Ocean since 1980 to provide reassurance and protection for British merchant vessels. From September 1987 until March 1989 the Armilla Patrol was supported by nine MCM ships. Although Britain shared America's determination to uphold the principle of freedom of navigation in the Gulf as an integral component of its policy of finding a negotiated settlement to the Iran-Iraq War, there was no attempt to formally integrate American and British activities. A primary British objective was to maintain neutrality and to encourage all countries involved in the Gulf, including the United States, to exercise restraint and to refrain from actions that could further escalate and widen the conflict.[93] And as if to underscore the independence of British operations and Britain's commitment to the Gulf states, Thatcher made a surprise visit in August 1988 to the Royal Navy ships patrolling the Gulf, shortly before the Iran-Iraq ceasefire went into effect. She also met briefly with United Arab Emirates Defense Minister Sheikh Muhammed al-Maktum.[94]

What differentiated the Iraq-Iran conflict from other Third World crises was the willingness of both superpowers and the West European allies to search for a diplomatic solution, primarily because ongoing hostilities were detrimental to their major interests. Britain played a central role, as President of the UN Security Council, in efforts to persuade Iran and Iraq to agree to a ceasefire. It initiated the process which culminated in the adoption of UN Security Council Resolution 598 that temporarily ended hostilities.[95] Although Britain's historical ties to the Gulf states facilitated its mediating role, the inability of the superpowers to turn the Gulf war into an East-West confrontation also helped. The West European allies had effectively demonstrated their ability to work together under the recently rejuvenated WEU and to cooperate with as well as distance themselves from the United States.

IRAQ'S OCCUPATION OF KUWAIT AND OPERATION DESERT STORM

Kuwait's deeply held apprehension about Iraq's military intentions was tragically realized on August 2, 1990, when Iraqi forces invaded. Iraq's claim to Kuwait was inextricably intertwined with British imperial designs in the Gulf and in India. Although Britain had managed to protect Kuwait from Turkish domination since 1899, Iraq contended that Kuwait had been an integral part of Basra Province under the Ottoman Empire and that Britain had drawn arbitrary boundaries to sever Kuwait from Iraq.[96] Consequently, when Kuwait achieved independence in 1961, Iraq refused to recognize the new state and threatened to invade it. Confronted with the possibility of war with British troops, the Iraqis accepted the Military Patrol Line, the boundary endorsed by the Arab League.

Alliances in the Iran-Iraq War, during which Kuwait gave approximately $30 billion in loans to Iraq, only postponed Iraq's aggression against Kuwait and may have actually contributed to Baghdad's decision to invade. Weakened economically by eight years of war with Iran, Iraq had first endeavored to secure a higher price for oil—around $25 per barrel. Although Iraq maintained that it had argued against keeping oil prices high since 1974, the sharp decline in oil prices in the 1980s to as low as $12 per barrel was seen as disastrous for heavily indebted Iraq. Accusing Kuwaiti officials of conspiring to maintain artificially low prices and of illegally taking Iraqi oil, Saddam Hussein claimed that Kuwait and other Arab states were weakening Iraq, thereby encouraging Israel and Iran to attack Baghdad.[97] This perception and Kuwait's refusal to seriously address Iraqi concerns, among other factors, prompted Hussein to occupy Kuwait.

Iraq's invasion of Kuwait and Operation Desert Storm altered profoundly the political and strategic environment of the Middle East and the Gulf, ushered in unprecedented international cooperation under UN auspices, underscored the growing irrelevance of NATO, highlighted intra-alliance strains, and engendered a post-Cold War situation replete with paradox and tragic irony. The crisis demonstrated the interdependence of developments in Europe and conflicts in the Third World. It also buttressed the often-disregarded view that problems in the Gulf were, at best, tangentially connected to Soviet designs. It further undermined the argument that Israel was America's most important ally in the region and an asset to U.S. national interests. Furthermore, it highlighted Europe's dependence on U.S. military might and influenced the allies to consider becoming more self-sufficient militarily, a move that further weakened NATO.

American soldiers stationed in Europe to defend the allies against the Warsaw Pact countries were sent to the Gulf. They were no longer needed in Europe because of German unification, broader European cooperation, and the signing of agreements among members of the Cold War alliances that provided for reducing the number of conventional weapons in Europe.[98] Also, the Warsaw Pact was formally disbanded on March 31, 1991. The Soviet Union was disintegrating politically and facing its severest food shortages since World War II, and the United States, which had assembled an impressive international coalition against Hussein under UN auspices, was embarrassed by the fact that it owed the UN $750 million.[99] Furthermore, while America was unquestionably the only country capable of a massive military response to Iraq's occupation of Kuwait, it was forced to ask Japan, Germany, and others for financial support. The contrast between America's military might and its relative decline in economic power was painfully illustrated by the paralysis and confusion that accompanied attempts to pass the national budget amidst a growing recession. Similarly, Thatcher, who had strongly backed President Bush's initiatives, was forced to resign as prime minister at the end of 1990 because of Britain's deteriorating economy, passage of the poll tax, and because of her reluctance to bring Britain into the new Europe. And even as most of the allies expressed nuanced support for American initiatives in the Gulf and eventually participated in Operation Desert Storm, trade disputes between the EC and America and Bush's attempts to build a North American trading bloc following the war continued to underscore the crucial nature of economic power in the post–Cold War period.

The U.S. response to Saudi Arabia's request for military assistance, and its massive military build-up in that country, while enjoying widespread international and domestic support, was viewed as a Cold War reaction based on how America had intended to respond to the Soviet threat to the region.[100] Although Bush's decision to deploy U.S. troops to Saudi Arabia seemed a prudent deterrent, the speed and size of the deployment raised questions about U.S. objectives in the Gulf. America's predilection for unilateral action was unchecked by the end of the Cold War and new international realities. Despite serious economic difficulties at home, the United States committed itself to an enormously expensive undertaking without first consulting its allies to ascertain their willingness to support what became known as Operation Desert Shield and, later, Operation Desert Storm.

While several arguments were advanced for how U.S. policy was formulated and implemented, it was clear that America's dependence on petroleum from the Gulf was a major factor influencing that policy.[101] It was also obvious that relatively inexpensive petroleum had propelled both the United States and Iraq toward military action in the Gulf, albeit for opposite reasons. To a large extent, both acted out of weakness. Iraq's indebtedness to Kuwait, among others, and the failure of the Reagan-Bush administration to implement national energy policies when energy prices were low were key ingredients of the Gulf tragedy. Iraq's use of force to settle disputes with its Arab neighbor galvanized international opposition against Baghdad and facilitated global support for the limited U.S. objectives of protecting Saudi Arabia and restoring Kuwait's independence.   .

The West European allies unanimously condemned the invasion; Britain, France, and the United States froze Kuwaiti assets; and the EC immediately imposed an embargo on oil imports from Iraq as well as on arms sales to Baghdad.[102] The allies also endorsed U.S.-led actions against Iraq in the UN Security Council. Nevertheless, rhetorical support was not matched by tangible military and financial contributions from all the allies. Furthermore, the allies were not fully convinced that the rapid military build-up, accompanied by hateful rhetoric in both Washington and Baghdad, was conducive to an efficient negotiated settlement of the conflict. Thus, their cooperation in the Gulf was partly designed to restrain America. Moreover, each country participated, at varying levels of commitment, in the international coalition against Iraq in order to achieve specific national objectives.

Although approximately twenty-six countries contributed militarily to Operation Desert Shield and Operation Desert Storm, the United States was by far the principal member. By early 1991 there were more than four hundred thousand American troops in the Gulf. Britain was America's staunchest ally and also the most supportive of military action against Iraq. Britain not only contributed thirty thousand troops, tanks, ships, and aircraft, but also allowed its forces to operate under U.S. command prior to the war. However, France and the other countries maintained control over their own forces until Operation Desert Storm began.[103] And while the European allies collaborated with the United States, they emphasized that their logistical support for, or economic assistance to, the Gulf countries was neither part of the American effort nor a NATO military campaign. Instead, they stressed that they were operating under the UN. Frustrated by the lack of allied cooperation, Thatcher argued that "we cannot expect the U.S. to go on bearing military and defense burdens worldwide, acting in effect as the world's policeman if it does not get a positive and swift response from its allies when the crunch comes."[104]

Having significant investments in Iraq, America's major allies, especially Germany and Japan, eschewed military action and were reluctant to divert attention from their economic objectives at home and abroad. Preoccupied with German unification, the principal goal of Bonn's foreign policy since the beginning of the Cold War, Germany viewed U.S. policy in the Gulf as inimical to its own particular interests as well as undermining the achievements of America's Cold War containment policy. Diverting billions of dollars away from Europe clearly threatened emerging democracies in Eastern Europe, and reduced the allies' ability to provide essential economic assistance to the Soviet Union. Nonetheless, intense lobbying by U.S. Treasury Secretary Nicholas Brady and Secretary of State James Baker eventually persuaded Japan and Germany to contribute billions of dollars to the coalition effort.

Both countries, however, refused to send soldiers to the Gulf, and emphasized prohibitions against military action abroad in their American-influenced constitutions. In Japan, Prime Minister Toshiki Kaifu's proposal to send "unarmed military personnel" to the Gulf encountered overwhelming domestic opposition as well as immediate protests from Japan's neighbors who feared the consequences of a new military role for Tokyo.[105] Furthermore, America's emphasis on the military option, especially prior to Bush's abortive decision to send Baker to Baghdad following passage of the UN Security Council Resolution authorizing force against Iraq, worried many of the allies, as well as American citizens and members of Congress. In a radio interview broadcast shortly before Bush's brief visit to Germany in November 1990, Kohl stated that "anyone who believes this can be solved militarily must think of the end, not the beginning, of the enterprise. What will the consequences be? How many victims will there be? And won't a political solution still have to be found afterward?"[106] Ironically, the European allies took the initiative in dealing with the massive refugee problem following the war. Washington responded shortly thereafter amid growing criticism of its abandonment of the Kurds with Operation Provide Comfort. Serious questions from the allies about the wisdom of Bush's policy and widespread concern about his impatience with economic sanctions were underscored by the Soviet Union's response to the crisis.

Unprecedented postwar superpower cooperation tended to obfuscate underlying Soviet and American differences. As in the case of the West European allies, Soviet support for U.S. initiatives restrained as well as strengthened Washington's actions against Iraq. Although Moscow voted for the UN Security Council Resolutions against Iraq, adhered to the international embargo, and condemned Iraq's violations of international law, Gorbachev stressed his preference for a negotiated settlement to the crisis. Constrained by dire economic and political problems at home, and more vulnerable to public opinion (partly because of his own reforms), Gorbachev adopted a low-risk, low-cost policy. In light of its experiences in Afghanistan, the Soviet Union refrained from militarily supporting U.S. initiatives. Moreover, Moscow's close relationship with Baghdad during much of the Cold War complicated its Gulf policy. The Soviet Union, similar to the European allies, depended on revenues from weapons sales to Iraq. In fact, Iraq owed the Soviets approximately $10 billion for arms sent during the Iran-Iraq war. Furthermore, Soviet military advisers and technical support personnel on long-term contracts remained in Iraq prior to Operation Desert Storm to maintain Iraqi tanks, planes, and sophisticated Soviet-supplied weapons systems.[107] Whether they were held hostage was unclear; but they were eventually allowed to leave.

Given the Soviet Union's geographic proximity to the Gulf as well as its large Muslim population, Gorbachev's collaboration with the West had to be balanced against geo-strategic implications of a large, permanent U.S. presence in the area. Instability in the Gulf, triggered by Iraqi or U.S. military action, was viewed as detrimental to Soviet interests. But the Gulf states were also concerned about the ramifications of war. Consequently, even as they encouraged Washington to pressure Baghdad to withdraw from Kuwait, the Gulf states improved relations with Moscow. Saudi Arabia established diplomatic relations with the Soviet Union, and Moscow allowed Saudi authorities greater access to Soviet Muslims. The Gulf states also contributed about $3 billion to the ailing Soviet economy. These developments underscored lingering Saudi concerns about the massive U.S. military buildup, as well as the Gulf states' desire to use the Soviet Union as a counterweight to the United States.[108] Thus, divergent and common Soviet and American interests engendered a set of dynamics within the anti-Iraq coalition that frustrated but also furthered U.S. military objectives in the Gulf. Other coalition partners also complicated U.S. policy.

Although Turkey, Egypt, Syria, and others sent military forces to Saudi Arabia, each country had its own reasons for doing so. Turkey, for example, worried about the growing irrelevance of NATO as well as the allies' refusal to permit it to join the EC, regarded the Gulf crisis as providing an opportunity for Ankara to demonstrate its importance to the West. Egypt succeeded in getting the United States to abrogate a $7 billion debt and, simultaneously, augmented its leadership position in the Arab world. Saudi Arabia and the Gulf States also canceled Egypt's debts. But America's decision to forgive Egypt's debt was strongly criticized by Japan after the war ended. Japan, increasingly assertive in economic affairs, believed that the United States had unilaterally allowed political considerations to play too great a role in its decision. Syria, regarded as a major supporter of terrorism against the United States and other Western countries, not only improved relations with the United States but was given approximately $2 billion by Saudi Arabia for sending troops to the Gulf. These alliances, together with the massive American military presence in the region, influenced Iraq to settle key issues that led to its eight-year war with Iran and to restore diplomatic relations.[109] By so doing, Iraq gave up all it had gained during the costly conflict with Iran.

The Gulf crisis also had serious ramifications for U.S.-Israeli relations and for the Palestinian-Israeli conflict. Israel, which had claimed to be an essential American ally, initially found itself not only relegated to the sidelines in the Gulf crisis but also confronted with the harsh reality of the massive transfer of sophisticated U.S. weapons to Saudi Arabia to improve its defense. Furthermore, Hussein's attempts to link Iraq's withdrawal from Kuwait to Israel's termination of its occupation of the West Bank and Gaza resonated in parts of the Arab world and created serious challenges for the international coalition opposing Iraq. Arafat's support of Iraq, though not of Iraq's invasion of Kuwait, created schisms in the PLO, but also helped to link the Gulf crisis to the Palestinian-Israeli conflict.

This linkage was inadvertently cemented by Israel's use of excessive force against Palestinian demonstrators at Temple Mount in Jerusalem. The deaths of over twenty Palestinians threatened the anti-Iraq coalition. In order to achieve its objectives in the Gulf and to be consistently supportive of the emerging international order centered around a rejuvenated UN, the United States departed from its traditional role of routinely vetoing UN resolutions against Israel. Stunned but defiant, Israel refused to fully cooperate with the UN investigation of the violence in Jerusalem.[110] Iraq's occupation of Kuwait, the massive military force used against Iraq to dislodge it from Kuwait, and Israel's disregard of international law in relation to occupation under the Fourth Geneva Convention effectively renewed international efforts to solve the Palestinian-Israeli conflict and brought U.S. policies in the Middle East closer to those of its European allies.

The United States, accustomed to acting unilaterally, had successfully assembled an unprecedented international coalition against Iraq. Apart from the trade-offs inherent in negotiations with diverse countries to obtain almost unanimous support for the UN resolution authorizing force to restore Kuwait's independence, American efforts ultimately propelled Bush toward talks with Iraq to settle the Gulf crisis.[111] After much debate about setting a date for discussions, U.S. Secretary of State Baker and Iraq's Foreign Minister Tariq Aziz met in Geneva in early January. Thus, paradoxically, America's determination to portray what was essentially a U.S. military campaign against Iraq as a global effort by enlisting widespread international participation, temporarily restrained Washington, while, simultaneously, broadening its options and legitimizing its use of force.

But negotiations with Iraq were largely perfunctory. The Baker-Aziz talks were clearly designed to pacify domestic opposition to the war as well as to consolidate European support for America's Persian Gulf policies. Personalization of the conflict and the escalation of hateful rhetoric by Hussein and Bush diminished the prospects of a diplomatic solution. More important, the Bush administration had decided as early as September 1990 to dislodge Iraqi troops from Kuwait militarily, despite official insistence that U.S. forces were in Saudi Arabia to prevent Iraq from attacking it. Bush had secretly approved a timetable for launching an air war against Iraq in mid-January, a fact that was inadvertently confirmed by General Michael J. Dugan who was dismissed as Air Force Chief of Staff because of his unauthorized comments. The plan also included a large scale ground offensive that would begin in February and would strike deep into Iraqi territory to outflank and encircle Hussein's army.[112] The failed Baker-Aziz talks were therefore greeted with relief by Washington. Furthermore, lack of progress toward a negotiated settlement was used by the Bush administration as evidence that Iraq was not willing to withdraw from Kuwait. Ironically, having concluded that Hussein was both inept and crazy, Bush concluded that the choice of peace or war was really Saddam Hussein's to make. Yet in what was described as a somber briefing to the NATO allies, America had insisted that an Iraqi promise to withdraw from Kuwait was not enough to stop an attack unless there were immediate signs of Iraqi troops leaving Kuwait.[113] European efforts to avert war as the UN deadline approached failed not only because the United States had eschewed negotiations but also because of Hussein's preoccupation with avoiding being humiliated by Bush and his rejection of EC peace initiatives. Consequently, European and Arab interlocutors were engaged in a dialogue with the deaf. Assured of America's military superiority, certain of victory, and determined to "kick the Vietnam syndrome" by demonstrating America's willingness to use "massive and decisive force" against Iraq, Bush marched confidently into war, seemingly oblivious of the political quagmire that would emanate from military success. The Europeans, although reluctant to fight, were unable to speak with one voice and to prevent war. Moreover, European peace initiatives underscored the fragility of the U.S.-led coalition, a factor that undoubtedly contributed to Bush's decision to start the war one day after the UN deadline expired.

Operation Desert Storm began with an unprecedented air assault on Baghdad. It was estimated that the destructive force of the explosives that were dropped on Iraq and Kuwait during the first 14 hours of the war exceeded that of the Hiroshima nuclear bomb. The relentless bombardment of Iraq, with some weapons that were previously untested in war, continued for the duration of the conflict and reduced that country to what a UN report termed "a pre-industrial age." In direct contradiction to U.S. attempts to obstruct diplomatic initiatives, Bush declared that the military action "followed months of constant and virtually endless diplomatic activity on the part of the UN, the United States, and many other countries."[114] But America's negative reaction to an attempted ceasefire brokered by the Soviet Union prior to commencement of the ground war was consistent with Bush's original intention to wage a massive and destructive military campaign against Iraq that clearly exceeded the UN mandate. Personalization of the conflict allowed the American-led coalition to destroy Iraq's water and power supply, its industrial infrastructure, and conveyed a sense of disregard about the widespread suffering of millions of innocent Iraqis, many of whom had been victimized by Hussein and purportedly had the sympathy of the Bush administration. American forces destroyed an estimated 75,000 fleeing Iraqi troops, many of whom were incinerated or crushed in their vehicles as they were bombed unmercifully on what was euphemistically called the "highway of death." The gruesomeness of this action raised questions about U.S. intentions in the Persian Gulf.

Despite misgivings among the allies about the wisdom of a military solution to Iraq's occupation of Kuwait, they ultimately supported U.S. military actions. Only a week prior to the war, 79 percent of the French and 70 percent of the Germans had opposed war in the Persian Gulf. Even in Britain, America's staunchest ally, only 49 percent of the population had supported freeing Kuwait by force.[115] However, when the war began the Europeans strongly backed their leaders. Britain and France actively participated in Operation Desert Storm. Spain and Britain permitted the United States to use their bases to increase the number of B-52 bombing raids against Iraqi ground forces in Kuwait. France allowed the bombers to overfly French territory, provided that they were not used to attack civilians and that they were not carrying nuclear weapons. Germany supplied shells for American M1-A1 tanks in Saudi Arabia as well as artillery shells for British forces in the Persian Gulf. On the other hand, France refused to give the coalition important technical information about radar jammers on French-made Iraqi Mirage jets. But given Iraq's ineffectiveness in the air war, withholding the information was inconsequential. Another development that underlined nuanced differences between the French and the other coalition partners was France's Defense Minister Jean-Pierre Chevènement's resignation following disagreements with Mitterrand concerning the extent to which the U.S.-led alliance had exceeded the UN mandate. Chevènement, a founding member of the Franco-Iraqi Friendship Association, had been an outspoken critic of the war. His resignation therefore strengthened the coalition. However, differences among the allies about the war's objectives, including Hussein's fate, influenced Bush to stop the war before the Iraqi forces were totally annihilated. This decision was apparently contrary to the wishes of General H. Norman Schwartzkopf, the general commander of the coalition forces, to continue the war.

Determined not to manage the war from Washington, as President Lyndon Johnson had been perceived as doing during Vietnam, Bush allowed the military maximum freedom of operation. By the time the temporary ceasefire was called, more than 72,000 Iraqis had been made homeless by "collateral damage" caused by the coalition's relentless bombing. Estimates of Iraqi soldiers killed ranged from 100,000 to 250,000, compared to about 125 allied casualties. Neither Iraq nor the allies seemed anxious to count the dead and wounded Iraqis. But as the euphoria of military victory faded, questions were raised about the appropriateness of the massive destruction of Iraq and America's accountability for the plight of Iraqi civilians. Pope John Paul II delivered a scathing denunciation of the war, calling it "a darkness that had cast a shadow over the whole human community."[116] The UN, which had authorized the use of force against Iraq, found itself in an awkward position after the war. Confronted with the destruction of Iraq's food supply, power generation, water purification plants, garbage disposal facilities, sewage treatment plants, and other essential services, the UN and other international agencies mounted a major international aid effort for Iraq's reconstruction. The EC, anxious to salvage the credibility of its collective foreign policy and to demonstrate its independence, announced within hours of the ceasefire that about $700,000 had been allocated to the Red Cross to purify and restore Baghdad's water supply—much to the surprise of the United States.[117]

In addition to "kicking the Vietnam syndrome," Bush had decided to use U.S. military power to establish a "new world order." In his State of the Union message, he declared that what was at stake was more than one small country; it was a big idea—"a new world order." American leadership was, in his view, indispensable in a rapidly changing world. Refuting the widely held notion that America was declining, Bush called upon Americans to prepare for "the next American century."[118] But the "new world order," constructed on the Middle East's shifting sands, was as ephemeral as the mirages of the Saudi desert. The fundamental problems of the region remained as intractable as they were before the war. And while the war temporarily diverted America's attention from its serious domestic problems and enhanced Bush's re-election chances in 1992, achieving the next American century required the President to make hard choices on economic and social issues. Yet he seemed unwilling or unable to make them. The outcome of the war was essentially a Pyrrhic victory for the United States and Kuwait. U.S. dependence on foreign oil, a major factor propelling Bush into war, remained virtually unchanged, and approximately five hundred of Kuwait's oil wells continued to burn and pollute the country. Furthermore, Kuwait lost about $5 million an hour due to the oil fires. America was confronted with the uncertainties unleashed by the massive bombardment of Iraq.

Faced with the dangers inherent in the Lebanonization of Iraq, which Bush encouraged by asking the Iraqis to overthrow Hussein, the United States was in the awkward position of inadvertently supporting Hussein by not assisting the Kurds and the Shi'ites who rebelled against him. Moreover, Iraq's civil war produced thousands of refugees in American-occupied southern Iraq, and roughly two million more in Iran and Turkey. Refused permission to enter Turkey, as many as one thousand refugees died each day in the cold and mud before international relief aid reached them. Although the United States was urged by Iran, the Iraqi rebels, and others, to intervene in Iraq's civil war, the European allies opposed it. For example, Mitterrand made it clear that the UN mandate did not extend to Iraq's internal turmoil.[119] However, deeply disturbed by the tragic and unprecedented refugee problem, Britain and France proposed establishing an enclave in northern Iraq for Kurdish refugees. Initially reluctant to interfere in Iraq's internal affairs, the United States supported the idea of "safe havens" for the Kurds. Allied troops, mostly American, were sent to northern Iraq to protect the Kurds from Hussein's army.

Having destroyed Iraq's military infrastructure not only to force Iraqi forces out of Kuwait but also to reduce Iraq's military threats to the region, the United States decided to become the major supplier of weapons to the region. The success of American technology in Operation Desert Storm stimulated both the demand by the Middle East allies for weapons and the willingness of U.S. companies to provide them. Instead of seizing the opportunity to mobilize international support for reducing arms sales to the Third World, the Bush administration approved a plan to allow the Export-Import Bank (Eximbank) to guarantee approximately $23 billion in loans for U.S. allies to purchase sophisticated conventional American weapons. Both China and the Soviet Union were forced to rethink their military strategies in light of Operation Desert Storm, and the military in each country was strengthened considerably in the war's aftermath. The "new world order" was indistinguishable from the pre-war situation. Operation Desert Storm did not significantly alter the fundamental redistribution of power that was based largely on economic might. And stability, a major U.S. objective in the Gulf, remained elusive.

NOTES

1. Michael Sterner, "Perceptions and Policies of the Gulf States Toward Regional Security and Superpower Rivalry," in *The Great Game: Rivalry in the Persian Gulf and South Asia*, ed. Alvin Z. Rubinstein (New York: Praeger, 1983), pp. 23–24.

2. Donald Hawley, *The Trucial States* (London: Allen and Unwin, 1970), p. 129.

3. Rosemary Hollis, "Great Britain," in *The Powers in the Middle East*, ed. Bernard Reich (New York: Praeger, 1987), p. 180.

4. Herman F. Eilts, *The Dilemma in the Persian Gulf* (Washington, D.C.: American Enterprise Institute, 1980), p. 6.

5. Catherine McArdle Kelleher, "The Federal Republic and NATO," in *The Federal Republic of Germany in the 1980s*, ed. Robert Gerald Livingston (New York: German Information Center, 1983), p. 14.

6. Richard W. Cottam, *Iran and the United States: A Cold War Case Study* (Pittsburgh: University of Pittsburgh Press, 1989), p. 4; and Anthony Parsons, "Iran and Western Europe," *The Middle East Journal* 43, no. 2 (Spring 1989): 220.

7. Everett Mendelsohn, *A Compassionate Peace: A Future For Israel, Palestine, and the Middle East* (New York: Hill and Wang, 1989), p. 172.

8. Sterner, p. 26.

9. "The Cooperation Agreement Between the Community and the Cooperation Council for the Arab States of the Gulf," *Bulletin of the European Communities* 21, no. 6 (1988): 97.

10. See Michael Cunningham, *Hostages to Fortune: The Future of Western Interests in the Arabian Gulf* (London: Brassey's Defense Publishers, 1988), p. 11.

11. Rodney Wilson, *Euro-Arab Trade: Prospects for the 1990s* (London: The Economist Intelligence Unit, 1988), pp. 9–10.

12. Georgina Watkins, "Hermes Goal is Cheaper Export Cover," *The Middle East Economic Digest*, November 28, 1987, p. 38.

13. Foreign Affairs Committee, House of Commons, *The Iran/Iraq Conflict: Minutes of Evidence, 20 April 1988* (London: HMSO, Her Majesty's Stationery Office, 1988), p. 122.

14. "France Wins Iranian Contract for Gulf Project," *Financial Times*, February 28, 1990, p. 6.

15. Cunningham, p. 24.

16. See President Reagan, "Arms Sales to Saudi Arabia," *Department of State Bulletin*, August 1987, p. 80; and "U.S. Arms Sales to Saudi Arabia," *Department of State Bulletin*, December 1987, pp. 76–77.

17. Andrew J. Pierre, *The Global Politics of Arms Sales* (Princeton, N.J.: Princeton University Press, 1982), pp. 84–86; and Alan Platt, "European Arms Transfers and Other Supplies," in *The Soviet-American Competition in the Middle East*, eds. Steven L. Spiegel, Mark A. Heller, and Jacob Goldberg (Lexington, Mass.: Lexington Books, 1988), p. 64.

18. Jonathan Fenby, "Boom in French Arms Sales to Arab Nations," *The Times* (London), October 14, 1981, p. 10a.

19. Geoffrey Howe, Foreign Secretary, *Britain and the Gulf—Together into the 21st Century* (London: Central Office of Information, 1989), p. 1.

20. George Younger, Defense Secretary, "Views on Mideast Arms Sales," *FBIS-WEU*, September 20, 1988, p. 2.

21. Cunningham, p. 24.

22. Toby Odone, "The U.K. and the Middle East," *The Middle East Economic Digest*, September 9, 1988, p. 9; Platt, p. 66; and Cunningham, p. 25.

23. Yitzhak Shamir, "Statement on Saudi Arms Deal," Tel Aviv IDF Radio in Hebrew, reprinted in *FBIS-Middle East*, January 27, 1981, p. N2.

24. Robert Bailey, "Middle East Spending Keeps World Arms Sales Buoyant," *The Middle East Economic Digest*, October 31, 1987, p. 26.

25. *Parliamentary Debates* (Commons), 6th ser., vol. 19, 1–12 March (1982), col. 267.

26. Edward Mortimer, "Europe Seen as a Counterbalance," *The Times* (London), June 3, 1980, p. 111a.

27. William G. Hyland, "The Atlantic Crisis," *Daedalus* 110, no. 1 (Winter 1981): 44.

28. William B. Quandt, "The Western Alliance in the Middle East," in *The Middle East and Western Alliance*, ed. Steven L. Spiegel (London: Allen and Unwin, 1982), p. 13.

29. "Political Cooperation: Lifting of Sanctions Against Iran," *Europe: Agence Internationale D'Information Pour La Presse* (cited as *Europe*), January 21, 1981, p. 3.

30. Stanley Hoffmann, *Dead Ends: American Foreign Policy in the New Cold War* (Cambridge, Mass.: Ballinger, 1983), p. 185.

31. Eduard A. Shevardnadze, "Speech to the Supreme Soviet," reprinted in *The New York Times*, October 25, 1989, p. A6.

32. "The Community's Reactions to the Invasion of Afghanistan," *Bulletin of the European Communities* 13, no. 1 (1980): 7–8.

33. James Oliver Goldsborough, *Rebel Europe: How America Can Live with a Changing Continent* (New York: Macmillan, 1982), p. 21; and Lawrence S. Ka-

plan, *NATO and the United States: The Enduring Alliance* (Boston: Twayne, 1988), p. 158.

34. Peter H. Langer, *Transatlantic Discord and NATO's Crisis of Cohesion* (Washington, D.C.: Pergamon-Brassey's, 1986), p. 35.

35. Edwina Moreton, "The German Question in the 1980s," in *Germany Between East and West,* ed. Edwina Moreton (Cambridge: Cambridge University Press, 1987), p. 249.

36. David Adamson, "EEC Drops Neutral Afghanistan Plan," *The Daily Telegraph,* March 25, 1980, p. 4.

37. "Protest Lodged with U.K. on Missiles Supplied to DRA," *FBIS-Soviet Union,* July 17, 1987, p. H1.

38. Philip Windsor, *Germany and the Western Alliance: Lessons From the 1980 Crisis* (London: International Institute for Strategic Studies, 1981), p. 19.

39. "Genscher Says Soviets Cannot Divide West on Afghan Issue," *FBIS-WEU,* January 28, 1980, p. J1.

40. Julius W. Friend, *Seven Years in France: François Mitterrand and the Unintended Revolution* (Boulder, Colo.: Westview Press, 1989), p. 197.

41. Richard J. Barnet, *The Alliance: America, Europe, Japan* (New York: Simon and Schuster, 1983), p. 408.

42. Zbigniew Brzezinski, "After the Carter Doctrine," in *Crosscurrents in the Gulf: Arab, Regional, and Global Interests,* eds. H. Richard Sindelar and J. E. Peterson (London: Routledge, 1988), p. 4.

43. Shahram Chubin, *Security in the Persian Gulf: The Role of Outside Powers* (Totowa, N.J.: Allanheld, Osman, 1982), p. 25.

44. Brzezinski, p. 6.

45. James R. Blaker, "The Out-of-Area Question and NATO Burden Sharing," in *NATO in the 1980s: Challenges and Responses,* eds. Linda P. Brady and Joyce P. Kaufman (New York: Praeger, 1985,) p. 41.

46. Shahram Chubin, "West European Perceptions of Europe's Stake in Persian Gulf-Indian Ocean Security," in *The Great Game: Rivalry in the Persian Gulf and South Asia,* ed. Alvin Rubinstein (New York: Praeger, 1983), p. 129.

47. Mark N. Katz, *Russia and Arabia: Soviet Foreign Policy Toward the Arabian Peninsula* (Baltimore: Johns Hopkins University Press, 1986), p. 145.

48. Mark N. Katz, "Iraq and the Superpowers," in *Iraq in Transition: A Political, Economic, and Strategic Perspective,* ed. Frederick W. Axelgard (Boulder, Colo.: Westview Press, 1986), p. 86.

49. Katz, "Iraq and the Superpowers," p. 87.

50. Jeffrey Schloesser, Political Military Officer in the Regional Affairs Office Bureau of Near East and South-Asian Affairs, "U.S. Policy in the Persian Gulf," *Department of State Bulletin,* October 1987, p. 41.

51. Roger F. Pajak, "Soviet Designs and Dilemmas in the Gulf Region," in *Crosscurrents in the Gulf,* p. 68; and Mohiaddin Mesbahi, "Soviet Policy Toward the Iran-Iraq War," in *Soviet Foreign Policy: New Dynamics, New Themes,* ed. Carl G. Jacobsen (New York: St. Martin's Press, 1989), p. 164.

52. Francis Fukuyama, *Gorbachev and the New Soviet Agenda in the Third World* (Santa Monica, Calif.: The Rand Corporation, 1989), p. 42.

53. Barry Rubin, "Drowning in the Gulf," *Foreign Policy,* no. 69 (Winter 1987–88): 130.

54. David E. Long, *The United States and Saudi Arabia: Ambivalent Allies* (Boulder, Colo.: Westview Press, 1985), pp. 6–7.

55. Youssef M. Ibrahim, "Saudi Arabia Beheads 16 Kuwaitis Linked to Pro-Iranian Terrorism," *The New York Times*, September 22, 1989, p. A1.

56. Michael Sterner, "The Gulf Cooperation Council and Persian Gulf Security," in *Gulf Security and the Iran-Iraq War*, ed. Thomas Naff (Washington, D.C.: National Defense University Press, 1985), p. 4; and Mohammed E. Ahrari, "Iran and the Superpowers in the Gulf," *SAIS Review* 7, no. 1 (Winter-Spring 1987): 157.

57. Lenore G. Martin, "Patterns of Regional Conflict and U.S. Gulf Policy," in *U.S. Strategic Interests in the Gulf Region*, ed. Wm. J. Olson (Boulder, Colo.: Westview Press, 1987), p. 10.

58. Martin, p. 11.

59. M. S. El Azharzy, "The Attitudes of the Superpowers Towards the Gulf War," *International Affairs* 59, no. 4 (Autumn 1983): p. 610.

60. Frederick W. Axelgard, *A New Iraq? The Gulf War and Implications for U.S. Policy* (New York: Praeger, 1988), p. 66.

61. Axelgard, p. 66.

62. "The Community and Events in the Middle East," *Bulletin of the European Communities* 13, no. 9 (1980): 7.

63. "Safe Shipping in the Gulf," *Europe*, September 29, 1980, p. 3; and Patrick Brogan, "U.S. Consults Its Allies on How to Protect Oil and Shipping in Threatened Gulf," *The Times* (London), September 27, 1980, p. 5ff.

64. "Iranians Call on Nine For Support Against Iraqi Aggression," *Europe*, November 28, 1980, p. 3.

65. Tareq Y. Ismael, *International Relations of the Contemporary Middle East* (Syracuse, N.Y.: Syracuse University Press, 1986), p. 123.

66. Hollis, p. 213.

67. Rubin, p. 122.

68. Richard W. Murphy, "Statement," in *U.S. Policy in the Persian Gulf*, Hearing Before the Subcommittee on Arms Control, International Security, and Science, and the Subcommittee on Europe and the Middle East, December 15, 1987 (Washington, D.C.: Government Printing Office, 1987), p. 11.

69. John Felton, "Introduction," in *The Iran-Contra Puzzle*, ed. Patricia Ann O'Connor (Washington, D.C.: Congressional Quarterly Inc., 1987) pp. 3–7.

70. Sohrab Sobbani, *The Pragmatic Entente: Israeli-Iranian Relations* (New York: Praeger, 1989), pp. 148–50.

71. Robert McFarlane, "Reasons for the Arms Sales and Expected Benefits," in *U.S. Policy Toward Iran*, Hearings before the U.S. Senate Committee on Foreign Relations, January 16, 1987 (Washington, D.C.: Government Printing Office, 1987), p. 36.

72. Ronald Reagan, "U.S. Initiative to Iran," *Department of State Bulletin*, January 1987, p. 65.

73. Anthony H. Cordesman, *The Gulf and the West: Strategic Relations and Military Realities* (Boulder, Colo.: Westview Press, 1988), p. 315.

74. Robert Art, "America's Foreign Policy," in *Foreign Policy in World Politics*, ed. Roy C. Macridis (Englewood Cliffs, N.J.: Prentice-Hall, 1989), p. 170.

75. *Parliamentary Debates* (Commons), 6th ser., vol. 120, 20 July–23 October (1987), col. 206.

76. "*El Pais* claims Government Authorized Arms to Iran," *FBIS-WEU*, November 12, 1987, p. 14.

77. "Company Reportedly Supplies Arms to Iran, Iraq, and the Republic of South Africa," *FBIS-WEU*, May 4, 1987, p. J3; and "Weapons Trade: Agreement Considered Secret," *Der Spiegel*, May 4, 1987, pp. 35–54. Abstracted in *FBIS-WEU*, May 6, 1987, p. J3.

78. "Arms from France for Iran," *FBIS-WEU*, September 24, 1987, p. 15; "Government Allegedly Knew of Iran Arms Sales," *FBIS-WEU*, January 16, 1987, p. K1; and "Chirac Spokesman Briefs Press on Arms Affair," *FBIS-WEU*, November 6, 1987, p. 7.

79. Richard L. Armitage, "Statement," in *U.S. Military Forces to Protect Reflagged Kuwaiti Oil Tankers*, Hearings before the U.S. Senate Committee on Foreign Relations, June 16, 1987 (Washington, D.C.: Government Printing Office, 1987), p. 86.

80. Richard W. Murphy, "Statement," *Department of State Bulletin*, July 1987, p. 59.

81. Murphy, pp. 60–61.

82. *Parliamentary Debates*, Commons, 6th Ser., vol. 120, 20 July–23 October (1987), col. 201.

83. Janice Gross Stein, "The Wrong Strategy in the Right Place: The U.S. in the Gulf," *International Security* 13, no. 3 (Winter 1988–89): 160.

84. Cordesman, p. 363.

85. "Federal Navy Will Not Act in Persian Gulf Area," *FBIS-WEU*, May 29, 1987, p. J1; and "U.S. Request for Minesweeping in Gulf Rejected," *FBIS-WEU*, July 29, 1987, p. H1.

86. Cordesman, p. 368; and "U.S. Request for Minesweeper Help in Gulf Rejected," *FBIS-WEU*, August 3, 1987, p. E1.

87. "French Fleet Mobilized," *Europe*, July 28, 1987, p. 2.

88. "French Involvement in the Gulf," *FBIS-WEU*, October 20, 1988, p. 4.

89. "Mr. Cahen Refers to the Role of WEU in the Gulf Crisis," *Europe*, September 26, 1987, p. 4.

90. Secretary of State for Defense, *Statement on the Defense Estimates, 1989, vol. 1* (London: HMSO, Her Majesty's Stationery Office, 1989), p. 19.

91. "Naval Ship Relieves Belgian Ship for Gulf Duty," *FBIS-WEU*, September 23, 1987, p. 6.

92. "Operational Coordination Between France and Italy, But the Missions Retain Their National Character," *Europe* , September 23, 1987, p. 3.

93. *Parliamentary Debates* (Commons), 6th ser., vol. 118, 17 June–3 July 1987), col. 484.

94. "Thatcher Makes Surprise Visit to Naval Force," *FBIS-WEU*, August 10, 1988, p. 3.

95. Geoffrey Howe, p. 3.

96. "Excerpts from Iraq's Statement on Kuwait," *The New York Times*, August 9, 1990, p. A10.

97. "Excerpts from Iraqi Document on Meeting with U.S. Envoy," *The New York Times*, September 23, 1990, p. A13.

98. See Alan Riding, "Designing the New Europe: Plenty to Argue About," *The New York Times*, November 19, 1990, p. A6.

99. Elaine Sciolino, "As U.S. Warms to UN, It Finds Unpaid Debts Embarrassing," *The New York Times*, September 13, 1990, p. A8.

100. Ted Galen Carpenter, "Bush Jumped the Gun in the Gulf," *The New York Times*, August 18, 1990, p. A15.

101. "Excerpts From Bush's Statement on U.S. Defense of Saudis," *The New York Times*, August 9, 1990, p. A7; and Zbigniew Brzezinski, "Redefine, Reformulate Persian Gulf Policy," *The Christian Science Monitor*, November 15, 1990, p. 19.

102. Clyde Haberman, "Trade Sanctions Against Baghdad Imposed by European Community," *The New York Times*, August 5, 1990, p. A1.

103. James LeMoyne, "Meshing the Parts of the Unwieldy War Machine in the Gulf," *The New York Times*, October 21, 1990, p. E2; and "A Strange and Motley Army," *The Economist*, September 22, 1990, pp. 45–46.

104. Craig R. Whitney, "Thatcher Warns Europeans on Slow Response to Crisis," *The New York Times*, August 31, 1990, p. A9.

105. Ferdinand Protzman, "Bonn, Heeding Critics in U.S., Will Provide Planes and Ships for Gulf Effort," *The New York Times*, September 15, 1990, p. A5; and Steven Weisman "Kaifu Outlines Proposal for Unarmed Japanese in Gulf," *The New York Times*, September 28, 1990, p. A4.

106. Philip Shenon, "Baghdad to Free Germans to Try to Split Gulf Alliance," *The New York Times*, November 21, 1990, p. A7.

107. Elaine Sciolino, "Soviet-Iraqi Tie: Marriage of Strained Convenience," *The New York Times*, September 9, 1990, p. A10; and Peter Schweizer, "Is Moscow Playing Cute on Kuwait?" *The New York Times*, August 22, 1990, p. A17.

108. "The Soviet Union and Saudi Arabia," *The Economist*, September 22, 1990, p. 46.

109. Philip Shenon, "Accords Reached by Iran and Iraq," *The New York Times*, November 17, 1990, p. A4.

110. Joel Brinkley, "Israel Promises No Help for UN," *The New York Times*, October 19, 1990, p. A6.

111. "Draft of UN Resolution Calling for Use of Force," *The New York Times*, November 27, 1990, p. A8; and R. W. Apple, "Surprise Overture: First Response by Iraqi Minister Is Positive," *The New York Times*, December 1, 1990, p. A1.

112. Thomas L. Friedman and Patrick E. Tyler, "From the First, U.S. Resolve to Fight," *The New York Times*, March 3, 1991, p. A1.

113. Michael Evans, "Promise of Pull-Out Not Enough to Halt Attack, NATO Is Told," *The Times* (London), January 11, 1991, p. 3.

114. "Transcript of Comments by Bush on the Air Strikes Against the Iraqis," *The New York Times*, January 17, 1991, p. A6.

115. Alan Riding, "For Europeans, Worry That War Could Hit Home," *The New York Times*, January 13, 1991, p. 2E.

116. Clyde Haberman, "Pope Denounces the Gulf War," *The New York Times*, April 1, 1991, p. A5.

117. George Brock and Peter Guilford, "EC Pledges $392,000 for Baghdad Water Supply," *The Times* (London), March 1, 1991, p. 1.

118. "Text of President Bush's State of the Union Message," *The New York Times*, January 30, 1991, p. A8.

119. Andrew Rosenthal, "Bush and Mitterrand United on Peace, Divided on Process," *The New York Times*, March 15, 1991, p. A7.

5

Central America: Nicaragua

Unlike the Middle East, the Persian Gulf, and southern Africa, where the West European allies have significant economic and political interests, Central America seemed relatively unimportant. Few Europeans believed that the 1979 Sandinista revolution directly threatened the NATO alliance. But President Reagan's ideological obsession with fighting communism in "America's backyard," his determination for America to "stand tall" in the world by demonstrating U.S. power and resolve in Nicaragua, and his emphasis on alliance solidarity in regional crises, transformed the Central American conflict into an alliance concern.

While the allies recognized the United States' legitimate interests in Central America, none of them shared Reagan's view that Nicaragua's policies constituted an "extraordinary threat." Nevertheless, as Nicaragua and the United States blundered toward military confrontation, the European allies viewed their involvement as providing a release valve for pressure generated by tragic miscalculations and hubris on both sides. Differences of opinion within the Reagan administration itself on how to address the issue only exacerbated problems between the United States and Western Europe. Furthermore, contradictions in Reagan's policies toward the region compounded the problem. Apart from the fact that waging a proxy war through the Contras against Nicaragua, a government with which the United States had diplomatic relations, was viewed by the allies as a violation of international law, America's support for the El Salvadoran government against rebels and its backing of rebels against the Nicaraguan government could not be reconciled. More important, Reagan's aggression against Daniel Ortega's Nicaragua inadvertently helped the Soviet Union to justify its invasion of Afghanistan. From the allies' perspective, the superpowers' behavior in both regions threatened European détente as well as specific national interests of Spain, West Germany, and to a lesser extent, France and Britain.

Although the Europeans (with the exception of France, which sold arms to Nicaragua shortly after Mitterrand became president) carefully avoided open confrontation with the United States in Central America, they nonetheless often pursued policies, individually or under the EC umbrella, that diverged from America's. The situation in Nicaragua symbolized a renewal of the Cold War that Europeans viewed as inimical to their national as well as collective interests. But it also represented an opportunity for Spain, France, and (to a lesser degree) West Germany to demonstrate their independence from Washington. Developments in Europe itself further complicated the allies' policies in Central America. With the most to gain from détente with Moscow, West Germany focused on developing stronger trade and cultural ties with Eastern Europe and on German unification. Simultaneously, however, it had to balance these objectives against its overall relationship with the United States and its membership in the NATO alliance. Spain, which was relatively unaffected by the Cold War, was primarily concerned with consolidating its transition from authoritarian rule to democracy, projecting a foreign policy toward Latin America to enhance its international image, and ending its isolation in Europe by joining the EC. Thus, Spain's attempt to pursue an independent foreign policy had to be reconciled with its economic interests in Europe as well as with its membership in NATO. France's initial overt opposition to U.S. policy in Nicaragua was moderated by its growing concern about Soviet activities in Afghanistan, Libya's invasion of Chad, and secessionist movements in Martinique and Guadeloupe.

From the beginning Britain was careful not to irritate the United States in an area where it had few interests. Less concerned than West Germany about détente, Britain wanted to maintain its special relationship with the United States and to enlist American support in its effort to prevent Guatemala from seizing disputed territory in Belize. Moreover, U.S. assistance to Britain during its war with Argentina over the Falkland Islands (Malvinas) undoubtedly moderated any criticism Britain may have had concerning U.S. policies in Central America. Anglo-American cooperation in the Caribbean following Britain's decision to grant independence to its territories in the 1960s also militated against significant variance between U.S. and British policies.

While the United States emphasized military solutions and eschewed negotiated settlements even as Reagan claimed to support the peace process initiated by the Central American states, the Europeans actively encouraged negotiations. Having participated in Spain's and Portugal's transition from authoritarian rule to democracy, European governments as well as the Socialist International (SI) were confident of their ability to find peaceful solutions to the Central American conflict. Nicaraguans, viewing Europeans as an alternative to the United States, tried to enlist their support, but sabotaged this strategy to some extent, by restricting the development of democracy in their country. Nevertheless, Europe's commitment to diplomacy and détente with the Soviet Union influenced the various countries to distance themselves from U.S. policies as well as from Nicaragua. Yet, the United States' relative decline vis-à-vis its allies influenced Washington to encourage the Europeans to play a greater economic and political role in a region from which the Monroe Doctrine had sought to exclude them.[1]

WESTERN EUROPE'S HISTORICAL TIES TO CENTRAL AMERICA

Historical links between Western Europe and Central America predate British colonization of North America. Under the Treaty of Tordesillas of 1494, Spain and Portugal effectively divided the region (and the world) between themselves and attempted to exclude other European powers. From then on developments in Latin America were inextricably intertwined with political, economic, and military changes in Europe itself. The settlement of North as well as South America by Europeans provided the most tangible link between Europe and the New World. Despite American efforts to reduce European influence in what it regarded as its sphere of influence, Spain, Britain, Germany, and France continued to pursue their own interests in Latin America until political and military realities in Europe and increased American power forced them to relinquish control over the region. Spain, the first European country to conquer and colonize Central America, was also the first to leave.

Spain's emergence as a significant military and political power in Europe was a direct outgrowth of its control over Latin America's gold and silver. Conversely, its decline resulted in part from its rivals' ability to successfully challenge Spain's dominance in the region. By 1825 Spain had lost most of its colonies in Latin America and had become a relatively insignificant country in Europe. Cuban nationalism and American expansionism in the late 1890s resulted in the Spanish-American War, which terminated Spain's political control in Latin America. Yet Spain's defeat coincided with increased Latin American interest in the former colonial power, prompted in part by U.S. intervention in the area. This trend was consolidated as Spain's internal problems and its civil war forced large numbers of Spanish citizens to immigrate to Latin America. Many of them became influential in the intellectual community and economic sectors of their adopted countries.[2]

Spain's decline in Central America, caused partly by British assistance to Latin American independence movements, was followed by increased British and German activity in the region. Throughout much of the nineteenth century, Britain was the dominant power in Central America. British commercial interests, backed by British military might, effectively controlled much of Costa Rica, Honduras, Nicaragua, and Guatemala. As the leading maritime nation, Britain was able to control Miskito province as an autonomous area of Nicaragua. Although Britain had promised to leave the Miskito Coast in the early 1780s, it decided to re-establish itself in the area in 1816 and remained until 1906. Under the Clayton-Bulwer Treaty of 1850 between Britain and the United States, both countries agreed to refrain from exercising dominion over the Miskito Coast or any part of Central America, and Nicaraguan sovereignty, much compromised by both Britain and the United States, was recognized as extending to the Miskito Coast in 1860. However, when the Nicaraguan government convinced Miskito residents to abdicate their autonomy, Britain did not hesitate to intervene to restore it.[3] Similarly, when Hondurans refused to repay their British creditors in 1872, British warships bombarded a Honduran port until the government complied with British demands. And when Guatemala claimed part of British Honduras (now Belize), Britain refused to discuss the issue. As Walter LaFeber stated, "the U.S. could proclaim the Monroe Doctrine, but Britannia's fleet and investors wrote their own rules."[4]

Compared with Britain, Germany's presence in Latin America was not as pervasive. Nevertheless, German influence increased as Spain withdrew and by the twentieth century Germany was able to compete with the United States for markets throughout the region. Commercial interests played a major role in determining Germany's foreign policies toward Latin America prior to the countries' independence from Spain. German merchants from the Hanseatic cities of Hamburg and Bremen, who had attempted to end Spain's trade monopoly, were among the first Europeans to recognize the new Latin American states.[5]

Having relatively few colonies, Germany concentrated on developing commercial ties with Latin America. German immigrants established local industries. German firms were involved in the coffee industry, shipping, and manufacturing. German religious organizations, principally the Moravians, became integrated into Nicaraguan society, especially along the Miskito Coast. But World War I temporarily diminished not only German but also British involvement in Central America and contributed to the United States' economic and political dominance in the region. This trend continued until after World War II. Even though Western Europe was devastated by the war and became increasingly dependent on American military protection, West Germany's preoccupation with economic recovery influenced it to reestablish economic relations with Central America in particular and Latin America in general. Whereas in 1950 West Germany imported approximately $2.4 million worth of goods from Central America, by 1954 German imports had escalated to $53.2 million, a figure which then doubled by 1958.[6]

Europe's renewed involvement in Latin America was apparent in the late 1960s when U.S. influence was being undermined by its domestic problems and the Vietnam war. The crisis of confidence created by an unpopular war prompted American policymakers to favor more isolationist policies precisely when the West European allies were becoming more assertive and confident of their ability to play a greater international role. Many Latin Americans, disillusioned by failed U.S. policy initiatives in the region, looked to Europe as an alternative to the United States. The combination of American decline, European ascendancy, and Latin American desire to pursue autonomous foreign policies facilitated Europe's renewed activity in what had been regarded as the United States' sphere of influence.[7] The allies attempted to avoid direct political competition with the United States in the Caribbean and Central America, despite their growing concerns about Washington's leadership of NATO. Yet the decline of the Cold War during the early 1970s and the movement toward a multipolar international political system enhanced the Europeans' maneuverability vis-à-vis the United States. As economic issues assumed greater significance in the international distribution of power, the Europeans became more confident of their ability to address Third World economic concerns. Furthermore, in order to protect European détente, the allies attempted to restrain the United States in its growing confrontation with the Soviet Union in Central America.

THE ALLIES' RESPONSES TO THE SANDINISTAS

Given the United States' direct involvement in Nicaraguan politics from 1848 until the Sandinista Revolution of 1979, nationalism in Nicaragua was almost inevitably anti-American in nature. When Jose Santos Zelaya's nationalism threatened Washington's interests, President William Howard Taft responded by backing a Conservative Party revolt that culminated in Zelaya's downfall in 1909. In 1912 U.S. marines landed in Nicaragua and stayed until 1933, with a brief interruption of eighteen months in 1925–26, thus giving Nicaragua the dubious distinction of enduring the longest U.S. occupation of any Latin American country during the twentieth century.[8] Resistance to American intervention, led by Augusto Cesar Sandino, consolidated not only Nicaraguan nationalism but also Nicaraguan anti-Americanism. Washington's support for the Somoza dynasty, which governed Nicaragua from 1936 to 1979, undoubtedly influenced the Frente Sandinista de Liberacion Nacional (FSLN) to be at least apprehensive about U.S. intentions. Consequently, when the Sandinistas came to power in 1979, they actively sought to diversify Nicaragua's international relations and attempted to enlist Western Europe's support to counterbalance the United States.

Although President Carter's policies toward the Sandinistas were similar to the Europeans', his approach was inconsistent with fundamental American attitudes toward radical change, especially when perceived within an East-West context. Despite America's own revolutionary tradition, U.S. foreign policy on political and economic transformation in the Third World has been essentially oriented toward the status quo.[9] Europeans, on the other hand, having experienced anticolonial upheavals and their own internal violent conflicts, emphasized the necessity of change and were more predisposed to accept socioeconomic and political factors as determining causes of revolution. Instead of pursuing what they regarded as counterproductive policies aimed at stopping revolutionary change, the Europeans attempted to provide nationalist movements with an alternative source of support, thereby minimizing their dependence on the Soviet Union and Cuba.

Among the West Europeans, the SI, led by Willy Brandt and Helmut Schmidt of West Germany, Felipe Gonzalez of Spain, Regis Debray of France, and Bruno Kreisky of Austria, openly disagreed with U.S. policy in Nicaragua and, even during the Carter administration, decided to support the Sandinistas. Akin to Mexico, the SI simultaneously wanted to prevent Nicaragua from becoming entangled in the East-West conflict and to reduce both U.S. and Cuban military activities in the region.[10] Initial contacts between the SI and the Sandinistas in 1977 coincided with widespread domestic opposition against Anastasio Somoza. By calling for the suspension of all economic and financial support for Somoza, and by providing organizational and financial support for the Sandinistas in mid–1978, the SI not only deepened European involvement in the Nicaraguan crisis but assisted in legitimizing internationally the Sandinistas' struggle against Somoza. Bruno Kreisky, Austria's prime minister, assumed leadership of the National Committee of Solidarity with Nicaragua. The Ebert Stiftung school in Costa Rica allowed the Sandinistas to use their facilities to prepare their blueprint for government, and Felipe Gonzalez led the newly created Committee in Defense of the Nicaraguan Revolution.[11] Since many of the SI's leaders were also national European leaders or were leaders of major political parties, escalating SI activities in Central America initially engendered serious conflicts between some of the allies and the United States when President Reagan took office.

An underlying cause of intra-alliance strains was that the European Socialist parties, such as the West German Social Democratic Party (SPD), the French Socialist Party (PS), and the Spanish Partido Socialista Obrero Español (PSOE), emphasized the North-South aspect of the Nicaraguan problem as opposed to the East-West view embraced by the Reagan administration. Many Europeans believed that the globalist approach favored by the United States overlooked the underlying causes of instability. The regional approach, advocated by the allies, focused on social injustice, political repression and denial of effective political choice, pervasive military power, and the growing militarization of society.[12] Thus, although the Europeans disagreed among themselves about the direction of change in Nicaragua, none of them, including Britain, supported U.S. military intervention as a solution. In addition to jeopardizing Western Europe's extensive ties with the Third World, using military force as an instrument of foreign policy was contrary to the allies' interest in maintaining détente with the Soviet Union and would have diverted attention from Europe's economic problems. Furthermore, Europeans opposed Reagan's attempts to elevate a relatively minor issue into an alliance crisis. Reagan the crusader showed no inclination to compromise with the "evil" Sandinistas, and was committed to overthrowing them in order to prevent Central America from falling into the Communist camp. Virtually declaring war against Nicaragua, Reagan accelerated military pressure on the Sandinistas by funding the Contras, whom he designated as freedom fighters and equated with Jefferson and Lafayette.[13] Although the Soviet Union and Cuba were actively involved in Nicaragua, the threat to the United States was clearly and deliberately exaggerated.

The West European allies, far removed from Central America, understood America's concern about regional instability but disagreed with its choice of instruments to solve the problems. They believed that funding the Contras could not achieve the overthrow of the Sandinistas, and were dismayed by the absence of pragmatism in U.S. policy. The allies also worried about the administration's political immaturity on Nicaragua, a fact demonstrated by the Iran-Contra scandal. What disturbed them most was America's confusion and contradictions on Central America. As William D. Rogers observed, it was how the U.S. behaved—how well it managed the crisis in Central America—which was really of importance to Europe. Obviously most of Europe would like to see the U.S. successful, confident, tactically sensible, rational, and avoiding excesses.[14]

Whereas the United States claimed that its strategies in Central America protected Western interests against the Soviet threat, many West Europeans did not share America's perception of the threat from Moscow. On the contrary, the allies generally believed that the United States itself was a threat to Western interests.[15] Confrontation with Moscow in Central America and elsewhere in the Third World was largely detrimental to the allies' interests. Therefore, when Assistant Secretary of State Lawrence Eagleburger headed the U.S. mission in 1981 to Bonn, Paris, Brussels, the Hague, and London to convince the Europeans that the Soviet Union and Nicaragua were providing military assistance to the guerrillas in El Salvador, he found little support among the allies. West Germany threw its weight behind the SI's initiatives in the region and France wanted the United States to concentrate its efforts on Afghanistan instead.[16] Yet Central America in general and Nicaragua in particular became an alliance concern because Reagan decided to make West European support for his policy in the region his first test of alliance solidarity.[17]

From the allies' perspective, Central America was not a priority. European support for American military intervention in Nicaragua was seen as strengthening pacifist movements in West Germany and elsewhere and generating strong anti-American sentiments throughout Europe at a time when America wanted more allied cooperation on Afghanistan, the Middle East, and the Persian Gulf.[18] In an effort to avert further military confrontation in Central America and to deemphasize the East-West aspect of the conflict, the allies supported the peace process, thereby providing an alternative to U.S. and Soviet approaches. However, since the Reagan administration was never serious about finding a negotiated settlement that took the interests of the parties into consideration, Europeans' preference for political solutions was neither consistent with U.S. expectations of its allies' behavior nor encouraged by Washington.

Yet the fact that many Europeans and Latin Americans shared underlying interests and common perceptions of the problem militated against U.S. efforts to dominate developments in Central America. Western Europe's objective of becoming an alternative to the superpowers for Central America was facilitated by the latter's need to decrease its dependence on the United States. This was particularly important to Nicaraguans, who wanted to diversify their international relations.[19] At the same time, the allies could demonstrate their independence from Washington and translate their growing economic power into political influence.

The convergence of European and Nicaraguan interests, especially in the early 1980s, was rooted in many political similarities between Western Europe and Latin America. Devastated by World War II and deprived of their great power status, many Europeans assumed the role played by the United States in the Third World prior to 1945. Like the United States during the period of decolonization in the 1950s and 1960s, the West Europeans now believed that Third World countries should not be dominated by the superpowers. Furthermore, the allies themselves wanted to create a new Europe in which U.S. political and military power would be drastically diminished. Central America and Western Europe were moving toward greater regional cooperation and shared a general disinterest in hegemonic aspirations. As medium powers, the West Europeans emphasized economic strength and adherence to international law and morality in a world dominated militarily by the United States and the Soviet Union. The Central American states, because of their limited military and economic capabilities, also supported principles of international law, nonintervention, and the peaceful settlement of conflicts.[20] And the Reagan administration's general disregard for humanitarian sentiments and international law strengthened the Central American-European alliance.

In many ways, the political diversity in Europe equipped the various leaders to better address the turmoil in Central America. Many West European leaders identified with political developments in Nicaragua because of their own experience with authoritarianism in Europe during the 1930s and 1940s. Socialists such as Willy Brandt and Felipe Gonzalez were strongly committed to promoting democracy in Central America because of their success in helping transform authoritarian European regimes into democratic societies. An underlying reason for their success was their ability to compromise with groups that had radically different economic and political views. The United States, on the other hand, had little experience with radical groups in mainstream politics. Even Canada's Conservative party in the 1980s was more liberal than the Democratic party in the United States. And despite America's rhetorical commitment to political diversity, the reality has been widespread political conformity. Inside the United States, no strong leftist movement has ever challenged the political system, and outside the country no forceful neighbor has ever required the United States to live alongside a political or economic system not to its liking.[21] Consequently, Americans became less tolerant of political systems that were significantly different from their own.

While several allies openly criticized U.S. policy toward Nicaragua in the early 1980s, they decided to harmonize their Central American policies, to the extent possible, through EPC. By so doing, individual European countries could avoid taking initiatives that would make them vulnerable to American pressure. Countries such as Spain and West Germany also viewed a broader EC approach to Central America as furthering their own objective of raising developments in the region to a major European concern. In addition to regular EC relations with Central America, attempts were made to coordinate various European programs in Latin America as a whole. For example, in 1984 the European Parliament created the Institute for European-Latin American Relations (IRELA) to promote and consolidate regional ties between Europe and Latin America. Initiated by West Germany, IRELA was a forum for dialogue and contact between the two regions and a source of information for governments and private organizations. But the lack of harmony that characterized EPC also plagued IRELA. France and Britain were not enthusiastic about IRELA, preferring instead to continue their bilateral relations with Latin America. Similarly, Spain was suspicious of the organization and perceived it as simultaneously advancing German interests and interfering with Spain's foreign policy objectives.[22] Consequently, each country pursued its own policy toward Nicaragua even as they tried to work through the EC.

Among the allies, Britain was the least critical of U.S. policy in Central America. In sharp contrast to Spain, Britain had few interests in the region and demonstrated little enthusiasm for developing closer links to the various countries. It continued to focus on Belize and the Caribbean islands, but even here Britain was content to delegate most of its responsibilities to the United States. In light of Central America's relative insignificance for Britain, British foreign policymakers were reluctant to disagree with the United States, especially when the latter evinced an intense commitment and sensitivity to the area. From Britain's viewpoint, there were far more important interests at stake elsewhere.[23] Furthermore, by opposing the United States in Central America, Britain would have risked damaging its relationship with the United States within NATO at a time when Germany and France were becoming the major political and economic players in Europe.

Prime Minister Thatcher was in broad agreement with Reagan's foreign policy objectives and, unlike the other European allies, had no ideological sympathy with the Sandinistas. Thatcher believed that the spread of Marxism in Central America had to be prevented, and tried to offer tangible support to the Reagan administration when possible. Britain was one of the few countries to send official observers to the 1982 Salvadoran elections, but refused to send official observers to the 1984 Nicaraguan elections.[24] However, like the other European countries, Britain articulated the position that the problems could be solved only through negotiations.

Drawing upon their country's own experience with anticolonial movements, British policymakers concluded that the most effective way to frustrate Soviet and Cuban aims in Central America was to recognize "that there will be revolutionary changes in the political atmosphere, Left and Right, and that it is not in our interest to distance ourselves from these movements or to force them to look only to the Soviet Union."[25] But compared to Spain and France, Britain carefully avoided close contacts with the Sandinistas, partly to avoid creating serious tensions within NATO. Britain did not have resident diplomatic staff at its embassy in Nicaragua from 1979 to 1984. A resident chargé d'affaires was appointed in mid-1984, and second and third secretaries were appointed in 1986 and 1988, respectively. The British ambassador in Costa Rica and three members of his diplomatic staff were accredited to Nicaragua. A defense attaché and a first secretary were accredited from Panama.[26]

Similar to its European partners, Britain believed that the underlying causes of conflict in Central America were longstanding social and economic problems and the absence of mechanisms whereby political views could be freely expressed or social justice obtained.[27] Consequently, Britain opposed military solutions and was quick to commend the Reagan administration for its initiative for economic development of the entire region. Humphrey Atkins, the Lord Privy Seal, noted that "if some of the poverty, some of the inequalities, and some of the economic difficulties of these countries can be tackled, stable governments, justice, and democracy will have a better future."[28]

Determined to pursue an independent foreign policy, France perceived itself as an alternative to both superpowers in Central America. Despite U.S. objections, France continued to develop commercial and political relations with Cuba, issued a joint declaration with Mexico that recognized the leftist guerrillas in El Salvador as a representative political force legitimately entitled to negotiate with the government, and, in direct opposition to the United States, sold small quantities of arms to the Sandinistas. The

French government under Mitterrand criticized American intervention in Central America, viewing it as abetting oppression in the region. Mitterrand argued that "instead of forcing the Latin American people to live under military dictatorships, it would be more intelligent of the West to help those people."[29] French policymakers openly disagreed with the United States for "encircling" Nicaragua and giving it a feeling of being surrounded by hostile powers. In order to avoid another Cuba, the French suggested that the alliance attempt to bring Nicaragua closer to the West and to find an internal solution through negotiations that included opposition forces. Obviously more apprehensive about U.S. policies than any Soviet threat, the French regarded their approach to Central America as the "only way to avoid an increased U.S. political and military presence in the region, and the danger of an eventual direct intervention which could provoke a similar reaction from the Soviet Union, through its allies in the area."[30] When informed that President Reagan did not approve of his policies, President Mitterrand asserted that the peoples of Central America had the right to determine their own fate and to refuse a life of misery and suppression by dictators and ruthless economic power-holders. Mitterrand declared his support for the revolt by these people and stated that "if that does not please the United States, and it clearly does not, it is just too bad."[31]

Unlike Britain, which showed relatively little interest in Central American developments, France had significant links to Nicaragua and El Salvador. Mitterrand himself was close to West Germany's Willy Brandt, the inspiration behind the SI's Third World policies, and was also a friend of a number of Latin American opposition leaders. Furthermore, Mitterrand's wife, Danielle, and his political adviser and Minister of Culture, Regis Debray, were keenly interested in Central America. French involvement was not only an expression of the Socialists' concern for Third World countries, but also a deliberate attempt by France to differentiate its strategies from those employed by Washington in dealing with East-West conflicts. The French Socialists had collaborated with the Sandinistas, many of whom were observers at the SI, and had encouraged the Nicaraguans to plead their case before the international community to protect their country from what they regarded as American aggression and internal destabilization. The French also advised the Sandinistas to show that they were open to negotiation and democratization.[32] While Washington was generally annoyed with French assertiveness and independence in Central America, it decided to ignore France's activities. However, when Mitterrand recognized the Salvadoran guerrillas and sold arms to the Sandinistas, the United States abruptly altered its position.[33]

France's cooperation with Mexico in Central America emanated in part from the fact that both countries wanted to pursue independent foreign policies, to be regarded as leaders of the Third World, and to prevent Central America from becoming a battleground in the new Cold War. Mexican

President José López Portillo traveled throughout Latin America to build a united front against the return of Cold War politics to the region, and visited Cuba on the eve of the 1980 U.S. presidential elections to demonstrate Mexico's autonomy in international affairs and to consolidate its position as a leader of the Third World.[34] Shortly after Mitterrand became president he decided to expand French influence in Latin America by strengthening ties with Mexico. France persuaded Mexico to join it in recognizing the rebel forces in El Salvador, a development that represented the first major international challenge to U.S. policy in Central America. France essentially suggested a division of labor within the Western alliance in El Salvador, and maintained that since the United States had severed ties with the Salvadoran leftists, some Western countries should support the guerrillas in order for NATO to have ties to the new regime if they were to win their struggle.[35] Although the United States did not accept France's assumptions, the fact that French Foreign Minister Claude Cheysson had telephoned to give Washington advance warning of the joint French-Mexican declaration apparently moderated America's response. Moreover, the United States hoped that, in return for its muted criticism of French statements on El Salvador, it would obtain France's support for the eventual installation of Pershing and cruise missiles in Europe.[36]

In 1981 France and Nicaragua signed an agreement that provided for the delivery of French military equipment to the Sandinista regime. The weapons sold included two Alouette helicopters, rockets and shoulder-fired rocket launchers, two patrol boats, and a dozen military trucks. Under the agreement, France trained ten Nicaraguan sailors in France. French Defense Minister Charles Hernu and other French Socialist leaders argued that the arms sales helped Third World nations to reduce their dependence on the superpowers and enabled them to avoid being entangled in the East-West confrontation. From France's perspective, it was preferable to offer the Sandinistas a non-Communist source of weapons than to force them to rely on Soviet and Cuban weapons. But the action proved too provocative for Washington, and the Reagan administration strongly condemned it. Partly in response to Washington's sharp disagreement, France decided to deliver the weapons on an installment basis between 1981 and 1983.[37]

New economic, political, and military realities in Nicaragua, the Caribbean, Africa, and in France itself influenced French foreign policymakers to modify their policy toward the Sandinistas by the mid-1980s and to assume a lower political profile in Nicaragua. A major consideration was the Sandinistas' deepening links to Cuba and the Soviet Union. A second factor was the lack of progress with democratic reforms in Nicaragua. Finally, France was having its own problems with leftist movements in Guadeloupe and Martinique and with Libyan intervention in Chad. These factors combined to make France less critical of U.S. policies in Central America.

Mitterrand realized that by openly opposing the United States in Central America, where France had comparatively few tangible interests, France risked jeopardizing its significant interests in Europe and Africa, the protection of which required good relations with the United States. The deteriorating French economy in the early 1980s could not be improved without U.S. cooperation. Consequently, broader alliance concerns became far more important than Nicaragua's derailed revolution. Moreover, France had to intervene militarily in Chad to protect it from Libyan aggression, and separatist movements in Martinique and Guadeloupe forced France to increase its military presence in the Caribbean.[38] Given these circumstances, France decided to rely increasingly on the SI and the EC in Central America.

West Germany's Central American policy was more complex than Britain's or France's. This was largely due to domestic political considerations, Bonn's dependence on both Washington and Moscow, and the importance West German foreign policymakers placed on economic and political relations with Latin America. Although the Social Democrats favored closer links with the Sandinistas, the fact that West Germany was ruled by a coalition government meant that compromises had to be made with the more conservative Christian Democratic Union party. In addition, each political party was represented by government-supported foundations that were active in Central America. Thus, Bonn could avoid conflict with Washington by allowing the foundations to assume greater foreign policy responsibilities. Business groups played a similar role. Given the pivotal role of business in West German politics and society, Bonn carefully avoided taking actions that would impede commercial relations. But these factors had to be weighed against West Germany's broader foreign policy objectives, the achievement of which depended on Bonn's ability to maneuver skillfully between Washington and Moscow. While Germany could not appear disloyal to the United States and the NATO alliance, it had to protect détente with the Soviet Union in order to accomplish its goal of unifying Germany and expanding trade with Eastern Europe. Overt support for violent American actions in Nicaragua would have engendered serious opposition from the Social Democrats and the Greens, thereby endangering American efforts to station nuclear missiles in West Germany. In light of these complex considerations, West Germany approached Nicaragua cautiously.

The Social Democrats were instrumental in Spain's and Portugal's transition to democracy, a factor that encouraged West Germany to become politically involved in Central America.[39] Augmenting this was Germany's objective of isolating Third World conflicts from East-West competition. Apart from engaging in a calculated division of labor within the Western alliance, Bonn perceived superpower conflict as detrimental to European détente and its own goal of gaining greater independence from both Washington and Moscow. Moreover, by focusing on the North-South dimension of world politics, West Germany was attempting to shift the emphasis from military power to economic power, thereby enhancing its own position in global political and economic affairs vis-à-vis the superpowers.

Consistent with these views, West Germany under Social Democrat (SPD) leadership provided political and organizational support to the Sandinistas, and when Somoza was forced out of office, Bonn approved an aid program for Nicaragua but suspended financial assistance to El Salvador. The Ebert Stiftung Foundation, which is connected to the SPD, opened an office in Managua. Recognizing that different political factions had united under the umbrella of the Sandinistas to overthrow Somoza, the West Germans attempted to work with the moderates in Nicaragua to help establish democracy. Hans-Juergen Wishnewski, minister of state in the chancellor's office, promised the new government full SPD support for Nicaragua's rapid reconstruction.[40] Believing that West German and alliance interests were being harmed by Reagan's Central American policies, Bonn advocated a negotiated settlement in El Salvador and endorsed the SI's efforts to establish contacts between the government and the guerrillas. However, increased U.S. military and economic support for El Salvador's government and strong opposition to negotiations with rebel groups influenced West Germany to moderate its position. When conservative Helmut Kohl became chancellor in 1982, West Germany decreased its aid to Nicaragua and minimized its differences with Washington on El Salvador. But whereas Kohl shared Thatcher's conviction that Europe should not interfere where American vital interests seemed to be at stake, Bonn continued to work through German foundations in Central America and the EC to achieve its objectives.[41]

Kohl and other West German political leaders believed that Washington's support for the Contras was counterproductive and dangerous. But instead of confronting the United States, Kohl attempted to "fill the gaps" caused by shortcomings in U.S. policies in the region by involving the EC. Consequently, West Germany immediately accepted Costa Rican President Luis Alberto Monge's invitation to the Euro-Central American conference in 1984,[42] and West Germany actively supported the Central American peace process.

Spain's political isolation in Europe influenced Spanish foreign policy-makers to develop stronger links with Latin America. Since Spain's decline as a major world power was directly related to its loss of colonies in the New World, there was a general tendency among Spain's leaders, including Franco, to view renewed relations with Latin America as the springboard for Spain's re-entry into international affairs. Spain openly disagreed with U.S. policy toward Cuba, and Franco strongly supported the Castro regime. Underlying this policy was a belief that Spain had a historical obligation toward Latin America regardless of the various governments' ideologies.[43]

During Spain's transition to democracy after Franco's death in 1975, Spain made a major effort to develop a new and more assertive foreign policy. Spain hoped that by cultivating relations with Latin America it would enhance its position in Europe. But there were other reasons for Spain's intensive search for foreign friends. Adolfo Suárez, the new Spanish leader, was attempting to consolidate his power domestically and to maintain the transition toward democracy by raising Spain's international profile.[44] Thus, the intensity of Spain's policy toward Central America depended on developments within both Spain and Latin America.

Spain's experience under Franco's dictatorship prompted opposition political groups such as Socialists, who shared their country's desire to develop political, cultural, and economic relations with Latin America, to collaborate with their counterparts in Central America. Working closely with the SI, Felipe Gonzalez assisted the Sandinistas in their struggle against Somoza. Several Spanish groups, including the Americanist lobby and the Institute for Latin American Cooperation, endorsed efforts to make both Spain and Nicaragua more independent of the United States. Yet the Suárez government (1976–81) refused to withdraw its ambassador from Nicaragua, unlike Britain, and continued to ship weapons to Somoza even as Spanish officials appealed for peace. It was estimated that ten thousand mortar shells and hand grenades as well as fifty thousand rounds of submachine gun ammunition were dispatched to Somoza's National Guard.[45] And despite the Spanish Socialists' close association with the Sandinistas, Gonzalez had to balance his policy in Nicaragua against Spain's reintegration into Europe when he became prime minister in 1982.

Although Spain endeavored to serve as a bridge between Europe and Latin America and to play a pivotal role in Central America, it was prevented from achieving these objectives by the United States, the West European allies, and the leading Latin American countries. Suggestions that Spain mediate the Nicaraguan crisis were rejected by the United States because they represented an indirect criticism of U.S. policy in Central America. Moreover, any Spanish involvement in the peace process had to be carefully weighed against the interests of countries such as Mexico, Colombia, and Venezuela, members of the Contadora group.[46] Spain's assertiveness and determination to implement an independent foreign policy also worried many of the European allies, particularly West Germany. Bonn was clearly concerned about Spain's new role in the Third World, and especially in Central America.

Spain's economic and political integration into Europe complicated the Socialists' approach to Nicaragua in particular and Latin America generally. Strong opposition to U.S. activities in Nicaragua would have fueled anti-American and anti-NATO sentiments in Spain precisely when Spanish policymakers wanted to use their country's membership in NATO as leverage to gain entry into the EC as well as to reduce the importance of Spain's bilateral relationship with the United States.[47] By antagonizing Washington, Spain would have diminished its own ability to achieve its major foreign policy objectives. Many EC members were apprehensive about Spain's perception of its role in Latin America and delayed its accession to the EC. A major consideration was the impact Spain's relations with its former colonies would have on arrangements worked out between Britain and France and their former colonies vis-à-vis the EC. On one hand, Spain wanted to minimize commercial difficulties that Latin American states would experience as a result of Spain's membership in the EC. On the other hand, Spain was not in a strong enough bargaining position to persuade the EC to accept a number of "mini-Lomés." Ultimately, Spain had to acquiesce to EC commitments to the ACP countries under the Lomé Treaty.[48] In return, the EC promised to cooperate with Latin America in areas of common interest, without being specific.

Spain's rapid economic growth in the late 1980s helped consolidate its ties with Western Europe. Most Spanish citizens were largely preoccupied with developments on the Continent. It was apparent that Spain's objective of serving as a bridge between Europe and Latin America could not be easily reconciled with its primary goal of ending its isolation from the rest of Europe. Pressure from Britain and France forced Spain to restrict immigration from its former colonies. Europeans were worried by Colombian drug traffickers' use of Spain as a distribution center for cocaine.[49] Furthermore, the political and economic transformation of Eastern Europe undermined Spain's goal of strengthening ties between the EC and Latin America. In addition, developments within Nicaragua during the mid-1980s influenced the European allies to modify their Central American policies.

Confronted by increased internal opposition to their policies and mounting military, political, and economic pressure from the United States, the Sandinistas proceeded to consolidate power and emphasized unity rather than pluralism or tolerance. Following the bombing of two bridges in northern Nicaragua by the Contras in March 1982, many large family farms were nationalized, the press was censored, and a general state of emergency was declared. Many Miskito Indians were evicted from their homes on the Atlantic coast and forced to flee to Honduras to escape the Sandinistas' scorched-earth policy. Approximately three to five thousand Indians were sent to labor camps in the Matagalpa-Jinotega area, where the Contras were most brutal, to pick coffee for the state. Thus, the Indians were victimized by both the government and the U.S.-supported guerrillas.[50]

Nicaragua was also victimized by U.S. actions. For example, the United States increased its military activities in Central America in early 1984, drastically reduced Nicaraguan sugar quotas in retaliation for alleged Nicaraguan subversive activities in the region, and mined Nicaragua's harbors. In February 1984 two Nicaraguan fishing vessels struck mines in the Nicaraguan port of El Bluff, on the Atlantic coast. In March the Dutch dredger *Geopointe*, the Panamanian ship *Los Caraibes*, and the Soviet tanker *Lugansk* were damaged by mines.[51] Arguing that Nicaraguan policies posed an "extraordinary threat" to the United States, the Reagan administration imposed a trade embargo against that country in 1985. These actions weakened the Sandinista regime and exacerbated many of the economic and political problems the Sandinistas helped to create. Although the French offered to clear the mines and the British deplored mining the harbors as a matter of principle, the West European allies were unwilling to confront the U.S. Instead, they decided to distance themselves from Nicaragua. Even the SI, a staunch supporter of the Sandinistas, urged Nicaragua to scale down the state of emergency, lift press censorship, allow opposition groups to freely organize within the country, and implement democratic reforms.[52]

Among the allies, West Germany and Britain, under conservative leadership, were the first to change their policies toward the Sandinistas. A key factor influencing the change in Bonn's policy was the assassination of German physician Albrecht Pflaum by the Contras in early 1983. Attention was focused not only on the personal tragedy but also on German aid to Nicaragua. The issue was divisive domestically and threatened relations between Bonn and Washington. In order to avoid conflict, Jurgen Warnke of the Federal Ministry for Economic Cooperation advocated terminating German aid to Nicaragua, which included withdrawing all German development specialists.[53] Bonn's conciliatory policy toward Nicaragua hardened as American pressure on the Sandinistas escalated and as Daniel Ortega severely restricted political and economic freedoms. When Ortega called West Germany an "accomplice in the extermination of the Nicaraguan people" during his visit to East Berlin in May 1985, West German-Nicaraguan relations were strained even further.[54] Germany responded by calling on the Sandinistas to respect human rights and to grant democratic freedoms to the Nicaraguans.

While the Ebert Stiftung Foundation, the Social Democrats' think-tank, continued to support the Sandinistas, it also emphasized respect for human rights and for balancing U.S. security concerns with self-determination. But the Konrad Adenauer Foundation and its Institute for International Solidarity, closely associated with the Christian Democrats, advocated increasing internal and external pressure on the Sandinistas to force them to "undo what has been done." Comparing the Sandinista regime to the Communist parties of Eastern Europe, leaders of the Adenauer Foundation believed that pressures from the Contras and support for internal opposition groups, the press, and the Catholic Church would eventually force the Nicaraguan government to implement democracy.[55]

France, faced with significant economic problems during the early 1980s, had to rethink many of its more radical policies. With the departure of the French Communist party from the governing coalition in 1984, Mitterrand developed a more pragmatic approach to the Soviet Union, the Third World, and the French economy. In light of the comparative strength of the American economy, France was reluctant to antagonize Washington. Furthermore, France's own troubles in the Caribbean influenced it to conduct joint military exercises with the United States on the Puerto Rican island of Vieques. (France had increased the number of military personnel stationed in the Caribbean from three thousand in 1981 to seven thousand in 1985.[56]) Although France continued to provide aid to Nicaragua, it strongly condemned restrictions on civil liberties as contrary to democratic principles, and reaffirmed its support for the peace process in Central America. Spain's response to developments in Nicaragua was not radically different from those of the other European allies.

As Spain's economic and political integration into the EC progressed, Felipe Gonzalez moved closer to the political center in Spain. Foreign Minister Fernando Moran, a strong Sandinista supporter, was replaced in 1985 by Francisco Fernández Ordonez, who was less critical of U.S. policy in Central America. Gonzalez, after traveling to the region, was worried about deteriorating economic and political conditions. In view of rising tensions between Washington and Managua, Gonzalez called for a rejuvenation of the peace process. Believing that the Sandinistas had drifted away from their initial plans, Gonzalez urged Daniel Ortega to move rapidly toward democracy. Spain also encouraged the Sandinistas to negotiate with the opposition, and increased its contacts with opposition leaders, including Alfonso Robelo.[57]

WESTERN EUROPE'S ECONOMIC RELATIONS WITH CENTRAL AMERICA

Western Europe's unwillingness to directly confront Washington in Central America was due in part to its relatively few economic interests in the region. In the twentieth century, West European trade with Latin America as a whole and Central America in particular has always been comparatively insignificant. During the early 1980s West Germany was the most important trading partner of the Latin American states. Approximately 3 percent of its total exports went to Latin America, compared to 2.6 percent of France's and 2 percent of Britain's. An expanding European market diminished Latin America's overall economic significance for Europe.

Spain, before joining the EC in 1986, was more dependent on Latin America, with 10 percent of its exports going to the region.[58] Isolated in Europe and relatively weak economically, Spain turned to Latin America for markets for its manufactured products and investments. Approximately two-thirds of Spain's direct foreign investments went to Latin America. However, Spanish investments comprised only 3 percent of total foreign investments in Latin America.[59] Spain's exports to Latin America consisted of machinery, transport, equipment, and various manufactured goods. Almost 95 percent of Latin America's exports to Spain were raw materials such as coffee, vegetables, tobacco, sorghum, sugar, and cocoa. By 1985 Cuba had surpassed Mexico and Venezuela as Spain's most important market. Spanish exports to Cuba doubled between 1984 and 1985. While Spain bought coffee and tobacco from Cuba, it sold Cuba freighters, industrial plants, steel, agricultural machinery, and chemicals. Spain was second only to Japan among the market economies supplying Cuba, and was the island's principal Western customer.[60]

Unlike Britain, which withdrew the Export Credit Guarantee Department's coverage of Nicaragua in early 1979 because of the economic problems resulting from internal conflict and the acute shortage of foreign exchange that followed,[61] Spain granted Nicaragua a $34 million loan in 1981 to enable it to import Spanish manufactured products. By early 1985, however, Nicaragua was unable to pay the interest on the loans, and Spain suspended credit until Nicaragua was able to pay the overdue interest and reschedule its debts.[62]

Despite its economic difficulties, Nicaragua was Spain's largest export market in Central America and its seventh largest in Latin America. Consequently, Spain and the other allies generally opposed economic sanctions as instruments of foreign policy. The United States denied the Nicaraguan airline landing rights in the United States and closed the market for spare parts for much of Nicaragua's machinery. Nicaraguan agricultural products, beef, and shellfish were barred from the United States. The European allies, particularly West Germany and Spain, opposed the economic embargo. Felipe Gonzalez rejected the economic boycott and recommended reopening the dialogue between the United States and Nicaragua, which had been suspended by the Reagan administration. West Germany's reaction was equally strong. Bonn not only disagreed with U.S. sanctions against Nicaragua but also offered to support the country within the framework of economic cooperation with Central America advocated by the EC.[63]

Attempting to deemphasize military solutions to Central America's problems, the EC focused more on economic solutions. By harmonizing their policies, the allies endeavored to diminish U.S. pressure against individual West European countries. And to counterbalance American efforts to isolate Nicaragua, the EC stressed the regional nature of the problem and included Nicaragua in all economic arrangements. Concerned about the negative economic impact its membership in the EC would have on Latin America in general, Spain tried to get special treatment for some of the region's products. It also encouraged its European partners to assist economic integration efforts in Central America by funding regional projects and programs.[64] The EC-Central America Agreement of November 12, 1985, which entered into force on March 1, 1987, created a joint committee to discuss priorities for future development aid projects, to promote Central American exports, and to initiate scientific cooperation. European markets were opened to Central American exports, and in 1986 the region registered a $560 million trade surplus with the EC.[65] Trade relations were assisted by various aid programs.

While direct bilateral assistance to the Sandinistas declined during the mid-1980s, Nicaragua continued to benefit from EC aid transfers to Central America. Additional assistance was provided by West German foundations and church groups, and private organizations from Britain, France, and Spain. For Britain and West Germany, which had refused to grant the Sandinistas substantive economic assistance until there was tangible evidence of movement toward free elections and democracy, the EC served as a buffer. Moreover, it allowed them to appear supportive of Washington's policies without really having to abandon their own approaches to Central America's dilemmas.

Britain, for example, showed very little enthusiasm for the Sandinistas. Thatcher refused to grant Nicaragua bilateral assistance, reminding Ortega that his country's economic problems resulted largely from misguided economic policies and the cost of running a vast military machine.[66] Nonetheless, Nicaragua received EC aid, of which Britain contributed approximately 20 percent. Britain also co-financed small development projects in Nicaragua with voluntary agencies such as Oxfam, Christian Aid, and CAFOD. During fiscal year 1987–88 Britain contributed about $71,000 to projects ranging from agricultural development and mother and child health programs to production and distribution of medicinal plants and building technology. Overall, Britain supported over forty nongovernmental organizations' projects in Nicaragua.[67] In response to the damage caused by Hurricane Joan in 1988, Britain provided humanitarian assistance to Central America, including Nicaragua, through international agencies such as the Red Cross and the UN Disaster Relief Office as well as through British voluntary agencies such as Oxfam.

Unlike Britain, West Germany initially gave Nicaragua a significant amount of economic assistance to rebuild the country following the devastating civil war. By late August 1979 planes loaded with food and medicine began arriving from West Germany. In order to reduce the acute housing shortage in Nicaragua, Bonn agreed to finance an apartment construction program, and offered credit for the acquisition of machines and technical equipment.[68] By 1983, however, developments within Nicaragua increased U.S. pressure on both Nicaragua and the European allies, and a more conservative government in Bonn resulted in diminished aid to Nicaragua. Jurgen Warnke, the minister for overseas aid and development, radically altered Bonn's guidelines on foreign assistance. He proposed (1) closer agreement with the United States, particularly on aid to Latin America; (2) greater emphasis on the East-West dimension, and much less on the North-South conflict; (3) an effort to foster free market economies; (4) aid to be made conditional on the recipients' positions in international forums; and (5) greater use of bilateral rather than multilateral channels for distributing aid.[69] Consistent with these policy proposals, in 1984 Bonn decided not to grant new development assistance to Nicaragua and to continue current projects only. West Germany linked future aid to Nicaragua's respect for stability in Central America and its implementation of democratic freedoms. Responding to these restrictions, which were seen as a result of U.S. pressure, several private West German voluntary organizations decided to donate medicine and medical equipment to Nicaragua and to participate in various projects.[70]

In early 1989 Kohl met Ortega in Bonn and reiterated earlier conditions for resuming German aid to Nicaragua. Kohl called on Ortega to give opposition political parties greater opportunities to compete in the 1990 elections, to strictly observe human rights, and to continue the dialogue with the church. But Bonn also agreed to participate in the UN observation of the peace process in Central America.[71] Following the February 1990 elections in Nicaragua, West Germany resumed development aid to Nicaragua.

Compared to Britain and West Germany, Spain, with limited funds for foreign aid, consistently supported Nicaragua, despite its serious misgivings about developments in the country. Spain's foreign aid projects tended to be overly ambitious and difficult to achieve. Felipe Gonzalez attempted to consolidate links between Spain and Latin America in general by mobilizing approximately thirty thousand volunteers with technical and professional skills to work on development projects for two to three years. The organization responsible for implementing this initiative was the Instituto de Cooperación Iberoamericano, and was given an annual budget of $15 million.[72] Unlike West Germany, which reduced its support for Nicaragua in 1983, Spain continued to fund various projects. In early 1985, for example, Spain and Nicaragua signed a complementary cooperation agreement under which Spain provided technical assistance to Nicaragua in the fields of health, public administration, cooperatives, agriculture, education, and local administration. Spain also granted fifteen scholarships to allow Nicaraguan experts to study in Spain for three months.[73] Thus, instead of focusing on the shortcomings of the Sandinista regime, Gonzalez decided to consider the people's suffering as well as the government's progress toward democracy. Gonzalez indicated Spain's interest in monitoring the 1990 elections, and articulated the view that by assisting Central America's economic reconstruction, Spain was contributing to regional stability and the establishment of democracy in Nicaragua.[74] Although the West European allies distanced themselves from Nicaragua, they supported Spain's assumptions and channeled aid to Central America through the EC.

EC aid to Central America increased from about $45 million dollars annually in 1984 to $127 million per year in 1988, an indication of the emphasis both Central Americans and Europeans placed on economic development. During the period of rapid militarization in the early 1980s, the Inter-American Development Bank and the Commission of the European Community jointly sponsored a meeting to discuss the economic development of Central American countries. Costa Rica's central bank governor Carlos Manuel Castillo estimated that approximately $20 billion would be needed by 1990 to recover the level of per capita income enjoyed by the region in 1980.[75] Violence was clearly detrimental to the economic stability of the entire region, and economic realities were inextricably linked to political upheavals. Consequently, the West Europeans and the Central Americans redoubled their efforts to improve economic conditions in all the countries, regardless of their political ideologies.

Major objectives of the EC aid programs included (1) encouraging the development of a regional economic system that would generate confidence and promote private enterprise, a free market, and domestic and foreign investment; (2) the expansion of intra-regional trade; and (3) the strengthening of the Central American Common Market. Given their own success, Europeans believed regional integration would help alleviate some of Central America's most difficult economic problems. In addition to aiding these long-term projects, the Europeans provided emergency food aid, assisted the repatriation and resettlement of refugees and displaced persons, and addressed issues such as energy supplies and external debt.[76] These efforts were integral parts of the larger objective—regional peace and stability. Despite significant political and economic changes in Eastern Europe and increased Western European investments in those countries, the EC's Commissioner for Latin America, Abel Matutes, indicated in early 1990 that additional funds would be allocated for Central America between 1990 and 1992.[77]

THE WEST EUROPEAN ALLIES AND THE PEACE PROCESS

Initiated by Latin American presidents, the peace process was immediately endorsed by the West European countries. In view of Reagan's preoccupation with Nicaragua, the allies were extremely concerned about the impact of hostilities in Central America on the Western alliance and European détente. Although the Reagan administration failed to demonstrate that it seriously supported the Contadora process and other peace initiatives, it could hardly condemn its allies for trying to achieve nonviolent solutions, partly because it was also rhetorically committed to peace. And when the Soviets' "new thinking" was applied to Central America, the United States was effectively isolated in terms of its support for the Contras. Furthermore, neither the American people nor Congress endorsed U.S. military involvement, directly or indirectly, in Central America—a reality that influenced the implementation of the Iran-Contra scheme.

European support for a political solution to the escalating Central American conflict in the mid-1980s led to the San José conference in 1984, which was attended by the member states of the EC, the Contadora group of countries (Mexico, Venezuela, Colombia, and Panama), and the Central American states. In their joint communiqué, the participants reaffirmed their commitment to the objectives of peace, democracy, security, and economic and social development in Central America. They articulated the view that the region's problems could not be solved by armed force, but only by political solutions emanating from the region itself. They also stressed that an effective way to reduce political tensions was to support actions intended to preserve regional economic integration.[78]

With dramatically improved superpower relations in the late 1980s and the Sandinistas under severe pressure because of Nicaragua's serious economic problems, conditions were conducive for a negotiated settlement. The Contras were widely regarded as a destabilizing force in Central America, and Honduras, which had provided a base for them, was now endangered by their presence. Regarded as guardians of democracy by the Reagan administration, the Contra rebels, in an ironic twist, sold their American-supplied weapons and ammunition to the leftist guerrillas in El Salvador, who were undermining a government staunchly supported by the United States.[79]

Despite ongoing problems with the Contras, the Central American states and the EC encouraged Nicaragua to proceed with free elections in February 1990. Even though President Bush reaffirmed the U.S. embargo against Nicaragua, and despite Nicaragua's decision to terminate its ceasefire agreement with the Contras, the Europeans worked assiduously to maintain the momentum for the 1990 elections. Felipe Gonzalez worked with Daniel Ortega to gain EC support for Nicaragua's democratization plan, but remained neutral in Nicaragua's electoral process.[80] France, West Germany, and other European countries provided material and technical assistance to Nicaragua for the elections. Former President Carter, highly regarded in Nicaragua for his peace efforts, and Elliot Richardson, a former U.S. Attorney General, were among the numerous international observers in Nicaragua to guarantee that the elections were fair.

Violeta Chamorro's victory demonstrated that Nicaragua had proceeded toward democracy. But the problems created by the Sandinistas' miscalculations and Reagan's support of the Contras remained. The European allies' approach was now endorsed by the United States. The ideological crusade of the Cold War seemed strangely irrelevant as dramatic changes in Europe and the Persian Gulf conflict of 1990 preoccupied U.S. policymakers. With NATO's future uncertain and America's leadership in Europe no longer assumed, Central American issues became largely peripheral NATO concerns.

NOTES

1. Lionel Barber, "Washington Sees Dual Role for EC in Latin America," *Financial Times*, April 25, 1990, p. 4.

2. Antonio Sanchez-Gijon, "Spanish Involvement in Latin America," in *The Latin American Policies of U.S. Allies*, eds. William Perry and Peter Wehner (New York: Praeger, 1985), p. 66.

3. Franklin D. Parker, *The Central American Republics* (London: Oxford University Press, 1964), p. 235; and Ralph Lee Woodward, *Central America: A Nation Divided* (New York: Oxford University Press, 1976), p. 121.

4. Walter LaFeber, *Inevitable Revolutions: The United States in Central America* (New York: W. W. Norton, 1984), p. 28.

5. Albrecht von Gleich, *Germany and Latin America*. Santa Monica, Calif.: Rand Corporation, p. 3.

6. H. Jurgen Hess, "West Germany and the Central American Crisis," *Fletcher Forum* 10, no. 2 (Summer 1986): 302.

7. Howard J. Wiarda, "Europe's Ambiguous Relations with Latin America," *The Washington Quarterly* 13, no. 2 (Spring 1990): 159.

8. Piero Gleijeses, "Nicaragua: Resist Romanticism," *Foreign Policy*, no. 54 (Spring 1984): p. 125.

9. Michael D. Barnes, "U.S. Policy in Central America: The Challenge of Revolutionary Change," in *A Widening Atlantic: Domestic Change and Foreign Policy*, ed. Andrew J. Pierre (New York: Council on Foreign Relations, 1986), p. 99.

10. Eusebio Mujal-Léon, "European Socialism and the Crisis in Central America," in *Rift and Revolution*, ed. Howard J. Wiarda (Washington, D.C.: American Enterprise Institute, 1984), p. 269.

11. Mujal-Léon, p. 271.

12. Wolf Grabendorff, "West European Perceptions of the Crisis in Central America," in *Political Change in Central America: Internal and External Dimensions*, eds. Wolf Grabendorff, Heinrich Krumwiede, and Jorg Todt (Boulder, Colo.: Westview Press, 1984), p. 287.

13. Richard H. Ullman, "At War with Nicaragua," *Foreign Affairs* 62, no. 1 (Fall 1983): 39.

14. William D. Rogers, "American Behavior and European Apprehensions," in *Central America and the Western Alliance*, ed. Joseph Cirincione (New York: Holmes and Meier, 1985), pp. 15–16.

15. Carlos Rico, "European Socialism, The Western Alliance, and Central America," in *Spain's Entry into NATO: Conflicting Political and Strategic Perspectives*, eds. Frederico G. Gil and Joseph S. Tulchin (Boulder, Colo.: Lynne Rienner, 1988), p. 96.

16. "Europe Gives Skeptical Reception to Haig's Red Scare Mission," *Latin America Weekly Report*, February 20, 1981, p. 5.

17. Charlotte Phillips Preece, *West European Policies Toward Central America: Another Source of Friction Within the Alliance?* (Washington, D.C.: Congressional Research Service, 1982), p. 2.

18. "Europe's View of U.S. in the Region," *Latin America Weekly Report*, April 6, 1984, p. 10.

19. "Nicaraguan Delegation Visiting European Countries," *Europe: Agence Internationale D'Information Pour La Presse* (cited as *Europe*), April 3, 1981, p. 4.

20. Mary B. Vanderlaan, *Revolution and Foreign Policy in Nicaragua* (Boulder, Colo.: Westview Press, 1986), p. 21; and Wolf Grabendorff, "Latin America and Western Europe: Towards a New International Subsystem," in *The European Challenge: Europe's New Role in Latin America* (London: Latin America Bureau, 1982), p. 45.

21. Grabendorff, "West European Perceptions," p. 393.

22. Howard J. Wiarda, "Europe's Ambiguous Relations," p. 165.

23. George Philip, "British Involvement in Latin America," in *The Latin American Policies of U.S. Allies*, eds. William Perry and Peter Wehner (New York: Praeger, 1985), p. 35.

24. David Thomas, "The United States Factor in British Relations with Latin America," in *Britain and Latin America: A Changing Relationship*, ed. Victor Bulmer-Thomas (Cambridge: Cambridge University Press, 1989), p. 80; and *Parliamentary Debates* (Commons), 6th ser., vol. 19, 14–23 December (1981), col. 214.

25. *Parliamentary Debates* (Commons), 6th ser., vol. 19, 14–23 December (1981), col. 218.

26. *Parliamentary Debates* (Commons), 6th ser., vol. 138, 24 October–4 November (1988), col. 36(w).

27. Foreign and Commonwealth Office, *The Central American Peace Process* (London: Foreign and Commonwealth Office, 1988), p. 1.

28. *Parliamentary Debates* (Commons), 6th ser., vol. 19, 24 October–4 November (1988), col. 210.

29. "France and Mexico See FDR as Key to Peace in Central America," *Latin America Weekly Report*, September 4, 1981, p. 1.

30. "France and Mexico," p. 1.

31. "Mitterrand Assails U.S. Critics," *The New York Times*, April 28, 1982, p. A4.

32. "Europe's View of U.S. in the Region," *Latin America Weekly Report*, April 6, 1984, p. 10.

33. "France's New Latinism Troubles the White House," *The Latin American Times*, March 1982, p. 30.

34. "Lopez Portillo Stakes His Claim to be Latin America's de Gaulle," *Latin America Weekly Report*, August 8, 1980, p. 1.

35. Preece, p. 4.

36. "France and Mexico See FDR," p. 1.

37. "France to Deliver Two Patrol Boats Soon," *FBIS-LAT*, June 16, 1983, p. 16; and "France's New Latinism," p. 31.

38. Roy C. Macridis, "French Foreign Policy: The Quest for Rank," in *Foreign Policy in World Politics*, ed. Roy C. Macridis (Englewood Cliffs, N.J.: Prentice-Hall, 1985), p. 68.

39. Eusebio Mujal-Léon, "The West German SPD and the Politics of Internationalism in Central America," *Journal of Interamerican Studies and World Affairs* 29, no. 4 (Winter 1987–88): 91.

40. "Secretary of State on Talks with Nicaraguan Representatives," *FBIS-LAT*, July 25, 1979, p. J3.

41. Nadia Malley, "Relations with Western Europe and the Socialist International," in *Nicaragua: The First Five Years*, ed. Thomas Walker (New York: Praeger, 1985), p. 489.

42. "Bonn Will Go to San José," *Latin America Weekly Report*, July 20, 1984, p. 4.

43. Benny Pollack and Graham Hunter, *The Paradox of Spanish Foreign Policy* (New York: St. Martin's Press, 1987), p. 69.

44. Jean Grugel, "Spain's Socialist Government and Central American Dilemmas," *International Affairs* 63, no. 4 (Autumn 1987): 603.

45. "One Million Dollars in Spanish Munitions Reach Nicaragua," *FBIS-LAT*, July 12, 1979, p. 14.

46. Neale J. Pearson, "Recent Spanish Foreign Policy Toward Central America," in *Latin America Contemporary Record*, ed. Jack Hopkins (New York: Holmes and Meier, 1986), p. 163.

47. Emilio A. Rodriguez, "Atlanticism and Europeanism: NATO and Trends in Spanish Foreign Policy," in *Spain's Entry into NATO: Conflicting Political and Strategic Perspectives*, eds. Frederico G. Gil and Joseph S. Tulchin (Boulder, Colo.: Lynne Rienner, 1988), p. 57.

48. "Cross Winds Buffet Spain's Bridge Between Europe and Latin America," *Latin America Weekly Report*, November 28, 1980, p. 6.

49. Alan Riding, "As Spain Heeds Europe's Call, the Americans Fret," *The New York Times*, May 10, 1989, p. A3.

50. Richard J. Payne, *Opportunities and Dangers of Soviet-Cuban Expansion: Toward a Pragmatic U.S. Policy* (Albany: State University of New York Press, 1988), pp. 94–95.

51. "Military and Paramilitary Activities in and Against Nicaragua (Nicaragua v. United States of America)," *International Court of Justice Reports, 1986*. Reprinted in *International Legal Materials* 25, no. 5 (September 1986): 1039.

52. "Socialist International Deal Leaked to Spanish Newspaper," *Latin America Weekly Report*, March 26, 1987, p. 11; and "Socialists Shift Position on the Region," *Latin America Weekly Report*, July 10, 1986, pp. 8–9.

53. Hess, p. 306.

54. "Government Criticizes Remarks by Ortega," *FBIS-WEU*, May 21, 1985, p. J1.

55. "Contadora: German Institute Views on Conflict," *Latin America Weekly Report*, June 13, 1986, p. 7; and "West Germany Against Sandinistas," *Latin America Weekly Report*, March 21, 1986, p. 6.

56. "First French-U.S. Maneuvers," *Latin America Weekly Report*, December 13, 1985, p. 9.

57. "Robelo Tells of Spanish Warning," *FBIS-LAT*, December 11, 1984, p. 14.

58. Wiarda, "Europe's Ambiguous Relations," p. 161.

59. "Trade and Investments Buttress Special Spanish-Latin Ties," *The Latin American Times*, July 1982, p. 36.

60. "Cuba: Becoming Spain's Best Customer," *Latin America Weekly Report*, October 18, 1985, p. 3.

61. *Parliamentary Debates* (Commons), 6th ser., vol. 119, 6–17 July (1987), col. 338.

62. "Spain Freezes Credit Line: Madrid Blames Financial, Not Political Factors," *Latin America Weekly Report*, March 29, 1985, p. 9.

63. *FBIS-LAT*, May 15, 1985, p. 8; and "Government Rejects U.S. Embargo of Nicaragua," *FBIS-WEU*, May 30, 1985, p. J2.

64. "Relations with Latin America: Conclusions Adopted by the Council and the Representatives of the Governments of the Member States," *Bulletin of the European Communities* 20, no. 6 (1987): 138–39.

65. "Central America," *Bulletin of the European Communities* 20, no. 6 (1987): 88; and "EEC to Participate in Aid Program," *Latin America Regional Reports: Mexico and Central America*, March 24, 1988, p. 7.

66. "Nicaragua's Ortega and Thatcher Speak Bluntly," *FBIS-WEU*, May 9, 1989, p. 8.

67. *Parliamentary Debates* (Commons), 6th ser., vol. 138, 24 October–4 November (1988), col. 25.

68. "FRG Promises Extensive Aid to Reconstruct Country," *FBIS-LAT*, August 14, 1979, p. P4; and "FRG Delegation Arrives, Will Discuss Areas of Assistance," *FBIS-LAT*, November 27, 1979, p. P2.

69. "West Germany: Hardening the Line," *Latin America Weekly Report*, March 31, 1983, p. 7.

70. "Munich Youth Group to Work in Nicaragua," *FBIS-WEU*, July 31, 1985, p. J3.

71. "Kohl to Ortega: First Democratization, Then Aid," *The Week in Germany*, May 12, 1989, p. 1.

72. "Gonzalez Looks to the New World," *Latin America Weekly Report*, May 6, 1983, p. 11.

73. "1985 Cooperation Agreement Signed with Spain," *FBIS-LAT*, February 5, 1985, p. P11.

74. "Prime Minister Promises Aid," *FBIS-WEU*, April 27, 1989, p. 25.

75. "Six Get a European Hearing," *Latin America Weekly Report*, September 30, 1983, p. 9.

76. "San José III: EC Aid," *Latin America Weekly Report*, February 19, 1987, p. 10; and "Community-Central American Dialogue," *Bulletin of the European Communities* 21, no. 3 (1988): p. 19.

77. "EC Plans Boost in Its Aid for Central America," *Financial Times*, April 11, 1990, p. 4.

78. "Joint Communiqué of the San José Meeting Between the European Community and its Member States, Portugal and Spain, and the States of Central America and the Contadora States, 28, 29 September 1984," Reprinted in *International Legal Materials* 24, no. 1 (January 1985): pp. 208–13.

79. Paul Lewis, "Contras Said to Sell Arms to Salvador Rebels," *The New York Times*, October 15, 1989, p. A11.

80. "Gonzalez Meets with Nicaragua's Chamorro," *FBIS-WEU*, November 20, 1989, p. 20.

6

Southern Africa: Angola, Namibia, and South Africa

Superpower rapprochement, German unification, the political transformation of Eastern Europe, reductions in Soviet assistance to southern African liberation movements, the general failure of socialism, Namibia's independence in 1990, and significant changes in South Africa in late 1989 and early 1990 profoundly affected the Western alliance's relations with southern Africa. Economic developments in Western Europe, the Warsaw Pact's disintegration, and NATO's marginal role in the new international strategic environment of the 1990s highlighted common interests as well as major differences among the Western allies in southern Africa. The Communist threat, which was used by both South Africa and the United States to enlist West European support for the status quo, was largely irrelevant because the Soviet Union itself favored peaceful resolution of conflicts and attempted to diminish its commitment to the region. But the end of the Cold War also made underlying divisions within the alliance more obvious.

Historical and cultural ties, economic interests, perceptions of the Soviet-Cuban threat, domestic political factors, and international public opinion combined to induce both cooperation and conflict among the allies in Angola, Namibia, and South Africa. The United States, with no major historical links to the region, often viewed political conflicts there in terms of East-West rivalry when the Communist threat was emphasized. On the other hand, the United States was also influenced by its own domestic racial experiences and tended to regard white minority rule in South Africa as a fundamental violation of democratic principles and human rights. Although the Europeans generally took a regional approach to southern Africa's crises, their historical ties with specific countries in the region and their diverging economic and political interests prevented them from developing a coherent

EC policy. West Germany took a special interest in Namibia, Portugal attempted to develop strong ties with Angola, and Britain and West Germany maintained their relations with South Africa. Each country's policies were influenced by different considerations; consequently, EPC was relatively ineffective. However, because a common European policy amounted to essentially the lowest common denominator, countries with substantial economic interests in South Africa, such as Britain and West Germany, clearly favored it. In light of America's failure to articulate a consistent, unambiguous southern African policy, the West Europeans generally pursued their individual national interests, hid behind EPC, and were content to allow the United States to deal with growing international criticism on issues such as sanctions against apartheid, Namibian independence, and the devastating civil war in Angola.

THE WEST EUROPEAN ALLIES AND ANGOLA

Soviet-Cuban involvement in the Angolan civil war following Angola's hastily arranged independence from Portugal directly influenced the United States to increase its diplomatic and military activities in the region. Not only did the massive infusions of Soviet military equipment and Cuban troops serve as a catalyst for the deterioration of U.S.-Soviet relations, they also triggered serious conflicts within the NATO alliance.[1] The Soviet-Cuban factor radically altered the political-strategic realities in southern Africa, forced South Africa to reconsider its options, prompted the United States and Britain to cooperate in resolving the Rhodesian crisis, and eventually became a bargaining chip in America's policy of linking Namibia's independence from South Africa to the withdrawal of Cuban troops from Angola. Unlike South Africa, where the Western allies shared essentially the same interests and used many similar foreign policy instruments in an effort to convince Pretoria to abolish apartheid, Angola exposed major differences among the allies, especially about the importance of Soviet-Cuban involvement and how to deal with the perceived threat. Whereas the Europeans recognized the new Angolan government, led by the Popular Movement for the Liberation of Angola (MPLA), the United States not only refused to establish diplomatic relations with Angola but also found itself in a politically awkward alliance with South Africa when it decided to give military support to the opposition group, the Union for the Total Independence of Angola (UNITA). But even as the United States backed UNITA against MPLA, Chevron, an American oil firm, was the Angolan government's main commercial ally and provided the country with the bulk of its foreign exchange by exporting Angolan oil to the United States. The United States, in fact, continued to be Angola's most important trading partner.

Whereas the United States emphasized military solutions, the West Europeans sought to expand trade with Angola and allowed it to attend the

Lomé Convention under which the ACP states enjoyed special economic arrangements with the EC.[2] Finally, as President Bush continued to provide military assistance to UNITA, Portugal decided to aid the Angolan government militarily by training Angolan pilots and repairing military equipment. France supplied Alouette and Ecureuil helicopters to the Angolan armed forces. From Europe's perspective, America's policy was essentially counterproductive, since it forced the Angolans to depend on the Soviet Union and Cuba. The allies, Portugal in particular, deemphasized the East-West component of the problem partly because of their historical and cultural ties to the region.

Having achieved its independence from Spain in the twelfth century, Portugal consolidated its power by forming an alliance with England under the Anglo-Portuguese Treaty of Windsor in 1386, and embarked upon systematic maritime expansion and colonization.[3] In the process of driving the Moors, who had conquered most of the country early in the eighth century, across the Straits of Gibraltar in the fifteenth century, Portugal initiated European colonization of Africa. When formal territorial boundaries were established during the Berlin Conference of 1884–85, Portugal was too weak to prevent Britain from colonizing areas between Mozambique and Angola, and faced serious threats of German expansion from German Southwest Africa (Namibia) until Germany was forced out of Africa following World War I. The tentative nature of Portugal's control of Angola was confirmed to some extent by negotiations between Lisbon and the Jewish Territorial Organization of London, which was interested in establishing an autonomous Jewish colony in Angola prior to the Balfour Declaration.[4]

Regarding Angola first as a source of slaves for Brazil and later as a supplier of raw materials, Portugal, relatively poor and underdeveloped, did little to advance its colonies economically or politically. As African countries mobilized independence movements, Portugal incorporated Angola and attempted to crush all nationalist movements. Using cheap African labor, the Portuguese strengthened their control over Angola's economy. Coffee and diamond exports increased sharply in the late 1950s, and the discovery of petroleum and iron made Angola attractive to Portugal as well as to other Western European countries. Consequently, France, West Germany, and Britain supported Portugal's colonial rule. Strongly opposed to what it viewed as European imperialism, the United States during the Kennedy administration supported Angolan nationalists such as Holden Roberto.

Divergent European and American approaches to the emerging Angolan war were shaped by Portugal's role in NATO as well as by America's commitment to national self-determination. Yet U.S. interests in the alliance were not easily reconciled with its opposition to colonialism. President Eisenhower elevated NATO concerns above political and economic conditions in Portugal's colonies. Reversing America's policy of abstaining on UN resolutions dealing with Angola's independence, President Kennedy approved a 1961 UN resolution, initiated by Liberia, calling for a UN inquiry into the Angolan situation.[5] However, as the Cold War escalated, differences between Portugal and the United States were resolved at the expense of Angola's independence. After the Berlin Crisis demonstrated the strategic value of refueling facilities in the Azores, Portugal was allowed to join NATO in 1949 primarily because NATO wanted access to the Azores. America's allies continued to assist Portugal diplomatically, economically, and militarily in its war against Angolan nationalists. NATO was therefore perceived by the Angolans as Portugal's partner in its struggle to maintain colonial rule.

Britain generally abstained on the anticolonial UN resolutions; sold two frigates, light aircraft, army jeeps, and military equipment to Portugal; and opposed taking any actions against what it viewed as a Portuguese domestic problem, especially in light of the negative impact such actions could have had on Portugal's role in NATO.[6] France, reluctant to grant its own colonies their independence and embroiled in the Algerian war for independence, supported Portugal in international forums and supplied it with aircraft, frigates, submarines, and armored cars. French oil companies were already in Angola, and France had obtained a tracking station for French missiles in the Azores. West Germany, despite its restrictive policy on arms transfers, supplied Portugal with Uzi guns from Israel, fighter bombers, light counterinsurgency aircraft, and ships.

Portugal's membership in NATO provided the allies with what appeared to be legitimate reasons for assisting Portugal militarily.[7] They could argue, as the West Germans did, that the weapons would be used within the "NATO area." This area, at least initially, was seen by the European allies as extending to their colonial territories, a view with which the United States strongly disagreed. Since Portugal regarded Angola as an integral part of national territory, restrictions such as Germany's were meaningless.

The allies shared many strategic objectives which were directly connected to Portugal's presence in Africa. Between 1965 and 1974, West European concerns were heightened by increased Soviet naval activities in the Indian and South Atlantic oceans and by Moscow's growing military assistance to African national liberation movements. Portugal consistently sought to involve the NATO alliance in its colonial struggle by placing southern African problems within the broader context of Western security interests. The closure of the Suez Canal in 1967 underscored the importance of the Cape route for allied shipping, and the West's growing dependence on strategic minerals from southern Africa was not overlooked. Bases in the Portuguese colonies were becoming increasingly useful. In fact, the naval base at Nacala in Mozambique had been constructed to American specifications so that it could be used by the U.S. Seventh Fleet, if necessary.[8]

NATO support for Portugal increased as African nationalists began to seriously threaten white minority rule throughout southern Africa. The protection of Western interests was closely identified with the perpetuation of white rule. Consequently, when Rhodesia under Ian Smith declared unilateral independence from Britain, Smith's efforts were supported by Portugal, South Africa, and Britain itself, despite British calls for international sanctions against Smith's regime. Britain ignored Portugal's violations of the sanctions, and continued to supply weapons to the NATO ally. By 1969, it was clear that the United States had decided the white minority regimes in southern Africa were entrenched for the foreseeable future. The now infamous National Security Council Memorandum 39, which stated that the liberation groups were ineffective, called for U.S. accommodation with the minority governments to foster political stability, economic security, and the strategic balance of power.[9] Consistent with this view, Portugal encouraged the European allies to invest in Angola and Mozambique, thereby further tightening NATO's commitment to the status quo in southern Africa. But the allies underestimated the extent to which the Soviet Union and Cuba would become involved in the conflict as well as how the Angolan war would destabilize Portugal.

Rather than being an integral component of the Soviet Union's global strategy, Cuba's policy toward Angola emerged because of Castro's distrust of the Soviets, his fear of the United States, and his commitment to African liberation movements. Soviet-American relations in the mid-1960s had improved to the point where Moscow and Washington had agreed on peaceful coexistence, although Washington continued to be overtly hostile toward Cuba. The growing Sino-Soviet schism had shattered the unity of the socialist camp, which Castro had regarded as essential for Cuban security. Furthermore, when escalating U.S. bombing raids in Vietnam in 1964 were not met with Soviet or Chinese retaliation, Castro concluded that neither the Soviet commitment to defend Cuba nor the rhetoric of Marxist-Leninist international solidarity was sufficient guarantee against military attack. Under these circumstances, solidarity with the Third World became increasingly important for Cuba. For almost eight years there was a sharp divergence between Soviet and Cuban policies in Africa. Two developments in 1974 contributed to their coordination of policies in Angola: (1) increased Chinese support for the National Front for the Liberation of Angola (FNLA); and (2) the U.S. decision to commence arms shipments to the FNLA through Zaire.[10]

The United States and the Soviet Union had an opportunity at the beginning stages of the Angolan civil war to agree on a mutually acceptable formula for transition from Portuguese control to independence. That formula was a coalition government comprised of the three major liberation movements. Negotiations among these groups resulted in the Alvor Agreements, which endorsed a tripartite transitional government. Neither Moscow nor Washington fully supported the compromise, each preferring to support its particular group.[11] As the civil war escalated, European and

American mercenaries and approximately six thousand South African troops joined the conflict against the Cuban-backed MPLA. Cuba responded with Operation Carlotta, eventually sending in about twenty-five thousand troops. It was estimated that 150,000 tons of military equipment were supplied by the Soviet Union. Included were automatic weapons, ammunition, explosives, anti-aircraft guns, mortars, rockets, and ground-to-air missiles.[12] Soviet-Cuban involvement had radically altered the Angolan conflict.

Furthermore, Portugal itself had changed, a development which created conflicting approaches to Angola within the alliance. Sent to Angola to preserve the integrationist concept, which viewed the colonies as territorially and politically integrated with Portugal, many Portuguese soldiers became disillusioned by the relative privileges enjoyed by the generals in Luanda while they fought what was widely seen as an unwinnable war. Many soldiers were radicalized by their interaction with Angolans, and turned their attention to ending authoritarian rule in Portugal. General Antonio Spinola, an important supporter of Portugal's Angola policy, articulated his view of the war's futility in a book, *Portugal and the Future*, which was a catalyst for a coup d'etat in Portugal on April 25, 1974.[13]

Portugal's gradual transition to democracy, increased Soviet-Cuban involvement in Angola, South Africa's participation in the war, U.S. withdrawal from Vietnam, the OPEC oil embargo, Watergate, and other factors combined to influence the NATO allies' southern African policies. Watergate and Vietnam not only created a certain degree of political paralysis and self-doubt in the United States but also greatly undermined European confidence in America's wisdom and ability to lead the alliance. Portugal alone among the allies had assisted American efforts to get military equipment to Israel during the 1973 Yom Kippur War. Even West Germany, had begun to move toward the Arab countries. And Israel was influenced by the war and its growing international isolation to form an alliance with South Africa. Because the Arab states needed African support in international forums, they linked Israel's cooperation with South Africa to its occupation of Arab lands. Dependent on Arab oil supplies and concerned about their relations with Africa, the European allies decided to distance themselves from Washington's policies in the Middle East as well as in Angola.

Restricted by the Clark Amendment from providing military assistance to groups opposed to the MPLA, the United States attempted to pressure its allies to be more active in Angola. But the allies, influenced by their own experiences in the Third World, decided to focus on a negotiated settlement and called upon all foreign troops to withdraw from Angola.[14] Although this approach satisfied Washington's demands, U.S. and European support for the OAU-backed tripartite solution articulated in the Alvor Agreements was basically irrelevant because the vast majority of African states had recognized the MPLA, due mainly to South Africa's military intervention in Angola on the side of the opposition. With the exception of West Germany, the European allies had also concluded that the Angolan war was really peripheral to Western security. Determined to serve as an alternative to the superpowers, especially the Soviet Union, the allies decided to work with the MPLA. But even as British Foreign Secretary James Callaghan tried to develop a common EC position on the Angolan conflict, France unilaterally declared its recognition of the MPLA as Angola's legitimate government on February 17, 1976. Ignoring U.S. concerns, the other European allies recognized Angola within four days.[15] The United States refused to recognize the Angolan government and continued to insist on a negotiated settlement to be induced by military pressure. Whereas the United States resumed military assistance to UNITA in 1985, the allies consolidated their economic and political ties with the Angolan government.

WESTERN EUROPE'S ECONOMIC AND POLITICAL RELATIONS WITH ANGOLA

Although the United States refused to recognize the MPLA, it negotiated with the Angolans on several matters, the most important being the phased withdrawal of Cuban troops from the country as a condition for Namibia's independence in 1990. The United States was also Angola's main trading partner throughout the civil war, despite American support for Angolan opposition groups. Economic relations between the two countries militated against U.S. efforts to pressure its European allies to terminate commercial ties with Luanda. Even though Assistant Secretary of State Chester Crocker suggested that Chevron, which produced about 58 percent of Angola's oil, might be operating against U.S. national interests, no attempt was made to force Chevron and its subsidiary, Cabgulf, to leave Angola. In fact, its production quadrupled between 1982 and 1989. It competed successfully against Agip of Italy, British Petroleum, Societé Nationale Elf Aquitaine of France, and Marathon Oil Company and Texaco of the United States.[16] Yet American refusal to deal pragmatically with Angola created economic opportunities for its European allies. When the United States restricted Eximbank credits and guarantees to American firms engaged in commercial relations with Angola, the French, British, Italians, Spanish, West Germans, and Portuguese were the principal beneficiaries of reduced American trade.[17]

Western Europe exported manufactured products as well as manufacturing equipment to Angola, and Luanda made a serious effort to expand its trade with Western Europe. Angola's admission to membership in the Lomé Convention in 1985 consolidated its economic links to the EC. Similarly, the Europeans supported Angola's application to join the International Monetary Fund and were generally positive about Angola's decision in mid-1987 to radically restructure its economy. Admitting that socialist policies had contributed to Angola's economic decline, President José dos

Santos outlined major reforms, including greater support for private enterprise in the major economic sectors, removing state controls and excessive bureaucracy, and encouraging Western investments. Several agreements were concluded between Angola and the EC, including one that allowed West European countries to fish in Angolan waters.[18]

While these developments strengthened Angolan-European relations at the multilateral level, the allies also tried to improve bilateral economic ties. British exports to Angola increased by about 30 percent in 1979, and approximately 250 British business representatives participated in a seminar held in Angola that year. Britain also sent a small team of English language teachers to assist the National Language Institute in Luanda, thereby slightly weakening Portugal's influence in Angola. When the Angolan government appealed to Britain for assistance during the drought that devastated much of southern Angola in 1981, Britain sent relief supplies.[19]

France also established commercial ties with Angola, and its state-owned oil company, Elf Aquitaine, was active in Angola's petroleum industry. When the Reagan administration's policies made it difficult for Angola to purchase American aircraft to replace its Boeing 707 aircraft that were prevented from flying over Europe because their noise levels violated European law, Angola decided to purchase new planes from the French Airbus company.[20]

Akin to Spain in Central America, Portugal attempted to restore its economic and political links to Angola, which were negatively affected by the long and costly colonial wars, the hastily arranged independence for Angola following the coup in Portugal, and the mass exodus of Portuguese citizens from Angola. The end of authoritarian rule in Portugal was accompanied by that country's integration into the EC, a factor which reduced Angola's importance to Portugal. Both countries diversified their economic relations. Portugal increased its trade with Europe, the Sudan, Nigeria, and South Africa, while Angola established important commercial links with Spain, Britain, West Germany, France, Italy, and the Netherlands. Whereas in 1973 the Portuguese colonies had supplied nearly 90 percent of Portugal's exports to Africa, by 1983 that share had dropped to 67 percent.[21] Nevertheless, Portugal became more involved in Angola in the mid-1980s. Several bilateral economic agreements were signed by the two governments, and Portugal served as Angola's interlocutor in the EC. Portugal resumed work at the Catambambe dam, and a partly-owned subsidiary of the Portuguese state railways, Ferbritas, repaired loading and unloading equipment at Luanda to alleviate the port's chronic congestion.[22] Portugal also helped to rehabilitate the Benguela railway, reconstructed the Lomaum hydroelectric dam, which had been sabotaged in 1982 by UNITA, and increased its investments in various industries. The Company for Financial Services, Administration, and Management, the principal agent for Portuguese investments in Angola in 1989, collaborated with the Angolan government on a number of projects.[23] Commercial relations were undergirded by improved political ties between the European allies and Angola.

Angola's dependence on the Soviet Union and Cuba prompted West European countries to try to provide an alternative to Communist influence. France, consistent with its policy of helping Third World countries to pursue independent foreign policies, established close ties with Angola when President Reagan expressed strong opposition to the MPLA. Mitterrand, shortly after his election, officially welcomed dos Santos to France and extended much-needed diplomatic and economic assistance to Luanda. The allies also opposed American policies toward UNITA.

The allies' positions on the Angolan conflict had not changed significantly since 1975, despite differences between various political factions in countries such as West Germany and Portugal. Many of Portugal's leaders had opposed their country's authoritarian government and its colonial policies. Furthermore, several of them were closely linked to Angolan nationalists through various Portuguese political organizations. The MPLA had established strong ties with the United Democratic Movement in Portugal, and was better known than its rivals. Consequently, Lisbon tended to favor the government in Luanda. But UNITA also found support in the opposition Popular Democratic party, which opposed Soviet-Cuban involvement in Angola.[24] Yet the Europeanization of Portugal resulted in a relative drop in interest in Angola. By 1987, however, relations between Portugal and Angola had improved, and President dos Santos urged Portugal to play a more active role in his country.[25]

Compared to Portugal, West Germany's political relations with Angola were more complex, due in part to coalition politics in Bonn. Chancellor Helmut Kohl, seemed to pursue a two-track policy in Angola by allowing Franz-Josef Strauss and Hans-Dietrich Genscher to articulate two different policies, with Strauss supporting UNITA and Genscher reassuring the MPLA of West Germany's determination to strengthen and expand its links with Angola. While Genscher went to Luanda to meet dos Santos and leading government officials, Strauss visited Jonas Savimbi, UNITA's leader, in the Kalahari Desert. A delegation from Strauss' Christian Social Union also met with Savimbi in 1987 at Jamba, proclaimed by UNITA to be the provisional capital of liberated Angola. And as Strauss called for the total withdrawal of Soviet and Cuban troops from Angola in order to permit the Angolans to develop their country, Genscher stressed respect for different political views, the principle of non-interference, and the importance of genuine nonalignment.[26] Bonn was supporting a government that the United States actively opposed. While this two-track policy may have been unintentional, it effectively helped to reduce Washington's pressure on West Germany.

THE ALLIES AND ANGOLA'S WAR WITH UNITA

Alone among the NATO allies, the United States believed that military assistance to UNITA was the most effective way to achieve a negotiated settlement of the Angolan conflict. At the same time, however, it strongly opposed violence by South Africa's African National Congress, which was attempting to persuade Pretoria to abolish apartheid and respect the human rights of 86 percent of the country's population. Preoccupied with frustrating Soviet-Cuban activities in southern Africa by military means, U.S. foreign policymakers seemed oblivious to African realities and the destructiveness of America's violent solution. Determined to support what he regarded as the forces of democracy and freedom fighters, President Reagan succeeded in 1985 in convincing Congress to abolish the Clark Amendment, which had prevented the United States from giving covert military assistance to UNITA and the FNLA since 1975. Reagan's policies were continued by President Bush who, before taking office in 1989, had assured Savimbi that he would receive "all appropriate and effective assistance" from the United States. But even as Bush congratulated UNITA for its courageous demonstration over more than a decade that solutions to Angola's problems could not be found through repressive military force, the administration provided Savimbi with about $15 million in military aid.[27] At the same time, the United States successfully negotiated an agreement between South Africa, Angola, and Cuba that resulted in Namibia's independence in 1990 and the phased withdrawal of Cuban troops from Angola. The radically altered international strategic environment of the 1990s seemed to convince the United States, South Africa, the Soviet Union, and Cuba that diplomacy, not military force, was the more cost-efficient strategy. The West European allies had reached this conclusion a decade earlier.

Taking a more regional view of the conflict, instead of the East-West perspective embraced by the United States, the Europeans were less concerned about Angola becoming a Communist state. From their viewpoint both superpowers had miscalculated, due partly to their inexperience in Africa. Furthermore, there was little incentive for the Europeans to oppose the MPLA. Commercial ties were uninterrupted, Cuban troops provided protection for the oil industry, and over 80 percent of Angola's trade was with the West. European involvement in Angola was consistent with broader European objectives of strengthening ties with former African colonies, protecting détente from superpower rivalries, building the European economic enterprise, uniting Germany, and providing the Third World with an alternative to the United States and the Soviet Union. Moreover, any appearance of collaboration with South Africa, which was UNITA's principal supporter, would have been politically disastrous. Consequently, the Europeans voiced strong opposition to South Africa's invasions of Angola as well as to U.S. support for UNITA. When Pretoria launched a major operation inside Angola in 1981, France voted in the UN Security Council to condemn South Africa, the United States vetoed the resolution, and Britain abstained, primarily to restore Western unity.[28] The alliance's divisions widened as South Africa escalated its military activities inside Angola and the United States decided to give covert assistance to UNITA.

Portugal's armed forces cooperated with the Angolan army in many areas. The Portuguese helped maintain and repair Angolan army helicopters, trained Angolan aircraft mechanics, collaborated with Angolans to maintain the air base at Lubango, instructed Angolan pilots at the Portuguese Air Force Academy, and Portuguese advised Angolan counter-insurgency units.[29] France sold the Angolan government armed Alouette helicopters and more advanced Ecureuil helicopters for operations against UNITA guerrillas. Spain began selling Angola Aviocar C-212 counter-insurgency aircraft in 1986; Belgium sold bullets and artillery shells; Britain, West Germany, and France competed for the radiocommunications equipment market; Switzerland supplied training aircraft; and Britain and West Germany sold trucks and jeeps to the Angolan armed forces.[30] There is no evidence to suggest that the allies, with the exception of the United States, assisted Savimbi, although France, which had managed to obtain the release of 133 Angolan prisoners held by UNITA and a French citizen imprisoned in Ciskei in exchange for a South African officer held by Angola, was accused by Savimbi of breaking unspecified promises.[31]

American and South African military aid to Savimbi escalated even as the Reagan administration negotiated with the Angolan government for the withdrawal of Cuban troops from Angola as a precondition for Namibia's independence. While Pretoria and Washington had a common interest in preventing Soviet-Cuban expansion in southern Africa, South Africa also wanted to maintain its dominant military and political position in the region, an objective it attempted to achieve by destabilizing neighboring countries. Reagan's decision to link the Angolan and Namibian issues bolstered South Africa's confidence in its regional strategy. The rationale behind this linkage was that the South Africans were unlikely to leave Namibia as long as the Cuban troops remained in Angola.[32] But as long as the Cubans were in Angola, South Africa could justify its support for UNITA as well as its control of Namibia. The war was too costly for Angola, a fact that enhanced Pretoria's leverage.

Determined to pursue the military option, even as Chester Crocker had obtained assurances from the Angolan government that the Cuban troops would be withdrawn, the South Africans penetrated deep into Angola in late 1987 in cooperation with UNITA forces. Following their victory over MPLA units at Mavinga, the South Africans advanced to Cuito Cuanavale, where MPLA had retreated. To protect Cuito Cuanavale and repulse the South Africans and UNITA, Cuba sent approximately fifteen thousand troops to reinforce the area in early 1988. Confronted by well-trained Cuban troops and rain, the South Africans suffered heavy casualties. The Angolan air force gained air supremacy, and MPLA and Cuban troops moved toward South African bases in Namibia. Surrounded by Cuban and MPLA troops, deprived of air cover, and worried about Cuban troops on the Namibian border where they could collaborate with the South West African People's Organization (SWAPO), South Africa decided to seriously negotiate with Angola in order to extricate its troops trapped in Cuito Cuanavale.[33] More important than the military defeat was the psychological shock and sense of vulnerability that Afrikaners experienced for the first time since the Boer War (1899–1902). Combined with the negative effects of international economic sanctions, the war in Angola forced Pretoria to reconsider its options.

Nevertheless, both South Africa and the United States continued to support UNITA even after Angola agreed to send the Cubans home and Bush had committed the United States to negotiate a ceasefire in Angola. In late 1989, as Bush prepared for the Malta summit with Soviet President Mikhail Gorbachev, a Central Intelligence Agency plane carrying U.S. weapons to UNITA crashed in Angola, thereby underscoring U.S. commitment to a military solution of the Angolan conflict.[34] However, the U.S.-brokered Namibian settlement and significant political changes in South Africa in 1990 weakened UNITA and facilitated a negotiated end to the Angolan civil war. With the end of the Cold War officially declared by the NATO allies in mid-1990, America had moved closer to the Angolan policies of its European allies. The United States, Portugal, and the Soviet Union played a major role in persuading UNITA and the Angolan government to formally terminate the conflict in May 1991.

NAMIBIA: THE CONTACT GROUP

Compared to Angola, where the allies' interests and policies diverged, there was widespread agreement among the NATO allies on Namibia's independence. Furthermore, both superpowers shared this objective. However, the allies were divided on the strategy of linkage proposed by the Reagan administration. Reagan's East-West emphasis prompted the Europeans, including Britain and West Germany, to distance themselves from U.S. policies. But there were differences among the Europeans, emanating in part from their different historical ties to and interests in Africa.

France, with no historical links to Namibia, evinced relatively little enthusiasm for an active role there. West Germany, on the other hand, regarded Namibia as a special issue because of its colonial ties to that country, ongoing cultural and family connections, and West German business interests in Namibia and South Africa. Yet for historical reasons Bonn often remained in Britain's shadow in relation to foreign policy initiatives on southern Africa.

Britain's extensive knowledge of and interests in South Africa and Namibia enabled it to assume leadership on Namibia within the EC. France suspected British and West German activism, believing that both countries were primarily concerned with protecting their mineral interests in Namibia.[35] Despite these differences, none of the allies viewed the Namibian issue as a threat to NATO's cohesion. Instead of directly confronting the United States over its linkage policy, the allies, including West Germany, simply abdicated responsibility for solving the Namibian problem.

West Germany's relationship with Namibia began in 1883. Adolph Luderitz, believing that the territory would rival South Africa as a source of minerals, established a coastal settlement in what Europeans called South West Africa. Advancing rapidly into the interior to establish control, in accordance with provisions of the Berlin Conference of 1884–85, Germany succeeded by 1890 in obtaining British recognition of its claim to German South West Africa. Competition for grazing land and German disregard for the economic and political rights of the African inhabitants eventually led to war between the Herero and German settlers. The Herero and other ethnic groups were convinced that the German presence, already irksome, would become increasingly oppressive.[36] The German decision to use the military to suppress a small disturbance precipitated a Herero uprising under Samuel Maherero's leadership during which about a hundred German settlers and traders were killed. The German army retaliated under the command of the ruthless General von Trotha, who regarded the campaign as one of extermination. Before the German government recalled him, over 70 percent of the Herero and Nama were exterminated. Thousands died in concentration camps or perished in the Namib desert trying to escape the conflict.[37] Germany's brief but brutal rule ended when South African soldiers occupied Namibia during World War I as part of the allied campaign against Germany. For the Namibians, however, South Africa's victory meant a prolonged and painful struggle to govern themselves.

In 1920 the newly formed League of Nations gave South Africa responsibility for administering Namibia, which was designated a Class C mandate by the League. The principal objective of the mandate system was to develop the former German and Turkish colonies to the point where they could become independent. But Pretoria perceived Namibia as an extension of its territory. When the United Nations was created in 1945 and the League of Nations was dissolved in 1946, Namibia's status became an important international issue because South Africa attempted to incorporate the territory as a fifth province. The UN condemned the action. South Africa ignored the UN, implemented its system of apartheid in Namibia, and exploited the country's mineral resources.[38] The Namibians responded by creating the Ovambo People's Organization, which was later transformed into SWAPO, and in 1966 began a guerrilla war for independence under SWAPO's leadership. South Africa's violation of the UN resolutions and international law was confirmed by the International Court of Justice, which in 1971 declared South Africa's occupation of Namibia illegal. The court's action followed a UN Security Council Resolution, supported by the allies, calling South Africa's presence in Namibia illegal. Western pressure prompted Pretoria to receive a special representative from the UN Secretary General in 1972 to discuss Namibia's independence.[39] But South Africa had no intention of relinquishing control over the territory.

Angola's independence radically altered South Africa's strategy in Namibia. Deprived of the buffer provided by Portugal's control of Angola, South Africa became more vulnerable to attacks by SWAPO guerrillas based in southern Angola and operating within Namibia itself. Deteriorating strategic and political conditions in southern Africa as well as Pretoria's intransigence influenced the NATO allies to contemplate sanctions against South Africa. Confronted with these developments, South Africa's Prime Minister Vorster initiated a two-track policy: The MPLA government in Angola had to be replaced and movement toward nominal Namibian independence had to be demonstrated. Consequently, Vorster secretly committed South African troops to a major offensive inside Angola and simultaneously convened a constitutional conference on Namibia at the Turnhalle building in Windhoek to draft a constitution that would lead to Namibia's independence.[40]

But South Africa's invasion of Angola triggered the unexpected Cuban and Soviet military response that further undermined South Africa's security and its position in Namibia. The British urged Vorster to negotiate with SWAPO. Carter's election, aided by a large black American vote, marked a major departure from the Western alliance's sympathetic view of South Africa's dilemmas. Vice President Mondale, UN Ambassador Andrew Young, and his deputy, Donald McHenry, demanded the abandonment of South Africa's scheme to transfer power in Namibia to the ethnically based, white-controlled government negotiated by the Turnhalle delegates.[41] Worried about a Soviet-backed "total onslaught" against South Africa and the escalating violence in Soweto and other major townships and cities, Vorster attempted to expedite Namibia's independence.

Regarding SWAPO as a gang of Communists, the South African government refused to include them in any negotiations on Namibia's future, trying instead to divide the black population. This approach was rejected by SWAPO, the NATO allies, and the Third World. In early April 1977, Britain, France, Canada, West Germany, and the United States (the Contact Group's members) reiterated the demands of UN Security Council Resolution 385, which called for free elections under UN supervision, the release of political prisoners, rejection of the Turnhalle arrangements, and the withdrawal of South Africa's military from Namibia.[42] Although Vorster met with the Contact Group in May 1977 and recognized the UN's authority in Namibia and other general principles outlined by the allies, the issues of Walvis Bay and South Africa's military activities in Angola against SWAPO ultimately derailed progress toward Namibia's independence. Among the European allies, West Germany had the most significant links with Namibia, and was therefore concerned about the outcome of negotiations with South Africa. Bonn generally initiated actions within the Contact Group until 1982, when the United States linked the Namibian and Angolan problems.

Namibia's proximity to and virtual integration into South Africa resulted in the former's economy being tightly controlled by the latter.[43] Nonetheless, West Germany, Britain, and France participated in Namibia's principal sector, mining. Britain's Rio Tinto Zinc, France's Minatome, and West Germany's Urangesellschaft were major companies mining uranium at Rossing. In addition to economic interests, family, historical, and cultural ties also helped shape Bonn's Namibia policy. Approximately twenty thousand Namibians of German ancestry maintained contacts with relatives in West Germany and German churches historically have been active in Namibia. Several West Germany nongovernmental organizations, financed partly by the Ministry for Economic Cooperation, operated in Namibia. German foundations, principally the Hans-Seidel Foundation, the Konrad-Adenauer Foundation, and the Otto-Benecke Foundation, contributed to various educational and training programs.[44]

Bonn's aid policy was complicated by divergent opinions within the coalition government. The Christian Social Union generally opposed giving any assistance that could benefit SWAPO, whereas the Free Democratic Party had developed a close relationship with SWAPO. For example, eleven experts from SWAPO were invited to West Germany by the Ebert Stiftung Foundation, associated with the FDP, to participate in a training program organized by the Institute for Cooperation with Developing Countries. Courses were offered in agriculture, economic planning, administration, and the promotion of trade.[45] Overall, West Germany attempted to maintain political neutrality by granting and administering aid through private organizations, particularly churches.

Although West Germany was officially committed to the various UN resolutions, especially Resolution 435, which provided for Namibia's independence, differences between the Foreign Office and the Christian Social Union prevented Bonn from having an unambiguous policy. Furthermore, West Germany's reluctance to work with SWAPO and its alleged support for the Turnhalle arrangement created confusion about Bonn's Namibia policy. Given the significant role of German business in foreign policy, it was assumed that the business community's endorsement of the interim government engineered by South Africa reflected official West German policy. Bonn rejected the West German Anti-Apartheid Movement's allegation that the government supported moderate political groups within Namibia in an effort to outmaneuver SWAPO.[46] Despite these internal political disagreements, Bonn joined its European allies in opposing Washington's decision to link the Namibian and Angolan issues because it feared that linkage would impede a Namibian settlement.

Ideologically committed to confronting the Soviet Union, Reagan and his band of true believers viewed southern African problems principally in East-West terms. The underlying causes of Soviet-Cuban involvement in the region were largely ignored, and a tacit alliance developed between Washington and Pretoria based upon their common perception of the Communist threat. The European allies, while not aggressively pressuring South Africa to implement basic human rights, understood that apartheid, not communism, was the problem. To the dismay of the allies, Chester Crocker proposed linking Namibia's independence to the withdrawal of Cuban troops from Angola and negotiations between the Angolan government and UNITA for sharing power. Even though Britain, France, West Germany, and Canada clearly wanted the Soviets and Cubans to leave Angola, they were convinced that linkage was unnecessary, counterproductive, and reflected a particularist Reagan administration concern that was largely irrelevant to Western interests.[47]

By early 1983 the linkage issue had created serious schisms in the Western alliance and had contributed to a stalemate in negotiations. The allies disassociated themselves from America's policy, and France announced that it was leaving the Contact Group. Faced with opposition from Britain, West Germany, and France, the United States decided to focus on direct negotiations with Angola and South Africa. The South Africans and Angolans concentrated on obtaining a ceasefire between them, and the United States and Angola discussed Cuban troop withdrawal. As Jaster observed, the initiative was advantageous to Pretoria because it essentially locked out the Contact Group and the UN from the negotiations. South Africa was more comfortable dealing with a sympathetic Reagan administration.[48] But this strategy could also be seen as an astute division of labor within the NATO alliance. Unlike the issue of apartheid, which engendered internal pressures on American foreign policymakers, Namibia seemed important but peripheral to most Americans. Lacking historical ties with the frontline states of southern Africa, the Commonwealth (with the exception of Canada), and much of the Third World, America was not overly concerned about external pressures. The allies, however, faced extreme pressures from the Third World but relatively little from domestic sources.

However, the linkage strategy was not essential for Angolan compliance with American demands, largely because the Angolan government also wanted to end the civil war and wished to send the Cubans home. The war was simply too costly. Angola not only cooperated with the Contact Group but also made a concerted effort to improve economic relations with Western Europe and the United States. Luanda had played a leading role among the frontline states in working for a settlement of the Namibian conflict within the UN framework. The MPLA had persuaded SWAPO's leader, Sam Nujoma, to accept the UN principles for a settlement. Finally, the Angolans and South Africans had negotiated secretly and had convened several meetings in the Cape Verde islands,[49] even as South Africa was militarily involved in Angola. The basic ingredients of a negotiated settlement were already in place. Nonetheless, superpower cooperation added urgency to the situation and facilitated a resolution of the Namibian question. A rapidly deteriorating domestic situation in South Africa, Cuba's resolve to directly engage the South African armed forces, and escalating international economic pressures, among other factors, had also convinced Pretoria that Namibia's independence would be in its interest, since Namibia's dependence on South Africa would enable the latter to control the former. Akin to Botswana, Lesotho, and Swaziland, Namibia had little choice but to cooperate with Pretoria. Moreover, by granting independence to Namibia, South Africa would enhance its image internationally.

The first U.S.-brokered agreement, the Protocol of Brazzaville signed in mid-December 1988 by Angola, Cuba, and South Africa, provided for the exchange of prisoners, for a Joint Commission to facilitate the resolution of disputes regarding the interpretation and implementation of the agreement, and implementation of National Security Council Resolution 435.[50] Subsequent agreements committed Angola, Cuba, and South Africa to cooperate with the UN Secretary General on a transition to Namibia's independence, on-site verification of Cuban troop withdrawal, respect for each other's sovereignty, and acceptance of responsibility not to allow their territory to be used for aggression or violence against other states.[51] At the end of 1988 Angola, Cuba, and South Africa agreed to a four-step peace process. The first step involved Angola and Cuba signing a treaty on the departure of Cuban troops. Step two dealt with the actual withdrawal of three thousand Cuban troops by April 1, 1989, and provided for the implementation of Security Council Resolution 435. A UN Transition Assistance Group would prepare for supervising Namibia's elections. Step three called for free and fair elections on November 1, 1989, and full independence for Namibia when the elected assembly adopted a new constitution. Step four dealt with the complete withdrawal of Cuban troops from Angola by July 1, 1991.[52] The new constitution was adopted on February 9, 1990, and Namibia became independent at midnight, March 20, 1990.

Despite their differences on the linkage issue, the West European allies collaborated with the United States and other countries to assist Namibia's transition to independence. They assumed responsibility for much of the cost of the UN's operation and participated in the United Nations Angola Verification Mission (UNAVEM). Portugal, however, was excluded from UNAVEM due to strong U.S. opposition, the official justification for which was that Portugal was the former colonial power in Angola. But the United States, still supporting UNITA militarily, worried that the Portuguese military "would adopt an attitude favorable to the Angolan government."[53] Portugal did not seriously object to its exclusion.

THE ALLIES AND SOUTH AFRICA:
CONVERGING POLICIES

Compared to Angola and Namibia, South Africa did not engender serious strains within NATO. Having considerable economic interests in South Africa, the United States, Britain, West Germany, and France adopted policies that were not radically different, despite varying levels of commitment to reform in South Africa. Compared to Britain and West Germany, America was confronted with more domestic cross-pressures. When problems in South Africa were perceived in the context of East-West rivalry and the expansion of communism, the United States, as it did during the Reagan administration, was more sympathetic and supportive of the white minority government. However, the East-West perspective was inconsistent with Americans' belief in moral foreign policies, their commitment to civil rights, and their desire to preserve racial détente at home. Thus, the tensions created by these contradictory approaches often resulted in confused, inconsistent foreign policy. Furthermore, Congress, more vulnerable to interest group pressure than the executive branch, sharply disagreed with the White House, especially during Reagan's administration. These serious internal divisions were exploited by the South African government as well as by the allies, who preferred a more evolutionary, conservative, status-quo approach to South Africa's problems. Lacking serious anti-apartheid constituencies, both West Germany and France could hide behind American policy, even as U.S. policies were singled out for criticism. The very openness of the American political system and its willingness to address the issue of apartheid put it at a disadvantage vis-à-vis its European allies and Japan. Despite the fact that Japan had been South Africa's leading trade partner since 1987, there were few protests against Japan and most Japanese citizens were largely unaware of and unconcerned about apartheid.[54]

Despite Britain's more extensive contacts with South Africa, a very strong and intensely committed anti-apartheid movement, and access to the African National Congress (ANC) and other South African groups with offices in London and elsewhere, British foreign policy toward Pretoria had been consistently moderate. Unlike the United States, where foreign policies fluctuated from one administration to the other, Britain's political system was generally more stable. Those who formulated and implemented British foreign policy came from similar class backgrounds and held similar political views. Furthermore, the structure of Britain's parliamentary system blocked access to those chiefly responsible for British foreign policy, the prime minister and the Cabinet.[55] Under these circumstances, a strong anti-apartheid movement could have only a marginal impact on the government's relations with South Africa.

Nevertheless, subnational initiatives by anti-apartheid groups influenced consumers to boycott South African products and pressured business to divest from South Africa. Moreover, Britain's relations with Pretoria were influenced by the Commonwealth and the Group of Seven industrialized countries. However, given America's leadership role in NATO and in the Group of Seven, as well as its superpower status and its stated objective of spreading democracy to the rest of the world, Britain could always follow in America's shadow. West Germany's South Africa policies were equally complex, yet quite straightforward when its underlying interests were scrutinized. Akin to Japan, and to a lesser extent Britain, commercial considerations largely determined West Germany's position on South Africa. Unlike the United States, with its huge internal market, West Germany and Britain were more dependent on foreign trade. These countries' international power was based on their economic competitiveness and access to world markets. Lacking strategic mineral resources, they argued against being denied access to South Africa's vanadium, cobalt, platinum, chromium, and other metals. However, given Pretoria's reliance on mineral exports, the allies were in a much stronger bargaining position in relation to South Africa. Nonetheless, neither Britain nor Germany exhibited an interest in imposing serious restraints on business activities.[56]

What seemed to complicate West Germany's policy toward South Africa were ideological differences between Bonn and the former East German government, divergent views and policy positions within the coalition government in Bonn, and West German sensitivity to racial issues. East Germany had renounced its German nationality and had associated West Germany with Nazi atrocities. West Germany's extensive trade ties with and investments in South Africa were regarded by the East Berlin government as evidence of Bonn's complicity in apartheid.[57] Differences between Genscher and Strauss, which provided flexibility for Kohl, made West Germany's policy on apartheid appear inconsistent and contradictory: while Genscher regarded the ANC as a legitimate opposition group, Strauss viewed it as a terrorist organization. But neither side advocated radical changes in South Africa, thus rendering their differences more rhetorical than substantive. And while protecting human rights in other countries was a significant issue in West Germany's foreign policy, Bonn's human rights concerns were actually more focused on victims of the Holocaust. Despite West Germany's sensitivity to racial issues in South Africa, German public opinion tended to be more sympathetic to the white minority. Compared to America's multiracial society, the West German society was largely ethnically and racially homogeneous. Consequently, while America's policies were shaped to some extent by racial considerations, Germany's were not. The important consideration for both Britain and Germany was to implement South African policies that addressed the issue of morality but did not adversely affect commercial relations. Political pressure groups in the United States and deeply held American values militated against Washington's adoption of that approach when apartheid was seen as a human rights issue.

With comparatively few economic interests in and historical links to South Africa, France was not seriously concerned about developments there. France's interests in Africa had been primarily confined to its former colonies. Although Mitterrand and the Socialists took a strong anti-apartheid position in 1981, France's influence on the alliance's relations with South Africa was marginal. Compared to Britain, France was relatively unaffected by Third World pressures.[58] However, French policy toward Pretoria became more controversial in 1986 during the short ascendancy of Jacques Chirac, who advocated views different from Mitterrand's. Nonetheless, France remained on the periphery of the South African debate.

Political changes in Eastern Europe, significant developments within South Africa in 1990 and 1991, and Soviet support for negotiations between the ANC and Pretoria created new challenges for the Western allies at a time when NATO itself was being radically altered. Furthermore, growing economic competition between Western Europe and the United States threatened to complicate alliance policies toward South Africa. However, President F. W. de Klerk's and Nelson Mandela's commitment to end apartheid through negotiation was consistent with the allies' strategies, thus providing them with an opportunity to coordinate their foreign policies toward South Africa.

Prior to 1974, the European allies pursued individual national policies toward South Africa and made no concerted effort to harmonize them. Britain's entry into the EC in 1973 and growing European assertiveness and involvement in world affairs prompted the allies to try to develop common European foreign policies.[59] Apart from allowing the Europeans to increase their maneuverability vis-à-vis the United States, EPC enhanced British influence within the EC. Viewed primarily as a British problem, South Africa was not a priority for the other countries. However, Portugal's hasty withdrawal from Mozambique and Angola in 1975 and growing Soviet-Cuban involvement in Angola changed the regional balance of power, thereby forcing West Europeans with major economic interests in South Africa to reevaluate their policies.

Instead of developing new approaches, the other European states basically adopted Britain's policies as EC policies. This strategy enabled Britain to spread responsibility to Western Europe for relations with South Africa. West Germany and Portugal, which essentially favored the status quo, could simply follow Britain's conservative policies within the broader context of the EC.[60] Whereas EPC provided the framework that allowed Britain and West Germany to downplay their extensive economic links to South Africa and to avoid taking actions against Pretoria that would jeopardize their interests, the United States stood alone, and was therefore more vulnerable to attack for its relations with Pretoria. Yet, within the context of EPC, West Germany and Britain pursued policies which were much more conservative.

HISTORICAL, POLITICAL, AND MILITARY TIES WITH SOUTH AFRICA

Religious intolerance in Western Europe and Dutch commercial interests in Asia combined to influence Dutch, French, and German Huguenots to settle in South Africa. The Dutch East India Company established a refueling station for its ships on the Cape of Good Hope in 1652, and shortly thereafter religious refugees and settlers began arriving from Holland. But if the Huguenots were determined to escape religious persecution, this objective was compromised to some extent because European military conflicts eventually spread to the Cape. Holland's defeat by France during the Napoleonic Wars resulted in the establishment of a British caretaker government on the Cape in 1795 at Holland's request. But when the Dutch later allied themselves with France against Britain, the British seized the Cape and made it a British possession.[61] Britain's opposition to slavery and its imposition of its laws, language, and customs on the Dutch settlers inevitably led to conflict and ultimately the founding of two separate republics by the Afrikaners (as original European settlers were called around 1800).

The discovery of gold in the Transvaal (one of the Afrikaner republics) in 1885 influenced Germans to invest in the gold mines, prompted large numbers of English settlers to move from the Cape to the Transvaal, and encouraged increased German immigration—developments which contributed to the end of the Afrikaners' independence. Growing German interest in the Transvaal, triggered in part by the new immigrants, was of concern to Britain's foremost imperialist in southern Africa, Cecil Rhodes. German efforts to prevent Rhodes from acquiring Delagoa Bay in Mozambique from Portugal and Germany's declared support for the Afrikaners heightened Anglo-German rivalry and sharpened British-Boer antagonism.[62] Tensions eventually led to a poorly conceived and executed plan by Rhodes, known as the Jameson Raid, to overthrow the Afrikaner government headed by Paul Kruger.

In light of the Jameson Raid, the Transvaal and the Orange Free State—the other Afrikaner republic—concluded a treaty for mutual protection, and Germany promised significant support in the event of hostilities between the Afrikaners and the British. When war erupted on October 11, 1899, German assistance was not forthcoming. After waging an incompetent military campaign against the Afrikaners, who had turned to guerrilla tactics because they were greatly outnumbered, Britain resorted to burning Afrikaner farms and putting the women and children into concentration camps, where as many as twenty-thousand died. Although defeated on the battlefields, the Afrikaners ultimately obtained exclusive political control, due largely to fundamental miscalculations by British policymakers.[63]

These historical links provided the foundation for political, military, and economic ties between the allies and South Africa. Germany's defeat in both world wars deprived it of its commercial foothold in South Africa until the late 1950s. Apartheid in South Africa made relations between West Germany and Pretoria very sensitive for the Germans, whose racial philosophies and nationalism had culminated in the Holocaust and the destruction of much of Europe. Furthermore, there are roughly seventy thousand South Africans of German ancestry, compared to approximately two million Africans with family and cultural ties to Britain. Britain, therefore, faced little competition from West Germany for the leadership role on South African issues. However, as a Commonwealth member, Britain is sensitive to Third World, Australian, and Canadian views on apartheid.[64] Britain's policies were rendered more complex than Germany's by these realities. British policymakers have therefore insisted on maintaining close diplomatic relations with Pretoria in order to protect British subjects as well as to persuade the minority regime to end apartheid.

None of the allies believed that severing diplomatic relations with South Africa would contribute to peaceful change. On the contrary, they emphasized the importance of maintaining communications between senior officials of South Africa and the West. During the Reagan administration, contacts with Pretoria became the centerpiece of U.S. foreign policy. An important feature of this approach, known as constructive engagement, was quiet diplomacy. Instead of conf-onting apartheid, as Carter did, Reagan quietly admonished Pretoria.[65]

While this policy was essentially the same as that practiced by Britain's Prime Minister Thatcher, it was America that was criticized most often for its friendship with Pretoria. Britain's interactions with South Africa were far more extensive and intimate. However, the political dynamics in the United States were not present in Britain. The two countries' historical experiences were radically different and their self-perceptions also diverged. Within the American context, the racial implications of a close relationship with a government whose racial laws were similar to those enforced in some parts of the United States until the 1960s had to be taken into consideration. By ignoring this reality, Reagan not only contributed to America's strong anti-apartheid reactions and the demise of constructive engagement but also suffered his first major political defeat in Congress, which passed the Comprehensive Anti-Apartheid Act over the president's veto.[66] The parliamentary systems of West Germany and Britain, among other factors, militated against similar occurrences in those countries. Nevertheless, changes in U.S. policy were ultimately felt in Bonn and London.

More controversial than political ties was the issue of military relations between the Western alliance and South Africa, partly because South Africa's access to weapons was seen as essential to its perpetuation of apartheid. Intensification of the Cold War and the Algerian conflict in the mid-1950s influenced the allies to consider South Africa's strategic value to NATO. Regarding itself as a bulwark of Western civilization and security, South

Africa had tried to convince the Western allies of its importance as a southern arm of NATO. This idea was attractive to the Reagan administration during the renewed Cold War. But South Africa's principal objective was not the defense of the West; rather, Pretoria endeavored to involve the West in the defense of apartheid. The West's concern with Communist expansion was exploited by the white minority regime, which had succeeded in convincing many Western leaders that black nationalism was tantamount to communism. During the Korean War and the Soviet blockade of West Berlin South Africa had provided air support for allied operations, thereby demonstrating its usefulness to the NATO alliance.[67]

Accepting the widely held assumption that the West's security depended in part on the Cape route being controlled by an ally, Britain strengthened its military relations with South Africa by signing the Simonstown Agreement with it in 1955. The treaty provided for joint naval exercises, arms transfers, and general collaboration on intelligence and defense matters. France, though not fully supportive of NATO, had its own reasons for developing military ties with South Africa. Confronted with guerrilla activities of the Algerian Front for National Liberation, France decided to cooperate with South Africa. Pretoria's experience with suppressing internal opposition to apartheid prompted the French to invite South African officials to Algeria. As the Algerian war progressed, the South Africans returned to Algeria to learn from the French army's experience.[68]

South Africa's determination to forcefully suppress internal dissent ultimately undermined Western support for the apartheid regime. When police officers fired indiscriminantly at black protesters at Sharpeville in 1960, Britain and the United States reassessed their military support for South Africa. Worried about its own domestic civil rights problems, and the Soviets' willingness to exploit them, the United States distanced itself from South Africa by voting for the UN Security Council arms embargo against Pretoria. Britain was more ambivalent, and attempted to use semantics to circumvent the embargo even as it professed to comply with it. Although improved East-West relations and new strategic realities influenced Britain to perceive South Africa's contribution to the Western alliance as negligible, the outbreak of the Six Day War and Egypt's decision to close the Suez Canal rekindled Western interest in the Cape route. Moreover, the Soviets had increased their naval presence in the Indian Ocean precisely when Britain was confronting the Rhodesian problem and as Portugal was conducting a war against Mozambique and Angola. However, after a brief but intense period of British cooperation with South Africa under the Conservative party in the early 1970s, British military relations with South Africa were reduced to cooperation in the area of military intelligence.[69]

If America was pressured into ending arms sales to Pretoria, France, Italy, and West Germany were generally not so constrained. France expanded its military ties with South Africa, and by 1969 was that country's principal arms supplier. That position remained largely unchanged even under Mitterrand. France's much-publicized embargoes on specific categories of arms were usually preceded by lucrative licensing contracts that allowed South Africa to produce weapons domestically.[70] However, the United States' failure to carefully monitor Israel's military relationship with South Africa, which developed following the 1973 Yom Kippur War, virtually guaranteed South Africa access to American weapons and military technology. Concerned about possible reductions in U.S. military assistance and congressional hearings, Israel decided to comply with the arms boycott against South Africa, although numerous loopholes remained in its policy.[71] Despite occasional violations of the arms boycott, the Western allies had effectively terminated overt military ties with Pretoria by 1988.

ECONOMIC RELATIONS WITH SOUTH AFRICA

Economic interests have always been of paramount importance in Western Europe's relations with South Africa. Similar to Japan, West Germany and Britain viewed trade as an essential ingredient of national power and adamantly opposed any efforts that would have significantly restricted commercial ties with South Africa. Unlike in the United States, where business groups tend to have an antagonistic view of government, there is a close partnership between private enterprise and the public sector in Western Europe and Japan. Dependent on exports to maintain healthy economies, the European allies attempted to separate economic issues from political considerations. And while anti-apartheid groups succeeded in forcing many European companies to assess their activities in South Africa, they were unable to effectuate changes similar to those achieved by their U.S. counterparts in relation to U.S. corporations. Deteriorating economic and political conditions in South Africa induced many European and American companies to reduce operations there, but the majority of European firms remained. High unemployment throughout Western Europe during the 1980s exerted considerable influence on foreign policymakers. Since many jobs in the EC, especially in Britain and West Germany, were directly and indirectly dependent on trade with South Africa, few policymakers supported actions that would have adversely affected economic relations with South Africa.

By 1988, Japan, West Germany, the United States, and Britain, in that order, were South Africa's major trading partners, accounting for more than two-thirds of all exports to South Africa. In 1987 the value of Japan's exports to South Africa stood at $1.882 billion, up from $1.357 billion in 1986. West Germany's exports totaled $2.545 billion in 1987, compared to $1.940 billion in 1986. U.S. exports in 1987 stood at $1.253 billion, a marginal increase over $1.144 billion for 1986. Britain's exports totaled $1.556 billion in 1987 and $1.250 billion in 1986. Imports from South

Africa in 1987 were $2.455 billion for Japan, $1.320 billion for the United States, $1.248 billion for West Germany, and $1.085 billion for Britain. Whereas Japan's imports from South Africa increased by 9 percent over 1986 imports, West Germany's declined by 1 percent, Britain's declined by 10 percent, and the United States experienced a 47 percent decrease.[72] Although it was difficult to obtain complete trade data, these figures indicate the extent to which countries allowed their trade relations to be affected by political developments in South Africa and international pressures for sanctions against Pretoria.

Britain continued to be the major foreign investor in South Africa. In 1988 Britain's share of all foreign assets in South Africa was 45 percent, more than the combined shares of Japan, the United States, and West Germany.[73] Neither Britain nor West Germany imposed restrictions on new investments, preferring instead to support a voluntary ban. Major British and West German companies continued to invest in South Africa. Whereas many American firms divested, German companies such as Daimler-Benz, Siemens, Volkswagen, and Bayerische Motoren-Werke (BMW) continued expansion programs begun in 1983. Daimler-Benz completed retooling its East London factory and announced plans for additional investments. BMW opened an $18 million headquarters building in Johannesburg.[74] Faced with mounting international pressure to pull their companies out of South Africa and impose economic sanctions against the minority regime, Britain adopted a Code of Practice for British firms operating in South Africa. The United States responded to international and domestic pressure by endorsing the Sullivan Principles, which were similar to the Code of Practice. Britain's influence within the institution of EPC and its acknowledged leadership role in South Africa enabled British policymakers to modify the Code of Practice and apply it to the EC. The EC's Code of Conduct, like the Sullivan Principles, called upon companies to (1) give all employees equal pay for equal work, (2) abolish segregation in the work place, (3) encourage the growth of black businesses, (4) recognize and bargain with trade unions, (5) improve the living conditions for blacks, (6) open supervisory and management jobs to blacks, and (7) provide transportation for black workers from home to work and back.[75]

The objective of the Code of Conduct was to nullify apartheid laws in European businesses, but an underlying motivation for adopting the code was to avoid imposing economic sanctions against South Africa. After reevaluating the code's effectiveness, the EC concluded in 1988 that (1) the level of companies' involvement with trade unions representing black workers had continued to increase, (2) companies were applying common pay scales for all employees, (3) over 95 percent of black workers had received wages at or above the level advocated by the code, and (4) many companies had specific policies of training and promoting black employees.[76] Unlike the United States, Britain and West Germany generally opposed economic sanctions as instruments of foreign policy, preferring instead what they called "positive measures."

Most European states, particularly West Germany and Britain, endorsed Reagan's view that sanctions against South Africa were counterproductive. But compared to the European allies, America's position on sanctions was more contradictory and selective. Sanctions were regarded as essential in the case of Nicaragua, but as ineffective in relation to South Africa. While this may have been a pragmatic approach, Reagan's overall policy toward South Africa strongly influenced Congress to impose sanctions against South Africa, despite the president's veto. Congressional participation in foreign policy, compared to almost no input from members of Britain's Parliament, caused American and European policies on sanctions to diverge. Both Kohl and Thatcher believed that punitive actions, instead of promoting peaceful change, actually hardened white attitudes, strengthened the right wing, compelled Pretoria to develop a siege economy, and undermined black empowerment.[77]

Concerned about growing international pressures, especially in light of America's sanctions against Pretoria, West Germany and Britain decided in late 1986 to join other EC countries in adopting a sanctions package that included a ban on (1) nuclear cooperation with South Africa, (2) new investments, (3) arms sales, (4) oil exports, (5) investment credits, (6) the importation of Kruggerands, (7) the export of computers, and (8) export credits insurance. Neither Britain nor West Germany fully supported this package, and both made compliance with several measures voluntary. A web of legitimate loopholes through which trade could be continued was created by qualified definitions and exception clauses, thus rendering the EC sanctions virtually meaningless.[78]

Thatcher's decision to lift the voluntary ban on new investments in South Africa in February 1990, following Nelson Mandela's release from prison, underscored Britain's reluctance to implement the relatively mild sanctions it had adopted. Believing that sanctions had contributed to de Klerk's decision to begin negotiations on South Africa's future political and economic systems, few anti-apartheid activists or policymakers advocated lifting them before "irreversible" changes were demonstrated. By the end of 1990, however, the EC, to the dismay of the ANC, had decided to lift the ban on new investments in South Africa in light of reforms implemented by Pretoria. In mid-April 1991 the EC ended all economic sanctions against South Africa. The allies' different perceptions of sanctions as well as the abolition of the final legal structures of apartheid in June 1991 posed serious challenges for U.S. policy toward South Africa.

NOTES

1. Richard J. Payne, "The Soviet-Cuban Factor in U.S. Policy Toward Southern Africa," *Africa Today* 25, no. 2 (April–June 1978):8.

2. Max van der Stoel, "Breaking the Laager: A Two-Track Western Policy Toward South Africa," in *Europe, America, and South Africa*, ed. Gregory F. Treverton (New York: Council on Foreign Relations, 1988), p. 73.

3. Antonio de Figueiredo, "Portugal's Year in Africa: From Empire into the EEC," in *Africa Contemporary Record*, ed. Colin Legum (New York: Africana Publishing, 1987), p. A232.

4. John Marcum, *The Angolan Revolution*, vol. 1 (Cambridge, Mass.: MIT Press, 1969), p. 3.

5. Marcum, p. 181.

6. Marcum, p. 184.

7. William Minter, *Portuguese Africa and the West* (New York: Monthly Review Press, 1972), pp. 133–36.

8. Christopher Coker, *NATO, The Warsaw Pact, and Africa* (London: Macmillan, 1985), p. 55.

9. Mohamad A. El-Khawas and Barry Cohen, *The Kissinger Study of Southern Africa* (Westport, Conn.: Lawrence Hill, 1976), pp. 105–6; and Richard M. Nixon, *U.S. Foreign Policy for the 1970s: A Strategy For Peace* (Washington, D.C.: Government Printing Office, 1970), pp. 83–89.

10. Richard J. Payne, *Opportunities and Dangers of Soviet-Cuban Expansion: Toward a Pragmatic U.S. Policy* (Albany: State University of New York Press, 1988), pp. 162–63.

11. Payne, p. 164.

12. Payne, p. 165.

13. Arthur Jay Klinghoffer, *The Angolan War: A Study in Soviet Policy in the Third World* (Boulder, Colo.: Westview Press, 1980), p. 31.

14. *Parliamentary Debates* (Commons), 5th ser., vol. 904, 26 January–6 February (1976), col. 410.

15. Nicholas van Praag, "European Political Cooperation and Southern Africa," in *European Political Cooperation*, eds. David Allen, Reinhardt Rummel, and Wolfgang Wessels (London: Butterworths Scientific, 1982), p. 137.

16. Kenneth B. Noble, "Angola to Open Last Area to Oil Production," *The New York Times*, April 24, 1989, p. D10.

17. Tony Hodges, *Angola to the 1990s: The Potential for Recovery* (London: The Economist Intelligence Unit, 1987), p. 26.

18. Agreement Between the EC and the Government of Angola on Fishing off Angola for the Period Beginning on 3 May 1987 (Brussels: September 25, 1987), p. 4; and Gerald J. Bender, "Washington's Quest for Enemies in Angola," in *Regional Conflict and U.S. Policy*, ed. Richard J. Bloomfield (Algonac, Mich.: Reference Publications, 1988), p. 199; and Keith Somerville, *Angola: Politics, Economics, and Society* (London: Frances Pinter, 1986), p. 147.

19. *Parliamentary Debates* (Commons), 5th ser., vol. 980, 3–14 March (1980), col. 1323; and *Parliamentary Debates* (Commons), 6th ser., vol. 13, 16–27 November (1981), col. 16.

20. "Dos Santos Meets with Mitterrand," *FBIS-AFR*, September 24, 1987, p. 5.

21. Figueiredo, p. A228.

22. Antonio de Figueiredo, "Portugal's Year in Africa: Old Ties and New Needs," in *Africa Contemporary Record*, ed. Colin Legum (New York: Africana Publishing, 1984), p. A140.

23. "Portuguese Investment in Various Sectors," *FBIS-AFR*, March 28, 1989, p. 14; "Petrogal to Study Oil Refinery," *FBIS-AFR*, February 22, 1989, p. 20; and "Portuguese Credits to Help Rebuild Lomaum Dam," *FBIS-AFR*, July 17, 1987, p. D1.

24. Carlos Gaspar, "Portugal's Policies Toward Angola and Mozambique Since Independence," in *Regional Conflict and U.S. Policy*, ed. Richard J. Bloomfield (Algonac, Mich.: Reference Publications, 1988), pp. 50–54.

25. "Dos Santos Previews Visit to Portugal," *FBIS-AFR*, September 24, 1987, p. 8.

26. Hans-Dietrich Genscher, "The Visit to Angola Is an Important Signal," *Newsletter*, no. 5 (Bonn: Institute for International Relations, 1987), pp. 7–8; and "FRG Parliamentarians Visit UNITA Headquarters," *FBIS-AFR*, August 11, 1987, p. D1.

27. David Rampe, "Bush to Continue Savimbi-Group Aid," *The New York Times*, January 13, 1989, p. A16.

28. James Barber and Christopher Hill, *The Uneasy Relationship: Britain and South Africa* (London: Heineman, 1983), p. 22.

29. "Portuguese Armed Forces Increase Cooperation," *FBIS-AFR*, March 8, 1989, p. 18.

30. James Brooke, "Angola Turning to West to Equip Its Military," *The New York Times*, December 23, 1987, p. A5.

31. "Savimbi Denounces France's Broken Promises," *FBIS-AFR*, October 13, 1987, p. 14.

32. Chas. W. Freeman, "The Angola/Namibia Accords," *Foreign Affairs* 69, no. 3 (Summer 1989): 141.

33. John A. Marcum, "Africa: A Continent Adrift," *Foreign Affairs* 68, no. 1 (1989): 165–66; and "RSA Cuito Cuanavale Advance Reportedly Stopped," *FBIS-AFR*, January 25, 1988, p. 6.

34. Robert Pear, "U.S. Sees Plane Crash Hindering Peace in Angola," *The New York Times*, December 1, 1989, p. A4.

35. Barber and Hill, p. 103.

36. Robin Hallet, *Africa Since 1875* (Ann Arbor: University of Michigan Press, 1974), p. 623.

37. Shula Marks, "Southern and Central Africa," in *The Cambridge History of Africa*, vol. 6, eds. Roland Oliver and G. N. Sanderson (Cambridge: Cambridge University Press, 1985), p. 464.

38. Nicholas H. Z. Watts, "The Roots of Controversy," in *Namibia: Political and Economic Prospects*, ed. Robert I. Rotberg (Lexington, Mass.: Lexington Books, 1983), p. 5.

39. Robert S. Jaster, *The Defense of White Power: South African Foreign Policy Under Pressure* (New York: St. Martin's Press, 1989), p. 60.

40. Jaster, p. 61.

41. Robert I. Rotberg, *Suffer the Future: Policy Choices in Southern Africa* (Cambridge, Mass.: Harvard University Press, 1980), p. 200.

42. Colin Legum, *The Battlefronts of Southern Africa* (New York: African Publishing, 1988), pp. 86–87.

43. See "Namibia: Financial Times Survey," *Financial Times*, March 22, 1990, pp. 15–18.

44. Henning Melber, *Federal Republic of Germany and Namibia* (Copenhagen: NGO Initiative on EC and Apartheid, 1987), p. 4.

45. Institute for International Relations, "Training Program for Experts from SWAPO," *Newsletter* no. 8 (Bonn, 1986), pp. 1–2.

46. Alexander Count York, *Explanation of Vote of the Federal Republic of Germany in the UN General Assembly*, (New York: UN, 1987), pp. 1–2.

47. Legum, *Battlefronts*, p. 270.

48. Jaster, p. 115.

49. Legum, *Battlefronts*, p. 159.

50. Agreement Signed by Delegations from Angola, Cuba, and South Africa in Brazzaville, Congo, December 13, 1988. Reprinted in *International Legal Materials* 28, no. 4 (July 1989): 951.

51. Principles for a Peaceful Settlement in Southwestern Africa, July 20, 1988. Reprinted in *International Legal Materials* 28, no. 4 (July 1989): 950.

52. Four Steps on the Road to Peace in Southwestern Africa, Reprinted in *International Legal Materials* 28, no. 4. (July 1989): 947–48.

53. "America Opposes Portuguese Troops in Angola," *FBIS-AFR*, March 9, 1989, p. 1.

54. For a comprehensive analysis of Japan's, West Germany's, and Britain's South Africa policies see Richard J. Payne, *The Nonsuperpowers and South Africa: Implications for U.S. Policy* (Bloomington: Indiana University Press, 1990).

55. James Barber, *Who Makes British Foreign Policy?* (London: Open University Press, 1976), p. 28; and Wolfram F. Hanrieder and Graeme P. Auton, *The Foreign Policies of West Germany, France, and Britain* (Englewood Cliffs, N.J.: Prentice-Hall, 1980), p. 273.

56. Lewis J. Edinger, *Politics in West Germany* (Boston: Little, Brown, 1977), p. 65.

57. Coker, p. 195.

58. Claude Wauthier, "France and Africa: Socialists Blaze a New Trail," in *Africa Contemporary Record*, ed. Colin Legum (New York: Africana Publishing, 1981), p. A236.

59. Martin Holland, *The European Community and South Africa: European Political Cooperation Under Strain* (London: Pinter, 1988), p. 30.

60. Van Praag, p. 134; and James Barber, Jesmond Blumenfeld, and Christopher Hill, *The West and South Africa* (London: Routledge and Kegan Paul, 1982), p. 1.

61. Harm J. de Blij, *South Africa* (Evanston, Ill.: Northwestern University Press, 1962), p. 28.

62. Leonard Thompson, "Great Britain and Afrikaner Republics," in *The Oxford History of South Africa, vol. II*, eds. Monica Wilson and Leonard Thompson (Oxford: Clarendon Press, 1971), pp. 312–13; and Jeffrey Butler, "The German Factor in Anglo-Transvaal Relations," in *Britain and Germany in Africa: Imperial Rivalry and Colonial Rule*, eds. Prosser Gifford and Roger Louis (New Haven, Conn.: Yale University Press, 1967), p. 190.

63. Rotberg, p. 32.

64. The Commonwealth Accord on Southern Africa, adopted at Lyford Cay, October 20, 1985. Reprinted in *Africa Research Bulletin*, November 15, 1985, p. 7811; and Dennis Austin, *The Commonwealth and Britain* (London: Routledge and Kegan Paul, 1988), p. 75.

65. Chester A. Crocker, "South Africa: A Strategy for Change," *Foreign Affairs* 59 (Winter 1980–81): 350.

66. Richard J. Payne, "Black Americans and the Demise of Constructive Engagement," *Africa Today* 33, no. 4 (1986): 71–90.

67. Jaster, p. 12.

68. Rajen Harshe, "France, Francophone African States, and South Africa," *Alternatives* 9, no. 1 (Summer 1983): 54.

69. Coker, p. 81.

70. Holland, p. 107.

71. United States Comprehensive Anti-Apartheid Act. Reprinted in *International Legal Materials* 26, no. 1 (January 1987): 90; and Consulate General of Israel, *Israel Cabinet Decision Regarding Relations with South Africa* (Chicago: Consulate General of Israel, 1987), p. 1.

72. Commonwealth Experts Group, *Statistics on Trade with South Africa* (Ottawa, Canada: Commonwealth Experts Group, 1988).

73. William Minter, *King Solomon's Mines Revisited: Western Interests and the Burdened History of Southern Africa* (New York: Basic Books, 1986), p. 216.

74. "Divesting from South Africa," *The CTC Reporter*, no. 23 (Spring 1987), p. 39; and John Tagliabue, "Germans Stay in South Africa," *The New York Times*, January 19, 1989, p. A24.

75. Code of Conduct for Companies from the EC with Subsidiaries in South Africa, as revised November 19, 1985 by the Ministers of Foreign Affairs of the Ten Countries of the European Community and Spain and Portugal.

76. "Report on the Application of the Code of Conduct," *Bulletin of the European Communities* 21, no. 2 (1988): 79.

77. Foreign and Commonwealth Office, *Perspectives on Africa* (New York: British Information Services, 1988), p. 14; and the Federal Government, *Reply to the Interpellation of the SDP Parliamentary Group on the Government Policy in Southern Africa* (Bonn: The Federal Government, 1983), p. 7.

78. Martin Holland, "The European Community and South Africa: In Search of a Policy for the 1990s," *International Affairs* 64 (Summer 1988): 418.

7

Post–Cold War Challenges

For more than forty years American foreign policy focused on containing Soviet expansion and strengthening the NATO alliance against Soviet military aggression. In an intensely ideological environment, both Washington and Moscow built nuclear weapons to deter each other from initiating a military conflict that could have brought the superpowers into a nuclear confrontation. Although the United States allocated approximately 50 percent of its military budget to NATO, principally for the protection of Western Europe, the overwhelming majority of military conflicts involving the United States and the Soviet Union occurred not in Europe but in the Third World, an area which became the central battleground for gaining ideological and military allies during the Cold War. While the nuclear stalemate and the U.S. conventional military strategy maintained stability and contained the spread of communism in Europe, the general American tendency, pronounced during the Reagan administration, to eschew negotiations and to emphasize military solutions to what were essentially socioeconomic and political problems in the Third World, ultimately undermined American as well as Soviet power within their respective alliances without resolving underlying causes of Third World instability.

The failure of communism, the political and economic transformation of Europe, the end of the Cold War, tighter linkages between domestic problems and foreign affairs, the ascendancy of economic power as the principal currency of international power in a radically altered strategic environment, and the reemergence of a Europe capable of rivaling the United States for the global leadership role presented serious challenges for American foreign policy. The end of the Cold War will force U.S. policymakers to address the complexities of ongoing Third World conflicts independent of the Soviet threat, and to more carefully and systematically differentiate among various countries and conflicts within the context of a well-defined, pragmatic hierarchy of American interests. This new challenge was tragically demonstrated by Iraq's occupation of Kuwait. Regions and countries once regarded by Washington as vital bulwarks against Communist expansion will decline in importance as America focuses on problems such as environmental degradation, drug trafficking, trade imbalances with other countries, and economic and political competition from Western Europe and Japan. A major post–Cold War challenge for U.S. policymakers will be to transform military relationships with many Third World countries into economic relations. More important, American policymakers will have to rapidly change basic objectives and operating principles that guided U.S. foreign and domestic policy throughout the Cold War. For decades anticommunism functioned as the main organizing principle and was used to justify defense budgets, alliances, disciplining critics of American foreign policy, and the allocation of foreign assistance. As Charles William Maynes observed, "deprived of this principle, American foreign policy will lack direction."[1] This new situation is fraught with danger as well as opportunity.

Both Western Europe and the Third World will also be confronted with serious challenges in the post–Cold War international system. Europe's economic rejuvenation and progress toward economic and political integration strengthened its confidence, thereby reducing its need for America's protection. But Europe's remarkable economic recovery and the long period of stability it has enjoyed since World War II were due partly to America's willingness to provide economic assistance through the Marshall Plan and to maintain the balance of power in Europe through its leadership of NATO. Europe's reemergence as a political and economic power, together with declining American military involvement in the region, created a paradoxical situation with which Europeans are wrestling. German unification, a stated objective of the Western alliance, raised serious questions about Europe's future stability. The question of how to deal with an economically powerful Germany in Central Europe is likely to continue as a major concern among Europeans, especially those who, imprisoned by history, continue to view developments conventionally. While these fears cannot be dismissed, it seems unlikely that Germany will become a military threat. The suicidal implications of nuclear war are all too obvious to Europeans who, during the postwar period, eschewed military instruments of foreign policy and focused instead on economic reconstruction. Nevertheless, managing relations with the new Germany will be a major concern in the post–Cold War world. The French are likely to continue emphasizing tighter economic integration in order to contain Germany, and the British will endeavor to strengthen their position in the area of foreign policy by promoting EPC. Economic alliances will continue to emerge and the activities of global corporations are likely to complicate state economic planning. Already apparent are the growing ethnic rivalries and the rebirth of suppressed nationalism throughout Eastern Europe and the Soviet Union. The West Europeans will undoubtedly be expected to assume greater political and economic responsibility not only in Europe but also in the Third World. President Bush's "new world order" envisioned such a development.

Although the end of the Cold War will not significantly reduce conflicts in the Third World in the short run—as was underscored by the 1990–91 Persian Gulf crisis—diminished superpower involvement in what are usually indigenous problems is likely to enhance these countries' ability to address the underlying causes of violence and instability. Instead of dismissing agitation for reforms as communism, leaders will be pressured to address the problems. They will be unable to manipulate the superpowers, if the United States and the Soviet Union continue to cooperate in order to resolve regional disputes, as they did in the Gulf Crisis.

Furthermore, political and economic changes in Europe and the widespread emphasis on economic power will undoubtedly inspire people in the Third World to initiate struggles for internal decolonization. While the Cold War indirectly contributed to ending external colonial control, it also created an environment in which internal oppression was largely condoned by the superpowers. More assertive Third World citizens are likely to continue demanding democratic reforms, restoration of human rights, political accountability, and economic development. Thus, the end of the Cold War will create new challenges for Western Europe, the Third World, and the United States. The United States will have to address Third World problems under domestic pressure to withdraw from different parts of the world and in a radically altered international economic and strategic environment. The United States itself will have to confront its relative decline vis-à-vis Western Europe and Japan.

Superpower competition in the Third World not only increased the risk of nuclear war but also influenced the United States and Soviet Union to concentrate most of their human and material resources on fighting the Cold War. This disproportionate allocation of resources for conflicts that were largely peripheral to American security ultimately contributed to the erosion of America's economic strength and the economic deterioration of the Soviet Union. Blinded by ideological considerations, both superpowers disregarded the obvious fact that they were saddling their citizens with intolerable financial burdens in order to acquire weapons of mass destruction that neither side could use without inflicting self-destruction. Little consideration was given to the imbalance between commitments and capabilities as each superpower competed for allies in the Third World and raced toward the elusive goal of nuclear dominance. In this ideological crusade, to question the wisdom of such a policy was unpatriotic and tantamount to heresy. In the meantime, however, domestic concerns were largely ignored, and both the Soviet Union and the United States allowed their preoccupation with virtually meaningless victories in the Third World to distract them from building their economies.

But even before the Cold War between the Soviet Union and the United States ended, the European allies and Japan were emerging as America's economic rivals in a world in which economic might was increasingly more important than military power, despite the U.S.-led coalition's victory in Operation Desert Storm. As Bergsten observed, "the ultimate paradox of the twentieth century would be a realization of the Marxist prophecy of an inevitable clash among the capitalist nations just as the political conflict spurred by Marxist ideology is waning."[2] The challenge for American foreign policymakers is how to deal with America's decline and increasing competition from Europe as well as Japan. The triumph of U.S. military might in the Persian Gulf crisis did not alter this reality.

America's political and military ascendancy following World War II emanated from its unsurpassed economic power. Its huge internal market and the global spread of its multinational corporations supported its structural power. The United States shaped the structures of the global political economy within which other countries, their political institutions, their economic enterprises, and their professional people had to operate.[3] But the United States' position also stemmed from the relative weakness of Europe and Japan, areas devastated by war. Consequently, America's international leadership role would also be affected by these countries' economic recovery. Thus, America's decline is relative and inevitable. This does not mean that America will be replaced in the short term by either Western Europe or Japan as the leading superpower. However, as the Persian Gulf conflict in 1990–91 demonstrated, America will no longer be in a position to make important international decisions unilaterally without taking the views of Japan and Western Europe into consideration. U.S. foreign policymakers will have to operate in a world characterized by polycentrism, where power is diffused not only among states but also among nonstate actors.[4]

Economic competition among the United States, Western Europe, and Japan will intensify, with the Soviet Union attempting to develop commercial ties with all of them to improve its deteriorating economy. Economic alliances will shift as the leading economic powers try to prevent the emergence of one dominant power. This task will be complicated by competition among multinational firms and their partnerships with other companies based in competing countries. Japan will have to address increased competition from Taiwan, Korea, and other Asian countries. And efforts within the EC to prevent Germany from dominating the other states are likely to result in alliances between France and Japan or Britain and the United States. But if the Western Europeans manage to surmount difficulties inherent in the economic and political integration of sovereign states, rivalry between the EC and the United States for superpower status is quite probable. Saddled by huge budget deficits and a financial disaster of unprecedented proportions in the savings and loans industry, America seemed almost resigned to allow the EC to seize economic leadership. Bush's "new world order" was constructed on the application of American military might; but the President seemed unable or unwilling to address decisively the country's economic problems. As Samuel Huntington pointed out, "a federation of democratic, wealthy, socially diverse, mixed-economy societies would be a powerful force on the world scene. If the next century is not the American century, it is most likely to be the European century."[5]

To meet this challenge American foreign policy will have to be more flexible and will have to embrace a broader view of national security. This implies that domestic institutions and attitudes will have to adjust in order for policymakers to effectively address the issues of the post–Cold War world. Perhaps the most difficult problem for Americans will be to accept the international reality of diminished American power without using force unnecessarily to compensate for its decline or retreating into isolationism. Domestic problems, neglected in part because of the Cold War, will influence many Americans to try to ignore the rest of the world. But while the economy, educational system, infrastructure, and so on must be rehabilitated to arrest America's decline, no major country will be able to pursue domestic policies without interacting with other nations in an increasingly interdependent world. An important challenge will be to restructure America's policy toward Western Europe and the Third World.

An assertive Germany, determined to implement its full sovereignty, is likely to clash with the United States as its trade with and technology transfers to the Soviet Union escalate. Germany's relations with the Soviet Union might be troublesome for America partly because they represent tangible evidence of the achievement of Russia's dream of joining Europe. The strength of Gorbachev's drive to create a common European home through which the Soviet Union and Eastern Europe would be reintegrated into European civilization and the world economy may have been underestimated by the United States.[6]

But while these developments indicated a decreased need for American military involvement in Europe, an idea favored by those in Congress and elsewhere who were awaiting "peace dividends" prior to the massive U.S. military deployment in the Persian Gulf in 1990, NATO was still needed. Political changes in Eastern Europe have created uncertainty and instability, and have rekindled long-suppressed nationalism. NATO's presence, although reduced, provides stability during the transition period. Even so, radical adjustments in America's policies toward Western Europe and the Soviet Union will have to be made. As Deputy Secretary of State Lawrence Eagleburger put it, "U.S. relations with Europe will become more complicated as Europeans formulate their own responses to Soviet initiatives, seek a more coherent political and economic identity, and generally adopt more assertive postures in dealing with the United States."[7] America will have to redefine its foreign policy interests, no minor task for a country whose postwar policies were based primarily on anticommunism. But the European allies will also confront difficulties as they attempt to develop common policies in a unified Europe.

Although NATO will provide security for Western Europe in the short term, the 1990–91 Persian Gulf crisis demonstrated that more inclusive security arrangements will be necessary. The Conference on Security and Cooperation in Europe provides a possible framework for creating new security institutions. Both the Soviet Union and the United States, along with the Europeans, would be represented. A narrower, but perhaps more workable, security arrangement is WEU. This organization was rejuvenated during the Iran-Iraq War and allowed the Europeans to cooperate with the United States outside the framework of NATO. WEU would essentially replace NATO. Germany could contribute ground forces while France and Britain would provide the nuclear deterrent, thereby maintaining military stability within Western Europe itself.

Developments in Liberia, Trinidad and Tobago, and the Persian Gulf in 1990 clearly demonstrated that Third World conflicts will continue in the post–Cold War world. The challenge for U.S. policymakers is how to respond to these problems. Direct U.S. military intervention is likely to be costly despite the absence of Soviet involvement. This is due in part to the proliferation of weapons in Third World countries. The end of the Cold War exacerbated this situation as both superpowers sold missiles, tanks, planes, and artillery to their clients.[8] Furthermore, several developing countries manufactured many of their own weapons. Iraq, for example, built chemical weapons and threatened to launch them against Israel, if threatened, and against U.S., Arab, and other forces in Saudia Arabia in the event of war in the Gulf. Although chemical weapons were not used during the war, Iraqi Scud missile attacks on Israel and Saudi Arabia demonstrated the dangers. The challenge for the United States was articulated by President Bush in his address to the Coast Guard Academy in mid-1989: "We must curb the proliferation of advanced weaponry. We must check the aggressive ambitions of renegade regimes. And we must enhance the ability of our friends to defend themselves. We have not yet mastered the complex challenge. We and our allies must construct a common strategy for stability in the developing world."[9] The Persian Gulf crisis, the first major conflict of the post–Cold War period, underscored this challenge. Yet the United States increased its sale of advanced weapons to its Middle East allies even as Iraq was forced to destroy weapons that escaped destruction in Operation Desert Storm as one of the conditions of the UN resolution that formally ended the war on April 11, 1991.

In addition to political instability in the Third World, American foreign policymakers will have to deal with issues such as poverty, immigration, illegal drugs, terrorism, overpopulation, and environmental degradation.

Confronted with their own domestic problems, Americans are likely to ignore socioeconomic and environmental problems in the Third World. Yet global issues will assume increasing importance in industrial countries. But as Joseph Nye observed, ironically, the current neglect of weak Third World nations may reduce America's power to influence them on transnational issues in the future.[10]

The United States' approach to the Third World will also be shaped to a greater extent by West European policies. As conflicts, famine, poverty, and environmental problems in the Third World increase, a more economically powerful and assertive Europe will be expected to play a greater role in addressing these developments. Contrary to the assumption that the Third World will be ignored during the post–Cold War period, evidence suggests that as East-West tensions diminish, North-South issues will become more prominent. As a leading power, a unified Western Europe will no longer want to hide behind the United States. It will find it more difficult to settle into its role as the armchair critic that offers advice but does not shoulder responsibility. Europe will have to accept greater responsibility toward the developing countries.[11] Current economic and political links between the EC and the Third World will be intensified as Europe struggles with expectations for it to become more involved in developing areas.

European security concerns in a world dominated by economic powers will become inextricably intertwined with Third World problems, many of which are rooted in the dismal economic conditions in those countries. The United States will face similar problems. However, it is unlikely that Europe and the United States will employ the same policies to deal with security concerns.[12] Preoccupied with its own economic decline, America might be tempted to rely on military intervention, especially in light of its success in the Gulf crisis. Europe, on the other hand, is more likely to use economic and diplomatic instruments and, when necessary, apply force under the auspices of the UN or regional organizations.

Europe's approach to problems emanating from the Mediterranean region provides an example of how Europe might respond to Third World problems. Increasingly alarmed by potential unrest in North Africa, officials from Spain, Portugal, France, and Italy promoted the idea of a conference on security and cooperation for the Mediterranean. (The Europeans are worried that deepening poverty in North Africa will encourage more Africans to seek jobs in Europe, thereby exacerbating tense race relations in France and Italy.) A Forum for Regional Cooperation in the Mediterranean was established to enable Spain, Portugal, Italy, and France to enter informal discussions with Morocco, Algeria, Tunisia, Libya, and Mauritania. Abel Matutes, who is responsible for Mediterranean policy at the European Commission, proposed a $3.3 billion package of assistance for the region.[13]

However, when conditions within Third World countries deteriorate into anarchy and widespread violence, Europeans will either encourage countries with connections to the region to intervene militarily or will participate in military operations through the UN. As the Liberian civil war intensified and civilians were massacred, five ambassadors from the EC called upon the United States to intervene, declaring that "the interdependence of nations no longer permits other nations to sit idle while one country plunges into anarchy and national suicide."[14] Europeans also stressed the UN's role in Operation Desert Storm, despite their support for the United States.

After having been paralyzed by U.S.-Soviet rivalry and general East-West tensions, the UN Security Council's role in resolving regional conflicts will be strengthened in the post–Cold War era. This trend was evident through the Iran-Iraq war, Namibia, and Afghanistan. Although the United States had traditionally opposed greater UN participation in the Middle East, Iraq's invasion of Kuwait and changing American attitudes toward Israel influenced the United States to change its policy. The Europeans, supporters of international law and institutions, will probably continue to advocate a greater UN role in resolving Third World problems. Germany, for example, is reluctant to act unilaterally in regional conflicts, and will attempt to involve its EC partners. But despite an enhanced UN role, the Europeans, Soviets, and Americans will continue to develop their own policies toward the Third World, and the conflict and cooperation which characterized relations between the three will continue, albeit in a more nuanced form.

Increased economic competition between the United States, Japan, and Western Europe is likely to occur in many parts of the Third World, especially in the more economically advanced countries. As the world's resources dwindle, the industrialized countries will become even more dependent on African, Latin American, and the Middle Eastern resources. Competition among the industrialized countries for Third World resources and markets will increase the developing countries' leverage, thereby further complicating post–Cold War international relations. And the Soviet shift to a market economy will inevitably bring it into competition and cooperation with the United States, Western Europe, and the Third World. For example, the Soviet Union and Third World countries may collaborate to obtain higher prices for diamonds, gold, petroleum, and other minerals.

The movement of U.S. industries to stable Third World states such as Mexico in order to compete with the Europeans and the Japanese is likely to continue, despite Americans' concern about how such relocations would affect their jobs and wages. And more efficient Japanese and European multinational corporations are likely to acquire leading American firms. But foreign acquisition of strategic industries such as Semi-Gas Systems, which was a major supplier of gas distribution and control systems to America's computer chip industry, will generate serious debate within the United States because economic issues will be increasingly identified as national security issues. In specific Third World regions the United States will have to rethink its policies, not only because of changed strategic realities but also because

Western Europe will pursue much more independent foreign policies that might conflict with U.S. policies.

A major challenge for the United States will be to learn how to adjust to the reality of being an ordinary nation. Sharing power with Japan and Western Europe is bound to engender insecurities in America. While it is difficult to predict how America will respond to this diminution of its international status, it is clear that U.S. policymakers will have to abandon their proclivity for unilateralism and embrace cooperation, as was demonstrated in the Persian Gulf conflict. Greater emphasis on multilateral diplomacy and collaborative foreign policy initiatives under the auspices of international and regional organizations will be essential in order for the United States to achieve its foreign policy objectives in the radically altered strategic environment of the post–Cold War era. In light of the fact that Third World countries comprise the majority in most international organizations, the United States will have to attempt to enlist their support.

NOTES

1. Charles William Maynes, "America Without the Cold War," *Foreign Policy*, no. 78 (Spring 1990): 8. See John D. Steinbruner, "Introduction," in *Restructuring American Foreign Policy*, ed. John D. Steinbruner (Washington, D.C.: The Brookings Institution, 1989), pp. 1–11.

2. C. Fred Bergsten, "The World Economy After the Cold War," *Foreign Affairs* 69, no. 3 (Summer 1990): 98.

3. Susan Strange, "The Persistent Myth of Lost Hegemony," *International Organization* 41, no. 4 (Autumn 1987): 565.

4. Joseph S. Nye, "Arms Control After the Cold War," *Foreign Affairs* 68, no. 5 (Winter 1989–90): 52.

5. Samuel P. Huntington, "The U.S.—Decline or Renewal?" *Foreign Affairs* 67, no. 3 (Winter 1988–89): 93.

6. See Jerry F. Hough, "Gorbachev's Politics," *Foreign Affairs* 68, no. 5 (Winter 1989–90): 32–33; and Jeffrey E. Garten, "Japan and Germany: American Concerns," *Foreign Affairs* 68, no. 5 (Winter 1989–90): 96.

7. Lawrence S. Eagleburger, "The Challenge of the European Landscape in the 1990s," *Department of State Bulletin*, October 1989, p. 37.

8. Robert Pear, "Prospect of Arms Pacts Spurring Weapon Sales," *The New York Times*, March 25, 1990, p. A11.

9. "Excerpts from Bush's Address on Foreign Policy at Coast Guard Academy," *The New York Times*, May 25, 1989, p. A8.

10. Joseph S. Nye, *Bound to Lead: The Changing Nature of American Power* (New York: Basic Books, 1990), p. 198.

11. Giovanni Agnelli, "The Europe of 1992," *Foreign Affairs* 68, no. 4 (Fall 1989): 69.

12. Debra Van Opstal and Andrew C. Goldberg, *Meeting the Mavericks: Regional Challenges for the Next President* (Washington, D.C.: The Center for Strategic and International Studies, 1988), p. 1.

13. Alan Riding, "Four European Nations Planning a New Focus on North Africa," *The New York Times*, July 30, 1990, p. A4.

14. "Liberian Rebels Advance to President's Doorstep," *The Pantagraph*, July 29, 1990, p. C13.

Selected Bibliography

Agnelli, Giovanni. "The Europe of 1992." *Foreign Affairs* 68, no. 4 (Fall 1989): 61–70.

Agreement Signed by Delegations from Angola, Cuba, and South Africa in Brazzaville, Congo, December 13, 1988. *International Legal Materials* 28, no. 4 (July 1989): 951.

Ahrari, Mohammed E. "Iran and the Superpowers in the Gulf." *SAIS Review* 7, no. 1 (Winter-Spring 1987): 157–68.

Albright, David, and Jiri Valenta. *The Communist States in Africa*. Bloomington: Indiana University Press, 1982.

Andelman, David A. "Struggle over Western Europe." *Foreign Policy*, no. 49 (Winter 1982–83): 37–51.

Art, Robert. "America's Foreign Policy." In *Foreign Policy in World Politics*. Edited by Roy Macridis. Englewood Cliffs, N.J.: Prentice-Hall, 1989, pp. 125–80.

Artner, Stephen J. "The Middle East: A Chance for Europe?" *International Affairs* 56, no. 3 (Summer 1980): 420–42.

Asobie, Humphrey. "The EEC and South Africa." In *Southern Africa in the 1980s*. Edited by Olajide Aluko and Timothy Shaw. London: Allen and Unwin, 1985, pp. 171–93.

Axelgard, Frederick W. *A New Iraq? The Gulf War and Implications for U.S. Policy*. New York: Praeger, 1988.

El Azharzy, M. S. "The Attitudes of the Superpowers Toward the Gulf War." *International Affairs* 59, no. 4 (Autumn 1983): 609–20.

Bailey, Robert. "Middle East Spending Keeps World Arms Sales Buoyant." *Middle East Economic Digest*, October 31, 1987, pp. 23–48.

Baker, James A. "Principles and Pragmatism: American Policy Toward the Arab-Israeli Conflict." Address before the American-Israel Public Affairs Committee on May 22, 1989. *Department of State Bulletin*, July 1989, pp. 24–27.

Barber, James. *The Uneasy Relationship: Britain and South Africa*. London: Heinemann, 1983.

Benvenisti, Meron. *1986 Report: Demographic, Economic, Legal, Social, and Political Developments in the West Bank*. Jerusalem: The West Bank Data Base Project, 1988.

Blinken, Antony J. *Ally vs. Ally: America, Europe, and the Siberian Pipeline Crisis*. New York: Praeger, 1987.

Bonvicini, Gianni. "Out-of-Area Issues: A New Challenge to the Atlantic Alliance." In *The Atlantic Alliance and the Middle East*. Edited by Joseph I. Coffey and Gianni Bonvicini. Pittsburgh: University of Pittsburgh Press, 1989, pp. 1–16.

Bosworth, Barry P., and Robert Z. Lawrence. "America's Global Role: From Dominance to Interdependence." In *Restructuring American Foreign Policy*. Edited by John D. Steinbruner. Washington, D.C.: The Brookings Institution, 1989, pp. 12–47.

Bowie, Robert R. "The Atlantic Alliance." *Daedalus* 110, no. 1 (Winter 1981): 53–69.

Boyd, T. Barron, Jr. "France and the Third World: The African Connection." In *Third World Policies of Industrialized Nations*. Edited by Phillip Taylor and Gregory A. Raymond. Westport, Conn.: Greenwood Press, 1982. pp. 45–65.

Boyer, Yves. "French Foreign Policy: Alignment and Assertiveness." *The Washington Quarterly* 9, no. 4 (Fall 1986): 5–15.

Brady, Linda P. "NATO in the 1980s: An Uncertain Future." In *NATO in the 1980s: Challenges and Responses*. Edited by Linda P. Brady and Joyce P. Kaufman. New York: Praeger, 1985, pp. 3–15.

Bundy, William P. "The 1950s Versus the 1990s." In *America's Global Interests: A New Agenda*. Edited by Edward K. Hamilton. New York: Norton, 1989, pp. 33–81.

Cahen, Alfred. *The Western European Union and NATO*. London: Brassey's Defense Publishers, 1989.

Calleo, David P. "The Atlantic Alliance: An Enduring Relationship?" *SAIS Review* 2, no. 4 (Summer 1982): 27–39.

———. *Beyond American Hegemony: The Future of the Western Alliance*. New York: Basic Books, 1987.

Carter, Jimmy. *The Blood of Abraham*. Boston: Houghton Mifflin, 1985.

Central American Peace Process: A Chronology. London: Foreign and Commonwealth Office, March 1988.

Cerny, Philip G. "Political Entropy and American Decline." *Millenium* 18, no. 1 (Spring 1989): 47–63.

Chace, James. "Europe and America: Double Isolationism." *SAIS Review*, no. 4 (Summer 1982): 5–20.

Chubin, Shahram. *Security in the Persian Gulf: The Role of Outside Powers*. Totowa, N.J.: Allanheld, Osman, 1982.

Coker, Christopher. *NATO, The Warsaw Pact, and Africa*. London: Macmillan, 1985.

Conlon, Paul. *Analytical Compendium of Actions Taken by Governments with Respect to Sanctions on South Africa*. New York: UN Center Against Apartheid, 1986.

"Contadora: German Institute Views on Conflict." *Latin American Weekly Report* (13 June 1986): 6–7.

Cook, Don. *Forging the Alliance: NATO, 1945–1950.* New York: Arbor House/ William Morrow, 1989.

Cordesman, Anthony H. *The Gulf and the West: Strategic Relations and Military Realities.* Boulder, Colo.: Westview Press, 1988.

Cottam, Richard W. *Iran and the United States: A Cold War Case Study.* Pittsburgh: University of Pittsburgh Press, 1989.

Cunningham, Michael. *Hostages to Fortune: The Future of Western Interests in the Arabian Gulf.* London: Brassey's Defense Publishers, 1988.

Dale, Reginald. "U.S./Europe: More Than an Ocean Between Them." *The Atlantic Community Quarterly* 23, no. 3 (Fall 1985):233–38.

David, Stephen R. "Why the Third World Matters." *International Security* 14, no. 1 (Summer 1989): 50–85.

"Delegation of the Parliamentary Assembly for Euro-Arab Cooperation to the Occupied Territories." *Europe: Agence Internationale D'Information Pour La Presse* (cited as *Europe*) 6–7 March 1989: 4.

Department of State. *Report to the Congress on Industrialized Democracies' Relations with and Measures Against South Africa, in Implementation of Sections 401 (b) and 506 (a) of the Comprehensive Anti-Apartheid Act of 1986.* Washington, D.C.: Department of State, 1987.

———. "U.S. Orders Closure of Palestine Information Office." *Department of State Bulletin* (November 1987): 43.

DePorte, A. W. *Europe Between the Superpowers: The Enduring Balance.* New Haven, Conn.: Yale University Press, 1979.

Duran, Esperanza. *European Interests in Latin America.* London: Routledge and Kegan Paul, 1985.

Dyson, Kenneth. "European Detente in Historical Perspective." In *European Detente: Case Studies of the Politics of East-West Relations.* Edited by Kenneth Dyson. New York: St. Martin's Press, 1986, pp. 14–55.

Eagleburger, Lawrence S., Deputy Secretary of State. "The Challenge of the European Landscape in the 1990s." *Department of State Bulletin* (October 1989): 37–40.

"Europe Gives Skeptical Reception to Haig's 'Red Scare' Mission." *Latin American Weekly Report* (20 February 1981): 5.

European Economic Community. "Statement on the Middle East 13 June 1980: Venice Declaration." *Bulletin of the European Communities* 13, no. 6 (1980): 10–11.

Feldman, Lily Gardner. *The Special Relationship Between West Germany and Israel.* Boston: Allen and Unwin, 1984.

de Figueiredo, Antonio. "Portugal's Year in Africa." In *Africa Contemporary Record.* Edited by Colin Legum. New York: Africana Publishing, 1988, pp. 230–41.

Foot, Peter. "Western Security and the Third World." In *The Troubled Alliance: Atlantic Relations in the 1980s.* Edited by Lawrence Freedman. New York: St. Martin's Press, 1983, pp. 135–47.

"Four Steps on the Road to Peace in Southwestern Africa." *International Legal Materials* 28, no. 4 (July 1989): 947–48.

Frey-Wouters, Ellen. *The European Community and the Third World: The Lomé Convention and Its Impact.* New York: Praeger, 1980.

Friend, Julius W. *Seven Years in France: François Mitterrand and the Unintended Revolution, 1981–1988.* Boulder, Colo.: Westview Press, 1989.

Gaddis, John Lewis. *Strategies of Containment.* New York: Oxford University Press, 1982.

Garfinkle, Adam M. *Western Europe's Middle East Diplomacy and the United States.* Philadelphia: Foreign Policy Research Institute, 1983.

Garten, Jeffrey E. "Japan and Germany: American Concerns." *Foreign Affairs* 68, no. 5 (Winter 1989–90): 84–101.

Garthoff, Raymond L. *Detente and Confrontation: American-Soviet Relations from Nixon to Reagan.* Washington, D.C.: The Brookings Institution, 1985.

Gil, Federico G., and Joseph S. Tulchin. "Introduction." In *Spain's Entry into NATO: Conflicting Political and Strategic Perspectives.* Edited by Federico G. Gil and Joseph S. Tulchin. Boulder, Colo.: Lynne Rienner, 1988, pp. 1–8.

Ginsberg, Roy H. *Foreign Policy Actions of the European Community.* Boulder, Colo.: Lynne Rienner, 1989.

Gleich, Albrecht von. *Germany and Latin America.* Santa Monica: The Rand Corporation, 1968.

Goldsborough, James Oliver. *Rebel Europe: How America Can Live with a Changing Continent.* New York: Macmillan, 1982.

Goodison, Paul. *The European Community Cooperation with SADCC.* Copenhagen: NGO Initiative on EC and Apartheid, 1987.

Grabendorff, Wolf. "West European Perceptions of the Crisis in Central America." In *Political Change in Central America: Internal and External Dimensions.* Edited by Wolf Grabendorf, Heinrich W. Krumwiede, and Jorg Todt. Boulder, Colo.: Westview Press, 1984, pp. 285–97.

Greilsammer, Ilan, and Joseph H. H. Weiler. *Europe and Israel: Troubled Neighbors.* Berlin: Walter De Gruyter, 1988.

Hall, Peter A. *Governing the Economy: The Politics of State Intervention in Britain and France.* New York: Oxford University Press, 1986.

Halliday, Fred. *From Kabul to Managua: Soviet-American Relations in the 1980s.* New York: Pantheon Books, 1989.

Hanrieder, Wolfram F. *Germany, America, Europe: Forty Years of German Foreign Policy.* New Haven, Conn.: Yale University Press, 1989.

———, and Graeme P. Auton, eds. *The Foreign Policies of West Germany, France, and Britain.* Englewood Cliffs, N.J.: Prentice-Hall, 1980.

Harvey, David, and Dexter Jerome Smith. "In Defense of Europe: the Western European Union Reinvigorated." In *Drifting Apart? The Superpowers and Their European Allies.* Edited by Christopher Coker. London: Brassey's Defense Publishers, 1989, pp. 135–48.

Hawley, Donald. *The Trucial States.* London: Allen and Unwin, 1970.

Heiberg, William L. *The Sixteenth Nation: Spain's Role in NATO.* Washington, D.C.: National Defense University Press, 1983.

Heller, Mark A. *A Palestinian State: The Implications for Israel.* Cambridge, Mass.: Harvard University Press, 1983.

Hermat, Guy. "The European Left and Central America." *The Washington Quarterly* 9, no. 2 (Spring 1986): 37–43.

Hess, Jurgen H. "West Germany and the Central American Crisis." *The Fletcher Forum* 10, no. 2 (Summer 1986): 297–315.

Hoagland, Jim. "Europe's Destiny." *Foreign Affairs* 69, no. 1 (1990): 33–50.

Hodges, Tony. *Angola to the 1990s: The Potential for Recovery*. London: The Economist Intelligence Unit, 1987.

Hoffmann, Stanley. "The Western Alliance: Drift or Harmony." *International Security* 6, no. 2 (Fall 1981): 105–25.

———. *Dead Ends: American Foreign Policy in the New Cold War*. Cambridge, Mass.: Ballinger, 1983.

———. "Gaullism by Any Other Name." *Foreign Policy*, no. 57 (Winter 1984–85): 38–57.

———. "The European Community and 1992." *Foreign Affairs* 68, no. 4 (Fall 1989): 27–47.

Holland, Martin. *The European Community and South Africa: European Political Cooperation Under Strain*. London: Pinter Publishers, 1988.

Hormats, Robert D. "Redefining Europe and the Atlantic Link." *Foreign Affairs* 68, no. 4 (Fall 1989): 71–91.

Hough, Jerry F. "Gorbachev's Politics." *Foreign Affairs* 68, no. 5 (Winter 1989–90): 26–41.

Howard, Michael. "A European Perspective on the Reagan Years." *Foreign Affairs* 66, no. 3 (1988): 478–93.

Howe, Geoffrey. "East-West Relations: The British Role." *International Affairs* 63, no. 4 (Autumn 1987): 555–62.

———. "Britain and the Gulf—Together into the 21st Century." London: Press Service, Central Office of Information, January 4, 1989.

Howoth, Jolyon. "The Third Way." *Foreign Policy*, no. 65 (Winter 1986–87): 114–34.

Huntington, Samuel P. "The U.S.—Decline or Renewal?" *Foreign Affairs* 67, no. 2 (Winter 1988–89): 76–96.

Hurwitz, Leon. *The European Community and the Management of International Cooperation*. Westport, Conn.: Greenwood Press, 1987.

Hyland, William G. "The Atlantic Crisis." *Daedalus* 110, no. 1 (Winter 1981): 41–69.

Indyk, Martin. "Reagan and the Middle East: Learning the Art of the Possible." *SAIS Review* 7, no. 1 (Winter-Spring 1987): 111–38.

Ismael, Tareq Y. *International Relations of the Contemporary Middle East*. Syracuse, N.Y.: Syracuse University Press, 1986.

Joffe, Josef. *The Limited Partnership: Europe, the United States, and the Burdens of Alliance*. Cambridge, Mass.: Ballinger, 1987.

Kaiser, Karl. "A View from Europe: The U.S. Role in the Next Decade." *International Affairs* 65, no. 2 (Spring 1989): 209–24.

Kaplan, Lawrence S. *NATO and the United States: The Enduring Alliance*. Boston: Twayne Publishers, 1988.

Kennedy, Paul. *The Rise and Fall of the Great Powers: Economic Change and Military Conflict from 1500 to 2000*. New York: Random House, 1987.

Khalidi, Walid. "Toward Peace in the Holy Land." *Foreign Affairs* 66, no. 4 (Spring 1988): 771–89.

Kieval, Gershon R. *Party Politics in Israel and the Occupied Territories.* Westport, Conn.: Greenwood Press, 1983.

————, and Bernard Reich. "The United States." In *The Powers in the Middle East: The Ultimate Strategic Arena.* Edited by Bernard Reich. New York: Praeger, 1987.

Kissinger, Henry A. "Reflections on a Partnership: British and American Attitudes to Postwar Foreign Policy." *International Affairs* 58, no. 4 (Autumn 1982): 571–88.

————. "Strains in the Alliance." *Foreign Affairs* 41, no. 2 (January 1983): 161–285.

————. *The Troubled Partnership: A Re-appraisal of the Atlantic Alliance.* New York: McGraw-Hill, 1965.

Klinghoffer, Arthur Jay. *The Angolan War: A Study in Soviet Policy in the Third World.* Boulder, Colo.: Westview Press, 1980.

Knudsen, Baard Bredrup. *Europe Versus America: Foreign Policy in the 1980s.* Paris: The Atlantic Institute for International Affairs, 1984.

Kohl, Helmut. "Our Liability Continues." In *Twenty Years of Diplomatic Relations Between the Federal Republic of Germany and Israel.* Edited by Otto R. Romberg and Georg Schwinghammer. Frankfurt: Tribune-Verlag, 1985, pp. 10–13.

Kupchan, Charles A. *The Persian Gulf and the West: The Dilemmas of Security.* Boston: Allen and Unwin, 1987.

LaFeber, Walter. *Inevitable Revolutions: The United States in Central America.* New York: Norton, 1984.

Laird, Robbin F. "The Soviet Union and the Western Alliance: Elements of an Anticoalition Strategy." In *Soviet Foreign Policy.* Edited by Robbin F. Laird. New York: The Academy of Political Science, 1987, pp. 106–18.

————, and Susan Clark. *British Security Policy: The Modern Soviet View.* London: The Institute For European Defense and Strategic Studies, 1987.

Langer, Peter H. *Transatlantic Discord and NATO's Crises of Cohesion.* Washington, D.C.: Pergamon-Brassey's, 1986.

Layne, Christopher. "Atlanticism Without NATO." *Foreign Policy,* no. 67 (Summer 1987): 22–45.

————. "Superpower Disengagement." *Foreign Policy,* no. 77 (Winter 1989–90): 17–40.

Leanza, Umberto. "Relations Between the European Community and Central American States." *Journal of Regional Policy* 8, no. 3 (July/September 1988): 383–92.

Legum, Colin. *The Battlefronts of Southern Africa.* New York: Africana Publishing, 1988.

Leighton, Marian. *The Deceptive Lure of Detente.* New York: St. Martin's Press, 1989.

Licklider, Roy. *Political Power and the Arab Oil Weapon.* Berkeley: University of California Press, 1988.

Lieber, Robert J. "The European Community and the Middle East." In *Crises and*

Conflicts in the Middle East. Edited by Colin Legum. New York: Holmes and Meier, 1981, pp. 92–98.

———. "Secular Changes in the Atlantic Alliance: Will NATO Fragment or Manage to Survive?" In *Fighting Allies: Tensions Within the Atlantic Alliance.* Edited by Walter Goldstein. London: Brassey's Defense Publishers, 1986, pp. 173–84.

Long, David E. *The United States and Saudi Arabia: Ambivalent Allies.* Boulder, Colo.: Westview Press, 1985.

"Lopez Portillo Stakes His Claim to Be Latin America's de Gaulle." *Latin American Weekly Report,* August 8, 1980: 1.

Louis, Wm. Roger. *The British Empire in the Middle East, 1945–1951.* Oxford: Clarendon Press, 1985.

Luard, Evan. "Western Europe and the Reagan Doctrine. *International Affairs* 63, no. 4 (Autumn 1987): 563–74.

Lustick, Ian S. "Israeli Politics and American Foreign Policy." *Foreign Affairs* 61, no. 2 (Winter 1982–83): 379–99.

———. *For the Land and the Lord: Jewish Fundamentalism in Israel.* New York: Council on Foreign Relations, 1988.

McNamara, Robert S. *Out of the Cold: New Thinking for American Foreign and Defense Policy in the 21st Century.* New York: Simon and Schuster, 1989.

MacQueen, Norman. "Portugal and Africa: The Politics of Re-engagement." *The Journal of Modern African Studies* 23, no. 1 (March 1985): 31–52.

Macridis, Roy C. "French Foreign Policy: The Quest for Rank." In *Foreign Policy in World Politics.* Edited by Roy C. Macridis. Englewood Cliffs, N.J.: Prentice-Hall, 1985, pp. 22–71.

Maier, Harry. "Drifting Together? New Challenges Facing the Two Alliances." In *Drifting Apart? The Superpowers and Their European Allies.* Edited by Christopher Coker. London: Brassey's Defense Publishers, 1989, pp. 171–80.

Mandelbaum, Michael. "Ending the Cold War." *Foreign Affairs* 68, no. 2 (Spring 1989): 16–36.

Marcum, John. *The Angolan Revolution: Volume 1 (1950–1962).* Cambridge, Mass.: MIT Press, 1969.

———. "Africa: A Continent Adrift." *Foreign Affairs* 68, no. 1 (1989): 159–79.

Martin, Lenore G. "Patterns of Regional Conflict and U.S. Gulf Policy." In *U.S. Strategic Interests in the Gulf Region.* Edited by William J. Olson. Boulder, Colo.: Westview Press, 1987, pp. 9–27.

Maynes, Charles William. "America's Third World Hang-ups." *Foreign Policy,* no. 71 (Summer 1988): 117–40.

Melber, Henning. *Federal Republic of Germany and Namibia.* Copenhagen: NGO Initiative on EC and Apartheid, 1987.

Mendelsohn, Everett. *A Compassionate Peace: A Future for Israel, Palestine, and the Middle East.* New York: Hill and Wang, 1989.

Mendl, Wolf. *Western Europe and Japan Between the Superpowers.* New York: St. Martin's Press, 1984.

Mesbahi, Mohiaddin. "Soviet Policy Towards the Iran-Iraq War." In *Soviet Foreign Policy: New Dynamics, New Themes.* Edited by Carl G. Jacobsen. New York: St. Martin's Press, 1989, pp. 163–81.

Miller, Aaron David. *The Arab States and the Palestine Question: Between Ideology and Self-Interest.* New York: Praeger, 1986.

Minter, William. *Portuguese Africa and the West.* New York: Monthly Review Press, 1972.

Moisi, Dominique. "French Foreign Policy: The Challenge of Adaption." *Foreign Affairs* 67, no. 1 (Fall 1988): 151–64.

Moran, Fernando. "Europe's Role in Central America: A Spanish Socialist View." In *Third World Instability: Central America as a European-American Issue.* Edited by Andrew J. Pierre. New York: Council on Foreign Relations, 1985, pp. 6–44.

Mujal-Leon, Eusebio. "European Socialism and the Crisis in Central America." In *Rift and Revolution.* Edited by Howard Wiarda. Washington, D.C.: America Enterprise Institute for Public Policy Research, 1984, pp. 253–302.

Murphy, Richard W., Assistant Secretary. "Statement," May 19, 1987. *Department of State Bulletin,* July 1987, 59–63.

Nassar, Jamal R. and Roger Heacock, eds. *Intifada: Palestine at the Crossroads.* New York: Praeger, 1990.

Neustadt, Richard E. *Alliance Politics.* New York: Columbia University Press, 1970.

Newman, David. "Introduction: Gush Emunim in Society and Space." In *The Impact of Gush Emunim: Politics and Settlement in the West Bank.* Edited by David Newman. New York: St. Martin's Press, 1985, pp. 1–18.

Nixon, Richard. "American Foreign Policy: The Bush Agenda. *Foreign Affairs* 68, no. 1 (1989): 199–219.

North Atlantic Treaty Organization. Declaration and Report Adopted at the 40th Anniversary Meeting of the North Atlantic Council, May 30, 1989. *Weekly Compilation of Presidential Documents* 25, no. 22 (June 5, 1989): 786–802.

Osgood, Robert E. *Alliances and American Foreign Policy.* Baltimore: Johns Hopkins Press, 1968.

Palmer, John. *Europe Without America? The Crisis in Atlantic Relations.* New York: Oxford University Press, 1987.

Pappé, Ilan. *Britain and the Arab-Israeli Conflict, 1948–51.* New York: St. Martin's Press, 1988.

Pardalis, Anastasia. "European Political Cooperation and the United States." *Journal of Common Market Studies* 25, no. 4 (June 1987): 271–94.

Parker, Franklin D. *The Central American Republics.* London: Oxford University Press, 1964.

Parliamentary Debates (Commons), 5th ser., vol. 747 (1966–67): 31 May–9 June 1967.

Parliamentary Debates (Commons), 5th ser., vol. 748 (1966–67): 12–23 June 1967.

Parliamentary Debates (Commons), 5th ser., vol. 749 (1966–67): 26 June–7 July 1967.

Parliamentary Debates (Commons), 5th ser., vol. 750 (1966–67): 10–21 July 1967.

Parliamentary Debates (Commons), 5th ser., vol. 861 (1972–73): 16–25 October 1973.

Parliamentary Debates (Commons), 5th ser., vol. 863 (1973–74): 30 October–9 November 1973.

Parliamentary Debates (Commons), 5th ser., vol. 904 (1975–76): 26 January–6 February 1976.

Parliamentary Debates (Commons), 5th ser., vol. 914 (1975–76): 28 June–8 July 1976.

Parliamentary Debates (Commons), 5th ser., vol. 980 (1979–80): 3–14 March 1980.

Parliamentary Debates (Commons), 6th ser., vol. 4 (1980–81): 5–15 May 1981.

Parliamentary Debates (Commons), 6th ser., vol. 9 (1980–81): 20–31 July 1981.

Parliamentary Debates (Commons), 6th ser., vol. 12 (1981–82): 4–13 November 1981.

Parliamentary Debates (Commons), 6th ser., vol. 13 (1981–82): 16–27 November 1981.

Parliamentary Debates (Commons), 6th ser., vol. 15 (1981–82): 14–23 December 1981.

Parliamentary Debates (Commons), 6th ser., vol. 19 (1981–82): 1–12 March 1982.

Parliamentary Debates (Commons), 6th ser., vol. 26 (1981–82): 21 June–2 July 1982.

Parliamentary Debates (Commons), 6th ser., vol. 84 (1984–85): 21–30 October 1985.

Parliamentary Debates (Commons), 6th ser., vol. 118 (1987–88): 17 June—3 July 1987.

Parliamentary Debates (Commons), 6th ser., vol. 119 (1987–88): 6–17 July 1987.

Parliamentary Debates (Commons), 6th ser., vol. 120 (1987–88): 20 July–23 October 1987.

Parliamentary Debates (Commons), 6th ser., vol. 122 (1987–88): 9–20 November 1987.

Parliamentary Debates (Commons), 6th ser., vol. 138 (1987–88): 24 October–4 November 1988.

Parsons, Anthony. "Iran and Western Europe." *The Middle East Journal* 43, no. 2 (Spring 1989): 218–30.

Payne, Richard J. *Opportunities and Dangers of Soviet-Cuban Expansion.* Albany: State University of New York Press, 1988.

———. *The Nonsuperpowers and South Africa.* Bloomington: Indiana University Press, 1990.

Pearson, Neale J. "Recent Spanish Foreign Policy Toward Central America." In *Latin America and Caribbean Contemporary Record*, vol. 4. Edited by Jack Hopkins. New York: Holmes and Meier, 1986, pp. 158–67.

Perlmutter, Amos. "Israel's Dilemma." *Foreign Affairs* 68, no. 5 (Winter 1989–90): 119–32.

Pfaff, William. *Barbarian Sentiments: How the American Century Ends.* New York: Hill and Wang, 1989.

Philip, George. "British Involvement in Latin America." In *The Latin American Policies of U.S. Allies: Balancing Global Interests and Regional Concerns.* Edited by William Perry and Peter Wehner. New York: Praeger, 1985, pp. 31–54.

President Reagan's Address to the Nation, November 13, 1986: "U.S. Initiative to Iran." *Department of State Bulletin*, January 1987: 65–66.

President Reagan's Statement, December 14, 1988: "U.S. Opens Dialogue with PLO." *Department of State Bulletin*, January 1989: 51.

President Reagan's Statement, June 11, 1987: "Arms Sales to Saudi Arabia." *Department of State Bulletin*, August 1987: 80.

Principles for a Peaceful Settlement in Southwestern Africa, July 20, 1988. *International Legal Materials* 28, no. 7 (July 1989): 947–48.

Pym, Francis. "British Foreign Policy: Constraints and Opportunities." *International Affairs* 59, no. 1 (Winter 1982–83): 1–6.

Quandt, William B. "The Western Alliance in the Middle East: Problems for U.S. Policy." In *The Middle East and the Western Alliance*. Edited by Steven L. Spiegel. London: Allen and Unwin, 1982, 9–17.

Reich, Bernard. *The United States and Israel: Influence in the Special Relationship*. New York: Praeger, 1984.

Robins, Philip. *The Future of the Gulf: Politics and Oil in the 1990s*. London: The Royal Institute of International Affairs, 1989.

Rogers, William D. "American Behavior and European Apprehensions." In *Central America and the Western Alliance*. Edited by Joseph Cirincione. New York: Holmes and Meier, 1985, pp. 11–16.

Rondot, Philippe. "France and Palestine: From Charles de Gaulle to François Mitterand." *Journal of Palestine Studies* 16, no. 3 (Spring 1987): 87–100.

Rummel, Reinhardt. *The Evolution of an International Actor: Western Europe's New Assertiveness*. Boulder, Colo.: Westview Press, 1990.

Schloesser, Jeffrey, Political-Military Officer in the Regional Affairs Office Bureau of Near East and South-Asian Affairs. "U.S. Policy in the Persian Gulf." *Department of State Bulletin*, October 1987, pp. 38–44.

Schmahling, Elmar. "German Security Policy Beyond American Hegemony." *World Policy Journal* 6, no. 2 (Spring 1989): 371–84.

Schmidt, Helmut. *A Grand Strategy for the West: The Anachronism of National Strategies in an Interdependent World*. New Haven, Conn.: Yale University Press, 1985.

Secretary of State for Defense. *Statement on the Defense Estimates of 1987*. London: HMSO, Her Majesty's Stationery Office, 1987.

———. *Statement on the Defense Estimates 1989*, vol. 1. London: HMSO, Her Majesty's Stationery Office, 1989.

Secretary Spay's Statement, May 17, 1987. "*USS Stark* Hit by Iraqi Missiles." *Department of State Bulletin*, July 1987: 58.

Shipping Research Bureau. *The European Community and the Oil Embargo Against South Africa*. Copenhagen: NGO Initiative on EC and Apartheid, 1987.

Single European Act. *Bulletin of the European Communities*, supplement 2/86.

Sloan, Stanley R. *The Atlantic Alliance and the Third World: Implications of Diverging U.S. and European Approaches*. Washington, D.C.: Congressional Research Service, 1983.

Smith, Michael. *Western Europe and the United States: The Uncertain Alliance*. London: Allen and Unwin, 1984.

Smouts, Marie-Claude. "The External Policy of François Mitterrand." *International Affairs* 59, no. 2 (Spring 1983): 155–68.

Snyder, Glenn H. "The Security Dilemma in Alliance Politics." *World Politics* 36, no. 4 (July 1984): 461–95.

Sobhani, Sohrab. *The Pragmatic Entente: Israeli-Iranian Relations, 1948–1988*. New York: Praeger, 1989.

Statement by Herbert S. Okun, U.S. Deputy Permanent Representative to the UN on January 5, 1988 before the Security Council on Israeli Deportations. *Department of State Bulletin*, March 1988, p. 82.

Steel, Ronald. "NATO's Last Mission." *Foreign Policy*, no. 76 (Fall 1989): 83–95.

Stein, Janice Gross. "The Wrong Strategy in the Right Place: The U.S. in the Gulf." *International Security* 13, no. 3 (Winter 1988–89): 142–86.

Steinbruner, John D. "Introduction." In *Restructuring American Foreign Policy*. Edited by John D. Steinbruner. Washington, D.C.: The Brookings Institution, 1989, pp. 1–11.

Stent, Angela. "Franco-Soviet Relations from de Gaulle to Mitterrand." *French Politics and Society* 7, no. 1 (Winter 1989): 14–27.

———. "The Soviet Union and Western Europe: Divided Continent or Common House?" *The Harriman Institute Forum* 2, no. 9 (September 1989): 1–8.

Strange, Susan. "The Persistent Myth of Lost Hegemony." *International Organization* 41, no. 4 (Autumn 1987): 551–74.

Thurow, Lester C. "America Among Equals." In *Estrangement: America and the World*. Edited by Sanford J. Ungar. New York: Oxford University Press, 1985, pp. 157–78.

Tikhomirov, Vladimir I. "The USSR and South Africa: An End to 'Total Onslaught'?" *Africa Report* 34, no. 6 (November- December 1989): 58–62.

Tillman, Seth. *The United States in the Middle East: Interests and Obstacles*. Bloomington: Indiana University Press, 1982.

Touval, Saadia. *The Peace Brokers: Mediators in the Arab-Israeli Conflict, 1948–1979*. Princeton, N.J.: Princeton University Press, 1982.

Treverton, Gregory F. *Making the Alliance Work: The United States and Western Europe*. Ithaca, N.Y.: Cornell University Press, 1985.

Tschirgi, Dan. *The American Search for Mideast Peace*. New York: Praeger, 1989.

Tucker, Robert W. "Reagan's Foreign Policy." *Foreign Affairs* 68, no. 1 (1989): 1–27.

Tugendhat, Christopher, and William Wallace. *Options For British Foreign Policy in the 1990s*. London: Routledge, 1988.

"U.S. Arms Sales to Saudi Arabia." *Department of State Bulletin*, December 1987, p. 76.

U.S. Congress. House. Committee on Foreign Affairs. Subcommittee on Europe and the Middle East. Roundtable Discussion on U.S. Policy Toward Europe. 99th Cong., 2nd sess., July 22, 1986. Washington, D.C.: Government Printing Office, 1986.

U.S. Congress. House. Committee on Foreign Affairs. Subcommittee on Europe and the Middle East. Roundtable Discussion on U.S. Policy Toward Europe. 100th Cong., 1st sess., December 2, 1987. Washington, D.C.: Government Printing Office, 1988.

U.S. Congress. House. Committee on Foreign Affairs. Subcommittee on Europe and the Middle East. Hearing on U.S. Interests in and Policies Toward the Persian Gulf. 96th Cong., 2nd Sess., March 24; April 2; May 5; July 1, 28; and September 3, 1990. Washington, D.C.: Government Printing Office, 1980.

U.S. Congress. House. Subcommittee on Arms Control, International Security and Science and the Subcommittee on Europe and the Middle East. Hearing on U.S. Policy in the Persian Gulf. 100th Cong., 1st sess., December 15, 1987. Washington, D.C.: Government Printing Office, 1988.

U.S. Congress. House. Subcommittee on Europe and the Middle East and the Sub-committee on International Economic Policy and Trade. Hearing on U.S.-European Community Trade Relations. 99th Cong., 2nd sess., July 24, 1986. Washington, D.C.: Government Printing Office, 1986.

U.S. Policy in the Persian Gulf: New Beginnings. Muscatine, Iowa: The Stanley Foundation, 1989.

Vance, Cyrus. *Hard Choices: Critical Years in America's Foreign Policy.* New York: Simon and Schuster, 1983.

Verbaan, Mark. "Namibia: The Road to Independence." *Africa Report* 34, no. 6 (November–December 1989): 13–16.

Walker, Edward S., Deputy Assistant Secretary. "FY1990 Assistance Request for the Middle East." *Department of State Bulletin*, May 1989, pp. 61–62.

Wallace, William. "Introduction: Cooperation and Convergence in European Foreign Policy." In *National Foreign Policies and European Political Cooperation.* Edited by Christopher Hill. London: Allen and Unwin, 1983, pp. 1–16.

Wallander, Celeste A. "Third-World Conflict in Soviet Military Thought: Does the 'New Thinking' Grow Prematurely Grey?" *World Politics* 42, no. 1 (October 1989): 31–63.

Weymouth, Lally. "Andrew Young Wasn't the Only One." *The Washington Post National Weekly Edition*, June 12–18, 1989, p. 23.

White House Statement, October 8, 1987. "Arms Sales to Saudi Arabia." *Department of State Bulletin*, January 1988, p. 41.

Wiarda, Howard J. *Ethnocentrism in Foreign Policy: Can We Understand the Third World?* Washington, D.C.: American Enterprise Institute, 1985.

Wilson, Rodney. *Euro-Arab Trade: Prospects to the 1990s.* London: The Economist Intelligence Unit, 1988.

Windsor, Philip. *Germany and the Western Alliance: Lessons from the 1980 Crisis.* London: International Institute for Strategic Studies, 1981.

Wolfers, Arnold. *Alliance Policy in the Cold War.* Baltimore: Johns Hopkins Press, 1959.

Wolffsohn, Michael. *West Germany's Foreign Policy in the Era of Brandt and Schmidt, 1969–1982.* Frankfurt am Main: Verlag Peter Lang, 1986.

Woodward, Ralph Lee. *Central America: A Nation Divided.* New York: Oxford University Press, 1976.

Young, Lord. "Creating a Single European Market: A British View." *The World Today* 44, no. 3 (1988): 38–40.

Zartman, I. William. *The Politics of Trade Negotiations Between Africa and the European Economic Community.* Princeton, N.J.: Princeton University Press, 1971.

Index

economic links to the Gulf, 107–12. *See also specific countries*

West Germany: aid to Portugal and Angola, 178; anti-apartheid movement in, 189; arms sales to Middle East, 112; Central American policy, 159–60, 163, 166–67; commerce with Central America, 164; and the Contact Group, 190; economic assistance to Nicaragua, 166; economic links to South Africa, 198–99; Namibia policy, 189; and NATO, 8–9; and Ostpolitik, 18; perceptions of Soviet threat, 13; policy toward Angola, 183; policy toward South Africa, 193; relations with Israel, 68, 71; relations with SWAPO, 189; relations with the Soviet Union, 116; role of Foundations in policy of, 159, 163, 189; ties to Namibia, 184, 187; trade with Warsaw Pact, 21; views on European Political Cooperation, 29. *See also* Germany

Wilson, Woodrow, and the Balfour Declaration, 74

Yamal gas pipeline, 20–21
Yom Kippur War, 42, 83

Zionism: Churchill's sympathy to, 75; as a growing force in Europe, 74; new, 87; strains in Anglo-American alliance due to, 75

About the Author

RICHARD J. PAYNE is Professor of Political Science at Illinois State University. He is the author of *Dangers and Opportunities of Soviet-Cuban Expansion: Toward a Pragmatic U.S. Policy* and *The Nonsuperpowers and South Africa: Implications for U.S. Policy*. Payne has written numerous articles for scholarly journals, including the *Journal of Politics*, *African Affairs* (London), and *The Journal of Developing Areas*.